Education in the Balance

Education in the Balance

Mapping the Global Dynamics of School Leadership

RAPHAEL WILKINS

BLOOMSBURY

LONDON • NEW DELHI • NEW YORK • SYDNEY

Bloomsbury Academic
An imprint of Bloomsbury Publishing Plc

50 Bedford Square	175 Fifth Avenue
London	New York
WC1B 3DP	NY 10010
UK	USA

www.bloomsbury.com

First published 2014

British Library Cataloguing-in-Publication Data
A catalogue record for this book is available from the British Library.

ISBN: HB: 978-1-7809-3682-6
PB: 978-1-7809-3779-3
ePub: 978-1-7809-3777-9
ePDF: 978-1-7809-3674-1

Library of Congress Cataloging-in-Publication Data
A catalog record for this book is available from the Library of Congress.

Typeset by Integra Software Services Pvt. Ltd.
Printed and bound in Great Britain

CONTENTS

PREFACE

This book arises, first, from my reflections on several years of international consultancy, focusing on the leadership of schools or school systems. I needed to understand how each local set of issues related to broader global patterns of change in education, and whether and how practices developed somewhere else might be relevant to the particular situation. That is complex, so alongside the process skills of consultancy I undertook a scholarly quest into global issues in education, and the ideas and conceptual frameworks that people use to describe and critique what is happening. So I have been thinking through the implications of the global 'big picture' patterns of change for education leaders, and for the people who support leadership development.

Secondly, I am interested in what is happening to school leadership in England. High levels of institutional autonomy are the stated intention of government. The nature of this autonomy, and the extent to which it will be vested in headteachers as the professional leaders of education, remain to be seen. To take full advantage of new possibilities, a critical mass of English headteachers will need to break free from recent very prescriptive assumptions about the work they are to do. Three mutually supportive developmental strategies may help. First, headteachers can take responsibility for generating a larger proportion of the research-informed knowledge of education practice, by making their schools research-engaged. Secondly, they can adopt a global perspective, as a counter to the inward-looking focus of recent policy priorities. Thirdly, they may take for themselves greater collective autonomy by giving teaching and school leadership more of the characteristics of an established and self-regulating profession.

I covered the first of these developmental strategies in my book *Research Engagement for School Development* (2011). I plan to address the third, the professionalization of teaching and school leadership, in a future work. This book focuses on the second 'leg of the tripod': adopting a global perspective. As well as potential wider benefits, an increased global perspective will lead to better school leadership in England. I have responded to recent requests to speak to international audiences on topics such as 'the globalization of school leadership', and have treated those lectures as 'reporting milestones' for the development of my thinking. This book sets out in more detail where that thinking has reached. It is a progress report of a journey which is still far from complete.

ACKNOWLEDGEMENTS

The author and publisher are grateful for permission to use material adapted and developed from articles previously published in the journals *Professional Development Today* and *Education Today*.

LIST OF ABBREVIATIONS

ARK	Absolute Return for Kids
BRAC	Bangladesh Rural Advancement Committee
BSF	Building Schools for the Future
CPD	Continuing Professional Development
DCSF	Department for Children, Schools and Families
DfE	Department for Education
EAZ	Education Action Zone
ICT	Information and Communications Technology
INEE	Inter-Agency Network for Education in Emergencies
IOE	Institute of Education, University of London
MDG	Millennium Development Goal
OECD	Organisation for Economic Co-operation and Development
Ofsted	Office for Standards in Education
PEAS	Promoting Equality in African Schools
SEC	Shanghai Education Commission
TAKE	Trust for the Advancement of Knowledge and Education
TCF	The Citizens' Foundation
TESSA	Teacher Education in Sub-Saharan Africa
TVEI	Technical and Vocational Educational Initiative
UNESCO	United Nations Education, Scientific and Cultural Organisation
WISE	World Innovation Summit for Education

CHAPTER ONE
Where Is Education Going?

Why does the school leadership landscape need re-mapping?

Education is increasingly affected by global issues and by international movements of people, policies, resources, ideas and information. At the same time, the leadership of schools and school systems has become more complex and is subject to rising expectations. These factors combined suggest that fresh thinking is needed about the opportunities and processes for developing the school leaders of the future. This book addresses that need. It aims to support the strategic leadership of schools and school systems, worldwide, by mapping global issues and developments so as to help leaders in three ways: first, to rationalize and reflect on their chosen pathways and options; secondly, to re-assess their own professional development interests and options; and thirdly, to look further ahead and consider what new kinds of leadership development opportunities should be opened up for future generations of school leaders.

The global changes affecting school systems are creating conditions of dynamism, complexity and uncertainty. Some school leaders lack a clear overall view of where all of these changes might be leading. Are they, as school leaders, destined to be reactive to uncontrollable developments, and if so can they choose from a range of options? Or can they proactively shape the future? Should they focus attention on the needs of their current institution, or should they spare time to consider educational well-being on a wider scale? As with most aspects of the work of school leaders, those who are able to take a wide view, and are reflective and use opportunities to generate information, will have a greater sense of ownership of their work, and a stronger voice in agenda-setting. Such assertion of influence by school leaders is made more possible by the trend in some countries towards greater school autonomy.

Assertion of influence by school leaders is also a necessary response to some of the global problems in education. That is to say, whether and to what extent these problems are solved will depend significantly on whether school leaders, individually and collaboratively, make it their business to address them.

That statement will elicit an angry or dismissive rejoinder from many headteachers and education commentators in England, who will point out that most of the headteachers they know are already stressed out coping with the urgent demands of their own institution, worrying about the next inspection, and working out the best alternatives to the collapsed support services which used to be provided by local authorities. In response to this reasonable objection, three points of clarification are needed. When I talk about school leaders impacting on global educational problems, I do not mean all or most leaders; I am not thinking only of England; and I am not supposing this will happen today or tomorrow.

In the English school scene there have always been pioneers, and in modern times that role within the state mainstream sector has often been exercised by making creative and original use of new policy contexts. Whether that context was the Technical and Vocational Educational Initiative (TVEI) of the 1980s, or Education Action Zones (EAZ) in the late 1990s, or in the current wave of reforms, some school leaders find ways to come up with innovative ideas and put them into practice. Also in England, both in the independent sector and the special education sector, some school leaders have had much less external pressure and much more thinking space within which to evolve and put into practice enlightened educational philosophies.

Turning to the global scene, the world's population of school leaders is immensely diverse, but it certainly includes many competent and morally committed individuals who combine leading their own, often elite, group of schools, with philanthropic community outreach to engage with the educational needs of poor and marginalized communities.

Most English state schools have an international link, and this book's advocacy of the power and mutual benefits of enhanced international professional networking among school leaders calls only for an incremental enhancement of current activity, on the part of a small but critical mass of pioneers.

Finally, to clarify the timescale underlying this book's argument, while significant changes can affect schools and their leadership within periods of, say, ten years, a re-conceptualization of school leadership is unlikely to happen quickly. The current generation of young professionals engaging with their first leadership positions, who may go on to hold system leadership positions in twenty years' time, and positions of widespread influence in thirty years' time, will be the ones whose visions and dispositions shape the next vital phase of global school development. The choice for current school leaderships is whether horizons and doors will be opened up or closed down for those future generations of school leaders.

'Here be dragons': *Terra incognito*

Changes in the big picture of education systems affect both the rules and the players. The old rules within which education leaders operated now only partially apply, but the new rules have not yet become established. In the past, most decisions about education were taken by national governments and educationists working within national systems. In the future, while nation-states are still very much alive, many decisions about education will be taken by international agencies, multinational companies and consumers, some of whom are more mobile and more assertive than earlier. Neither the old players nor the new have an accurate map of the terrain that lies ahead, nor do they have very good maps on which to locate the dynamics of the current education policy context.

These limited perspectives will limit choices. The combination of new decision-makers (with new patterns of accountability), and the future being 'uncharted', has implications. Too many decisions will be taken from a local, institutional, project-specific, or corporate-headquarters perspective, based on knowledge of the past, and on knowledge of those aspects of context which are familiar, but without knowledge of all of the options and choices available, and without knowledge of the indirect effects of the choices selected. For example, this pattern of decision-making may prioritize the interests of specific groups and sectors, or the development of individual schools (or chains of schools owned by the same organization), without full regard to the consequences for the education system as a whole. Taking decisions in the absence of full information always implies unknown opportunity costs. In the case of education and school systems, there is a shortfall both in analysis and debate regarding what other options might be pursued; what greater benefits might be achieved through different patterns of investment; and hence what doors are being closed for future generations, and what problems are being stacked up for future governments.

If current maps are out of date, new ones need to be made. New maps would widen the choice of paths that are available, and give better indication of the kind of terrain that lies ahead. There are several stages to making new 'maps' of the future education landscape. It is necessary to adopt a global perspective, and, in developing that perspective, to look with percipience at what is really going on, and to apply criticality to accounts which foreground a single viewpoint. It is necessary to develop conceptual frameworks which enable decision makers to locate their stances, beliefs and choices in relation to the broad context, and in relation to different viewpoints. As well as identifying problems and issues, it is also necessary to find possible solutions: a map showing only very difficult terrain is of little use unless it also enables possible lines of approach to be evaluated, even if they have not been tried before. To do this, it is necessary to understand the interconnections between the spatial, temporal and power dimensions of education change.

The use of the term 'mapping' in this book is purely figurative: the 'maps' are presented through text and argument rather than diagrammatically on outlines of continents and countries, although there are many factors relevant to education that show interesting patterns when depicted that way. At the macro level, Ansell (2005) used world maps showing patterns of infant mortality, youth literacy and Internet access to illustrate her exploration of the impact of global issues on young people's lives, while at the meso level, maps were essential to Brock's (2011) study of the effects of local government reorganization on school choice in Hull and the East Yorkshire area of the UK.

Maps provide apparently objective reference material for the development of viewpoints and strategies regarding what it is that needs to be changed, but for this book's purposes it is just as important to emphasize the subjective nature of map-making. Harley (1989) drew attention to the way that 'maps serve a mediating function between the deployment of power, on the one hand, and the construction of knowledge, on the other' (Harley 1989 p 423). Harley argued that the technical production of maps is governed by their cultural production, and this 'interplay of social and technical rules is a universal feature of cartographic knowledge' (p 430). Such 'rules' include ethnocentricity: placing one's own location at the centre of a map, 'adding geopolitical force…to representation,…(helping) to codify, to legitimate and to promote the world views which are prevalent' (p 430). On the other hand, this subjective abstraction and foregrounding may create the condition where, to borrow a line from a novel by Michel Houellebecq, 'the map is more interesting than the territory' (Houellebecq 2012 p 48).

Harley (1989) also pointed out the 'hierachicalisation of space' in map-making. So, applying that idea to sites where learning may take place, in a large-scale map it might be common to see schools, libraries and churches separately identified and perhaps coloured, while homes and workplaces, regardless of physical size, are consolidated into undifferentiated grey patches. Maps are related to the exercise of power. As Harley observed, 'the map becomes a juridical territory: it facilitates surveillance and control' (p 439), and the process of mapping generates power. Acknowledging these subjectivities in map-making questions this book's perspective, and later in this chapter I present my standpoint.

Education in the balance

Education is 'in the balance' in three senses. First, national and international circumstances, and the suite of education policies pursued by numerous governments, have created conditions in which aspects of the education system are approaching 'tipping points'. These might lead to beneficial mould-breaking advances, or to destructive steps backwards, or most probably a combination of the two. In either case, what transpires may differ markedly from what policy-makers intend. As schools are given yet more autonomy and as private-sector involvement in school provision increases, the choices made by school leaders and by the private-sector leaders of chains of schools will, whether consciously or not, be an increasingly important factor in determining whether education moves forwards, backwards or sideways.

The choices that have to be made at all levels involve striking balances between competing demands, and this is the second sense in which education is 'in the balance'. These competing demands include the different educational needs between aspiring urban and underdeveloped rural communities; between economic development and social justice; between global mobility and cultural identity; between tradition and innovation; or between valuing what is easily measured and finding ways to measure what is valued. Drawing attention to these choices does not necessarily mean advocating the kind of safe, middle-of-the-road stances that governments tend to adopt: the new leaders of education in schools and the private sector may be more willing to adopt the radical fresh thinking on which true innovation depends. Discussing these issues involves considering the aims, processes and content of education, leading to the third sense in which education is 'in the balance': finding the balanced 'diet' of learning and experience that will define the educated person in the modern world. By 'educated person' I am thinking not only of school students, and adult learners in general, but also members of the education profession including school leaders, who should perhaps epitomize the term.

In making choices and striking balances, a question is whether the current trajectories of development will widen or narrow the gaps and divisions in societies and in school systems. Another question is, to what extent globalization and internationalism will lead to a belief among those living in countries that are placed lower in competitive league tables that the only way 'up' is 'out'? That is to say, whether the main route to advancement is seen to be to adopt standardized global values and ways of thinking, and whether doing so necessarily represents mobility away from the cultural identity of early moorings. To the extent that this is the case, it may be worth asking whether new routes to advancement should be encouraged, which give greater respect and value to cultural identities.

This book is about school leadership, so it is concerned with education for the 3–19 age range, carried out through school systems: 'schools', however defined, are the main institutional infrastructures at the local level through which the leadership of school-age education takes place. That focus does not imply a conventional view of 'education' as 'schooling', i.e. formal learning taking place in an institutionalized setting. To the contrary, one of the arguments presented through the following chapters is that addressing key educational issues depends on bridging the divides between formal and informal learning, and between schools and the communities to which they are connected, and between regular permanent educational provision and education to deal with crises and displacements. In the future, the leadership of mainstream schooling could become a pivotal source of infrastructural capacity, human capital and willpower to bridge those divides.

This book embraces a broad understanding of education and its relationship with culture, agreeing with Brock (2011) that 'education embraces formal and informal domains'; and more specifically adopting the proposition of Martin (2011) that Education is the process of 'encounter' between individual capacities and culture, *in which both are changed* (pp 2–3). This recognition that the impact of education is two-way, affecting not only the learner but also those with whom the learner is in contact, including their teacher, family and community, is fundamental to understanding educational change. The impact of the learner's learning on their context is lifelong, affecting the organizations that employ them, entertain them and provide them with services. At one level, this is obvious: societies that educate their citizens are changed by so doing. This resonates with the 'human capital' rationale for investing in education development, which is taken as the norm by many governments and agencies. It also exposes the other side of the coin: while schooling is often seen as part of the answer to society's difficulties, it may also be part of the problem. As Youdell has observed, 'Schooling is implicated in the making of particular sorts of people, as well as in the making of educational and social exclusions' (Youdell 2011). Alexander and Potter (2005) edited a provocative collection of viewpoints seeking to make schooling relevant to modern society: the spirit of the collection, and many of the contributions, also resonates with this book's position.

A view of education: Brock's challenge

The negative effects of formal schooling on the achievement of broader educational aims feature strongly in Brock's analysis *Education as a Global Concern* (Brock 2011), which is the flagship volume in the series of books *Education as a Humanitarian Response*, published by Continuum, two more of which are cited later. Brock's ideas have influenced my approach to the issues covered in this book. I like his interest in education geography, adding this emerging discipline to others to illuminate issues. I do not disagree with the fundamentals of his analysis in any important respect, except that I take a more positive view of the achievements, actual practices and underlying motivations of formal schooling. The major contribution of Brock's work is to explain the nature of a set of problems that need to be addressed, to emphasize how significant is the proportion of the world's population whose educational needs are not being met appropriately and to argue that the solution 'depends on repairing the dislocation between the formal system and civil society wherein the non-formal and informal majority of learning takes place' (Brock 2011 p 142). One of my intentions in writing this book is, in a complementary rather than contesting way, to answer Brock's challenge by exploring how school leadership, collectively, could develop in directions which would help to operationalize his agenda of 'repair'.

In England, the use of the term 'school leadership' has become overplayed as a description of a role that has been subjected to massive central direction and political interference. Which of the following best describes what a *leader* should be doing? Should their main purpose be to make marginal operational adjustments to an inherited system, to achieve small efficiency gains, as externally prescribed? Or should a leader decide what needs to be done, design systems to achieve it, implement those systems and further develop them as necessary? In reality, the main expectation placed on headteachers of state schools in England is that they will manage their institution so as to drive up its productivity, especially in students' attainment scores, without having any real say over the kind of education offered, how it is provided, how it will be judged and how it is managed. Some headteachers feel constrained not only by the boundaries of this agenda: they feel that to keep their jobs they must do this micro-management with the style, manner and attitudes that conform to current systemic expectations. This perception of overbearing constraint is not strictly reflective of the reality, nor is it fair to the actual intentions of either the present or previous government, but the perception is common and must be treated as a real phenomenon. I meet headteachers who say 'I do not like the person I have had to become in order to succeed in my job'.

Underlying that sentiment is the mismatch between the demands of results-driven operational management and the educational beliefs and values that drew people to work with children and to want to be headteachers. It suits governments to emphasize that headteachers are 'leaders' because it makes them accountable: if results are poor, it is the fault of the headteacher, not the fault of the policies within which they had to operate. It suits headteachers also, because the connotations of being a 'leader' (in contrast, say, to 'performance manager', 'fire-fighter', 'delivery-operative') are, even in the most constrained and challenging circumstances, more generative of motivation, self-respect and creativity. Much of the professional development provision specifically aimed at current or future headteachers is, nevertheless, anchored into a policy agenda that emphasizes delivering short-term improvements in performance, and discourages debate about the fundamental purposes and design of the school system. That is why I think it is helpful to adopt a completely different starting point, and to explore future directions for school leadership development starting from global issues, educational values and the long view.

Brock's (2011) analysis provides a foundation for developing such a perspective. Brock identifies the educational elements within the Millennium Development Goals, how they have been elaborated by UNESCO and the major reports on progress published in the first decade of the current millennium. Brock sees 'education' as three overlapping circles: formal education, provided by schools and universities; 'non-formal' education, which he equates to the organized teaching and learning that goes on in institutional settings such as workplaces and churches; and 'informal' education, which he equates with the involuntary learning of everyday life. Brock's thesis is that the full benefits of education are only achieved where these three forms are operating with mutual complementarity, and that the emphasis on formal schooling, and neglect of the other forms of education, amounts to a serious problem in the way the Millennium Development Goals are being implemented (Brock 2011).

Brock's (2011) concept of 'education as a humanitarian response' identifies six groups: the mainstream; those dislocated by natural disasters and conflicts, including refugees and displaced persons; those excluded, for example by extreme remoteness, or because they are living in illegal settlements, or because they are incarcerated or enslaved; those included intermittently such as orphans and vulnerable children; those who are mobile such as nomads and economic migrants; and the group defined by Brock as 'the marginalised majority' – the rural and urban poor. Brock argues that if education is a human right, the system should take better account of the needs of all of these groups (Brock 2011).

Brock considers that formal education has 'ingrained functions' including political and social control, and allocating life paths, in addition to developing skills for economic growth (Brock 2011 p 140). Brock offers the rather chilling conclusion that the best chances of

> repairing the dislocation between the formal system and civil society ... are in situations where the formal system has not yet gained a nationalist grip or where it has been loosened by some kind of disaster ... [where there is] the opportunity to bring the forms of education together to achieve sustainable development rather than mere reconstruction' [p 142]. [Similarly, among] 'the rural majorities of less developed countries there are spaces where innovation can be introduced in the interests of enhancing cultural capacity, ... such spaces are much less evident in the urban cultures of more developed countries'.
>
> (Brock 2011 p 146)

'Bringing the forms of education together' involves generating new partnerships to develop cultural capital, which is the ability of a society to embrace cultural change. This involves the 'contrived, convoluted and compartmentalised world of formal education learn(ing) from the more organic world of civil society' (Brock 2011 p 142).

Brock also introduces a quite separate argument, concerning the advancement of Millennium Development Goals 7 and 8, which cover sustainable development and environmental conservation (MDG 7), and 'developing an open, rule-based, predictable non-discriminatory trading and financial system' (MDG 8). Brock's solution is to propose that the curriculum covers these issues to 'educate about important global concerns' (Brock 2011 pp 141, 151). This argument does not sit very comfortably with his main exposition against the limitations of formal schooling including its function of 'political and social control'. Arguments of the form '... therefore children must be taught xyz' invite the objection that however morally justified 'xyz' might appear to be, this is simply seeking to replace one form of political and social control with another.

Is Brock's challenge relevant only to developing countries?

When I first became absorbed by the *Education as a Humanitarian Response* series of books, including Brock (2011), and the series writers' interests in education in emergencies, in post-conflict zones and in contexts where the basic infrastructures of school provision are seriously underdeveloped, I assumed that the disjunctures between formal school systems and community-based education that I was reading about were relevant mainly to developing country contexts. On reflection I became more aware that the fundamentals of Brock's argument are also relevant to England.

Chapter 2 looks at the impact of certain policies which were intended to address inner-city education problems in London, which on examination appeared to be remarkably unempathetic to the cultures and community characteristics of the groups who were supposed to benefit from them. I think also of the perceptions and issues surrounding the education of Traveller children, and the reasons why parents choose Elective Home Education (D'Arcy, forthcoming 2014). Kraftl (2013) reports the findings of his (UK) study of education in ten care farms, five forest schools, thirty home-schooling groups, six human scale schools, five Steiner schools and three Montessori schools, providing a reminder that the school education scene in England is more diverse than ministerial sound bites might imply.

I have seen imaginative forms of education in the special education sector, where they can flourish because it has remained outside the spotlight of political attention. For example, the Ruskin Mill Educational Trust (www.ruskin-mill.org.uk) uses facilities including converted cloth mills, a glassworks, a mixed farm, a trout farm, a market garden and a woodland to provide a residential curriculum based on traditional crafts, for students combining learning difficulties with challenging behaviour. Why are such beneficial experiences not more available to the educational mainstream? Indeed, since the implementation of the Education Reform Act 1988, English mainstream state education has been effectively devoid of the option of a practical skills-based education, of the kind that would meet the needs of a not insignificant sector of the population, who may instead simply be labelled as 'disaffected'. Reflections along these lines make me wonder whether the need to look afresh at the relationships between formal schooling and civil society does, perhaps, apply to a developed system such as in England, albeit to a different extent to contexts where the challenges are greater and resources fewer.

Ozga and Lingard (2007) commented:

> There is clearly something missing from this dominant conception of education policy as human capital development – the all pervasive globalised educational policy discourse today:…a normative vision of what educated individuals…might look like in this new globalised world.
>
> (Ozga and Lingard 2007 p 68)

The 'something missing' may include a diverse curriculum relevant to individuals and communities. In England, despite massive central government intervention and public investment in education, the attainment gap between different socio-economic classes remains wide, and a significant sector of the population is alienated from required competitive engagement in a predominantly academic curriculum which does not match their aptitudes or interests.

An apology for formal schooling

Brock's (2011) perceptions are challenging in a positive way, but there is a case for speaking up for the contribution of formal schooling in order to redress a slight imbalance in his argument. Just as the three poles of a tripod prop each other up, so there is a relationship of mutual dependency among the three elements of education: formal schooling; informal family and community learning; and structured skills development training in workplaces and similar settings.

Schools have existed for centuries, and represent a distinctive form of place and space which is deeply embedded into culture. Home, schoolroom, workshop, place of worship, shop and cafe, for example, have shared connotations as places for living, learning, manufacture, spirituality, trade and social eating, respectively. Those shared connotations include basic purposes and what kinds of activities and behaviours are appropriate in each place. Different places signify different mindsets and different roles to be enacted. Throughout much of human civilization, the role concepts of teacher and learner are profoundly connected to the place concept of schoolroom. That is why, where circumstances allow, a young person doing their homework may make a small area within their home 'school-like' for that purpose. That is why, in a flood relief camp I had the privilege of visiting at Tatta in Sind, the volunteers providing education had made a tent look as similar as possible to the schoolrooms they remembered.

For all their downsides, schoolhouses can have positive connotations as places where children will find security; food and water; and caring adults and the companionship of a peer group; quite apart from the learning that may occur. For the host community, having a place that passes as a schoolhouse has connotations of stability, a future and identity of being a responsible and self-respecting society. It has to be acknowledged that they can also have negative connotations as places lacking basic facilities in which there is harsh punishment and little learning of any practical value. In parts of the world where poor school attendance, especially by girls, is a major problem, it is now accepted that quality is the key to quantity: improving the experience offered by school is the way to improve participation. The level of formal learning and professional development achieved by teachers is the main factor affecting the quality of the education on offer, and the level of formal learning achieved by parents influences the extent to which they can support their children to take advantage of their opportunities. In those two ways alone, formal schooling contributes significantly to education. The third major factor in quality education is the strength of relationship between school and community, which to some extent can compensate for deficiencies in the other factors. Shared notions of 'school', and the physical presence of a school as an organization and as a facility, are important elements in these relationships.

Brock's (2011) analysis associates formal schooling with national governments and their agendas in ways that may slightly overstate the case, and which may not adequately reflect the dynamic relationships between governments and the education profession, and between state and independent sectors of education.

Schools have a longer history than the active involvement of most national governments in education. The idea that education should develop the whole person and should involve a broad and balanced curriculum, including maths, mother-tongue language, humanities, other languages, other 'recent' subjects such as science and commerce, physical development, arts and some practical skills development, was widely established before most governments took on education responsibilities, and all curriculum development since could be seen as marginal adjustment to inherited ideas that are embedded in culture.

The notion that parents should have some say in how their children are educated is quite widespread, and the overall effect of parental choice tends to be to favour traditional models of formal schooling. This is one of the puzzles for educators who want to argue both for educational innovation, and for education to strengthen democracy, and one of the reasons why school systems change quite slowly. Another factor weakening the association of formal schooling with national government is the existence of the independent school sector, which is enormous in some regions, such as in Pakistan and India. I have seen examples of the wide and often enlightened range of philosophies and practices which can be found within 'formal schooling', which have been developed by school leaders regardless of governments of the day.

Responding to Brock's challenge with new pedagogies

The notion of 'pedagogy' is central to formulating a coherent response to Brock's challenge. Otherwise the response might be a bundle of strategies, either without a systematic underlying rationale, or with a rationale that is essentially political rather than educational. Of course politics can never be taken out of education, because decisions about education involve value judgements that impact on society. Pedagogies are based on sets of beliefs about the nature and processes of teaching and learning. Bringing in consideration of pedagogy makes it easier to think through the working relationships between the politician and the educator, and how they might best complement each other through their shared occupancy of the driving seat of school system development.

'Pedagogy' is a slippery term which varies both in usage and in connotations. Chapter 4 includes a summary of relevant debates and positions. Given Brock's views about the relationships between formal and informal education, I need to clarify two matters regarding my own usage of the term. I follow the tradition of using 'pedagogy' in respect of learners of all ages, on the grounds that all teaching and learning strategies should have regard to relevant attributes of the learner, which include their age and experience, whether the learner is aged 4 or 64. So I find unhelpful the promotion by Knowles (1970) of the term 'andragogy' when talking about the learning of adults, so as to give 'pedagogy' the restricted and somewhat pejorative usage of 'teaching children'.

Secondly, the utility of 'pedagogy' as a concept is greatest where it is taken to combine 'the science and art of teaching and learning', with a particular philosophy of education. That is to say, the 'science and art' are not considered in isolation from the purposes to which they are directed, and the values and ethical considerations surrounding their application. Any particular 'pedagogy' may be based on good or bad 'science', and may be directed to worthy or reprehensible ends, but the term 'pedagogy' itself is neutral. On those grounds, I reject usages of the term which equate it to restrictive, controlling practices of the kind that Freire described as 'banking' (Freire 1970). Chapter 4 explores also the case for articulating pedagogies of radical educational reform which are not embedded within left-wing political ideologies.

An English contribution to global debate

Comparative education develops understanding of other countries' systems and circumstances, including through international collaborations and cross-cultural conversations. Each contributor participates from the standpoint and perspective of their own identity, which includes their culture, although as I explore more fully in Chapter 3, there may be disadvantages in using too embracing a definition of 'culture'. It is neither possible nor desirable to suppress individual identities, and indeed they are what enrich cross-cultural conversation.

The process of dealing with issues of identity, whether for comparative educationists, or for young people growing up in a globalized education system, is rather one of developing multi-layered affiliations. This is the sense of belonging (in different ways and to different intensities) at one and the same time to various sources of identity: for example, to family, profession, religion, political party, institution, city, nation, continent, and world. The list of such factors, and the weighting attributed to each, will reflect what it is that is important to an individual, and forms the components of their identity. For some individuals, factors might include social class, or the school or university they attended, or a regiment they served in. This approach is intended to replace contradictions with complementarities: to replace 'Do I choose to be an X or a Y?', with 'This is how I combine being both an X and a Y'.

While emphasizing the positive embracing of multiple identities, deciding 'who I am and who I want to be' inevitably invites the more negative identification of groups and categories from whom I wish to differentiate myself. Hoque (forthcoming 2014) is exploring, through a series of ethnographic studies, British-Islamic identity among third-generation Bangladeshi teenagers in East London. Hoque is investigating the roles of language, birthplace, skin colour and religion in constructing personal and collective identities. Sheppard (2013) has explored issues of cultural identity, particularly in relation to curriculum content, for mixed-race 'third culture' students attending a British international school in Vietnam. Sheppard's concern is with the extent of a school's ethical obligations towards the emerging cultural identity of children who come from a home combining two cultures, and are then immersed in a school where the curriculum is strongly orientated towards a third (in this case, British) culture.

Interaction and reflection generate multiple affinities; also greater awareness of what is distinctive not only about one's own system, but also about one's own position and viewpoint within that system. My own perspective is shaped by the first twenty-five years of my career having been in the English education system while maintaining scholarly interest in comparative education. More recently my work has been mainly international, with opportunities to gain first-hand experience of the issues being addressed in other systems, and the perspectives of those involved. In this book, I combine my reflections on those experiences with the perspectives of nationals of the countries concerned, as conveyed through publications, dissertations, theses produced by international students at the Institute of Education and direct conversations with people I have worked with in their own contexts.

The scholarship cited in this book includes relevant sources written in English by nationals of the systems discussed. English language books and journals are prominent within the literature of education leadership. In this field, writers of global stature who influence the thinking of other researchers and writers come from many national systems. As well as academic literature there is a vibrant professional literature. Supporting the local generation of practitioner contributions to professional literature that meet international standards, and so can be published and presented at the major international conferences, would ensure that the agenda for debate, and the cultural perspectives included within it, become more balanced. International mobilities and communications are fostering the emergence of global professional learning networks, which provide ever-increasing opportunities for cross-cultural dialogue.

Where does this book fit into literary fields?

This book adopts a broad understanding of education, giving attention to the connections between schooling, community and culture. It draws on some of the concepts of education geography to bring a spatial aspect to the analysis, highlighting the implications of education developments for places, and is also distinctive in its focus on the professional development needs of school leaders.

In addition to normal sources of scholarship, the book also refers to some unpublished theses, dissertations and work in progress by international students at the Institute of Education, University of London, as well as drawing on my own first-hand experience of international consultancy, which gives added attention to some of the 'real-life' practicalities of education change in specific contexts. I take an independent, critical stance in relation to currently orthodox views of globalization and school leadership while combining that with recognition of leaders' needs to take practical actions in contexts as they find them rather than as they might wish them to be. In these ways the book aims to offer a thought-provoking overview of education change worldwide, highlighting the positioned and contested nature of the viewpoints that currently dominate debate, and a structured reflection about the knowledge, skills and attributes required of school leaders in the future, and how they might be developed.

This book is intended to be of interest to individuals in a broad range of education leadership positions, including headteachers, school governors, trustees and proprietors in the UK and internationally; staff in ministries of education, in local school district administration globally; and people working in international development agencies. It may also be of interest to researchers and academics in the fields it covers. The book may appeal to participants in Masters programmes in education, especially in education leadership, comparative education and international development. It seeks to contribute to the field of education geography and may also be of interest to undergraduate and postgraduate students and university staff working in that sub-discipline.

An aim for this book is that it provides bridges between several related but different fields, as summarized below.

- Books about education policy, including critical and positioned perspectives. Mostly these tend not to deal directly with issues of school leadership and school leadership development.

- Books about globalization, both general and specifically on the globalization and internationalization of education. These provide a general background for this book's distinctive arguments for greater school leadership efficacy in impacting on educational problems.

- Books about the philosophy and future purpose of schooling and education, some of which form an important element of the scholarly base upon which this book builds. Continuum's *Education as a Humanitarian Response* series is closely related to the aims, purposes and positioning of this book, which adds the dimension of how school leadership can best contribute to that 'humanitarian response'.

- Books about school leadership, which while abundant, tend to foreground the school effectiveness movement, and ideas emanating from, for example, Ontario, Victoria, Philadelphia, Chicago and UK's New Labour. This book, in contrast, is positioned in favour of contextualized, bottom-up development emphasizing professional rather than managerial approaches to leadership.

- Books about comparative education, which, while again providing background, tend to focus either on the disciplinary development of comparative education as a field of study, or on comparative treatments of specific education issues, or on multinational quantitative studies, not including school leadership. This book complements that literature by being more focused on the issues of school leadership and school leadership development.

- Books about geography. In common with much school leadership writing, this book draws eclectically on academic disciplines, but seeks where possible to benefit from the spatial insights of geographical works. Education geography is an emerging sub-discipline, covering many topics related to educational provision for children and young people. At the time of writing, not much attention has yet been paid within this field to school leadership.

Overview of subsequent chapters

This final section gives an overview of each of Chapters 2–9. The next chapter, Chapter 2, serves two main purposes. First, it introduces some of the analytical lenses of education geography and illustrates their application, showing that an appreciation of spatiality can assist the critical appraisal of education policies. Secondly, it provides a bedrock for the book's argument that the issues for school leadership, viewed from certain perspectives, bear comparison across markedly different global contexts. This is illustrated by an extended case study of the policies applied by the previous UK government to deal with inner-city education problems in London. In each of Chapters 2–9, an insight from geography that can be applied to school leadership is highlighted. Chapter 2 presents the importance of understanding the characteristics of the place in which leadership is to be exercised, and in particular, how the people in that place perceive and experience the spaces they occupy.

Chapter 3 moves from local to global scale, by examining the significance of international perspectives for school leadership. The chapter explores understandings of internationalization and globalization as they apply to school leadership and the development of school systems. It examines the relationship between education policies and culture, and uses examples of education in contexts of ethnic conflict to illustrate the complexity of school leaders' moral responsibilities. The chapter advocates a cosmopolitan outlook and the promotion of global citizenship. The spatial issue highlighted is the need to understand and respect the spaces occupied by people in different countries and cultures, and how those spaces accompany migrant populations.

Chapter 4 turns to the question of what can be done to address educational problems. How can the leadership of one school connect with global-scale issues, especially issues that seem to defy the efforts of national governments and the international community? Can leaders of learning based in one system impact in any valuable way on educational needs in a different country and culture? This chapter considers the modern tendency towards activist strategies at every scale of education, from activism within the curriculum in individual classrooms, to outreach by schools within their own communities, to cross-system collaborations between schools, and to activist strategies used by major international agencies. The spatial issue highlighted in this chapter is how school leaders, using activist strategies, can have impact on spaces of exclusion and disconnection.

Chapter 5 explores the possibilities for taking further steps towards achieving effective interconnections and mutual benefits between formal and informal learning. This concerns the relationships between and among schools, homes, workplaces and civic spaces, and the part that school leadership can play in nurturing those connections for the purpose of enabling learning. Perspectives on this issue are affected by different views of the relationship between schooling and society and by different philosophies of education. To bring coherence to these numerous factors, the chapter takes as a central theme the notion of capacity-building and the infrastructures that support it, and what school leaders can do to build such infrastructures. This chapter explores the changing balance between education as a function of civil society, as a universal public service provided by governments on the basis of need and as a commodity provided in accordance with market forces. The exploration begins by clarifying the scope and connotations of 'education', and applies the ideas of networks and spatial practice to how school leaders build educational infrastructures.

Chapter 6 is concerned with innovation, and in particular how both the meaning of and opportunities for innovation are context-specific. Something that is standard in one place may be innovative in another, and what is practical and acceptable in different places are both variable. This means that school leaders who want to work in new ways have to design pragmatic solutions for specific circumstances. The chapter offers a framework for considering the 'problems' to which innovations provide 'solutions'. It examines the conditions necessary for successful innovation, and what school leaders can do to foster these. The chapter highlights educational innovation as a process which co-creates new spaces and new mobilities.

Chapters 4, 5 and 6, as introduced above, concern why and how school leaders carve out particular kinds of spaces for themselves, for the forms of education they advocate, for the services they lead and for community engagement. Chapter 7 takes this deeper by considering the impact of prevailing orthodoxies which form part of the exercise of power. Dominant viewpoints which provide the underlying rationale for policies embrace both facts and values. Highly selective messages drawn from research give the impression that dominant forces are simply acting on scientific evidence. Certain values, such as belief in the benefits of market forces, competitiveness and wealth generation are foregrounded in official dialogue to the exclusion of others. Thus there is an ongoing battle over ideas, truth and values, in which school leaders cannot avoid being engaged on one side or another. This requires a sense of 'permission' to stand up for alternative 'truths' and alternative values where there is good reason to do so. Chapter 7 highlights the process of transitioning spaces of prescription into spaces of negotiation.

Chapter 8 considers what is already happening, and what further steps might be taken, towards giving the global community of education leaders stronger professional identity. This identity concerns perceptions by self and others, and practical infrastructures so that perceptions are underpinned by realities. The chapter argues that school leadership should not be seen as a separate profession from teaching, but instead should be making a strong contribution as an integral part of a teaching profession which includes school leadership. This contribution embraces the ways in which new knowledge about educational practice is generated. The chapter argues that school leadership and school leadership development are, at their heart, educative processes, and for that reason it is meaningful and generative to consider a 'pedagogy of global school leadership'. Chapter 8 highlights the creation of professional spaces and their sustenance through networks.

Finally, Chapter 9 draws together the implications of the book's argument for the forms of professional development, and forms of professional collaboration, that might be helpful to future generations of school leaders. Leadership development must prepare leaders not only to respond to the changing demands of the future, but also to play their part in creating that future. The chapter argues that, in addition to gaining breadth of experience at an early career stage, different forms of international professional networks could support school leadership development, as well as supporting practice. Networks for research, professional learning and reflection will give leaders professional standing and capability; networks with linked schools, international agencies and philanthropic organizations will enable activist problem-solving in specific situations; and networks for lobbying governments, the international community and opinion-formers in multinational companies will enable school leaders to contribute to shaping future policy.

CHAPTER TWO

Places and Spaces of School Leadership

Spatiality, movement and power

The spatial dimension provides an important analytical lens for understanding the issues and opportunities for school leadership in a fast-changing world. Spatiality has four relevant elements, the first of which is location. Places, that is to say, physical locations and the human cultures that occupy them, show variety, representing different starting points, possibilities and choices of direction for development. It would be possible, while stopping short of determinism, to follow some way in the footsteps of Fleure (1919), and on place characteristics alone delineate for the field of education certain locations which, under current conditions, amount to regions of ease, and in contrast other locations presenting regions of various kinds of difficulty.

The second element of spatiality is movement, that is to say the mobility of people, money, ideas and data, which has always had an influence on school education, but has increased exponentially in scale and impact in recent times. Places are static (in the sense of having fixed location, rather than in the sense of being unchanging), whereas movements are by definition dynamic, and the interaction of these two elements is the main generative force behind two further elements of spatiality. The third is networks: individuals and organizations are nodes in the networks to which they belong, and both nodes and networks take different forms, reflecting a range of roles, information flows, levels of agreement and power dynamics. The fourth element is spaces, that is to say, the perception, experience, meaning-making and symbolism of places generated in the minds of the people who occupy them (and in the minds of people excluded from them).

School leaders make certain kinds of spaces. This involves understanding how spaces are experienced by others, and even before that, greater consciousness on the part of the leader of how they themselves experience and change the spaces they occupy. The combination of space-making and networking is one of the keys to the opportunities for school leaders, collectively, to address the big issues in education. Each school leader is working directly with three levels of spaces: the spaces they create for themselves as an individual, such as their mental and personal spaces; the spaces they create for learning within the institution they manage; and the spaces they can influence and co-create within the communities that interact with their school. Where schools are linked internationally, as many are, the leaders of the paired schools are networked into each others' sets of spaces. This offers the potential for international webs of infrastructural connection with the capacity to overcome the dislocations identified by Brock (2011) as problematical. These new networks have the power to make linkages among many educational contexts, from mainstream formal schooling in well-resourced institutions, to informal and community-based education in emergencies and in contexts lacking rudimentary facilities. Understanding and working within the dynamics of power relations is necessary to addressing those dislocations effectively, so in a suite of analytical lenses, perspectives on power relations are an adjunct to perspectives on spatiality.

School leadership understands starting points

Starting point and direction of travel are central to the idea of 'leadership', just as it is important to be clear about who is being led, how and through what activities. It may sound simple to say that leaders must know where they are starting from, but the last chapter noted the selective and biased nature of map-making. The cartographer marks features according to their own understanding: features that they notice and believe in their own scheme of things to be significant. Then they say to someone in that landscape, 'You are *there*', which means 'this is how I have classified your position in relation to other positions which I consider to be the most relevant reference points'. As Harley (1989) noted, mapping is a tool in the exercise of power.

School leaders who believe that education can be compared with engineering will follow their own 'map' and will look at a new situation with a view to diagnosing 'what needs to be fixed' to correct its deficiencies. School leaders who, by contrast, believe that education is better compared with human relations and creative cultural pursuits rather than with engineering, will be less confident about imposing their own perspective and agenda. They will be more interested in understanding how people see the places and spaces they occupy, and in co-constructing the map which depicts starting point, route and destination. So there will always be more than one starting point: those of the leader, of the led, and of third parties who influence the rules of the game. In debates about managing change, a certain weight of opinion favours meeting people where they are, and aligning direction of travel both to their motivation and their agency.

Taylor (2009, 2011) noted that the multidisciplinary nature of both geography and education as fields of study ensures that any description of 'education geography' as a sub-discipline will be messy and complex. Taylor (2011) drew attention to the range of spatial scales of studies, from micro (individual learner), to meso (neighbourhood, local authority), to macro (national and international), and to the scope for studies of children to give more specific attention to children in their capacities as learners. One way to make sense of global changes in education is to visualize how the spaces in which learning happens are being affected by movements and cultural dynamics over time. The point about these changing learning spaces is that they are nested within each of the scales to which Taylor (2011) drew attention. Ministries of education, or other legal frameworks, provide the spaces within which school systems operate; within which institutions manage campuses; within which middle leaders affect their faculty, department, year group or annex; within which teachers and students negotiate the daily minutiae of space-making. These processes incorporate ever-changing power relationships. The combination of these factors points towards posing a series of questions about educational phenomena:

- What is going on here (processes and outcomes over time)?
- How are *mobilities* influencing this development?
- How are *moorings* (see later section) influencing this development?
- How are *power relations* influencing this development?
- How are *places* being changed?
- How are *spaces* being changed? Whose spaces?
- What *networks* are instrumental to this development?
- What educational opportunities or interests are being advanced by these processes?
- What educational opportunities or interests are being limited by these processes?
- Why? What rationales or motivations appear to be influential?

I do not propose to adopt these questions as a method, although there is no reason why such a method might not be applied to reviewing systematically particular issues within education. For this book's purposes, these questions are more useful as a list of additional factors to consider alongside the other factors that inform school leadership work. Leaders working wholly or mainly within a single national system, concerning themselves with the questions leading where, and leading how, will often frame their thinking within the fields of education policy and school improvement. Leaders whose concerns are more predominantly international may frame their thinking additionally, or alternatively, within the fields of comparative and international education, or in some cases in the specialized field of education in emergencies. For all of these groups of school leaders, the 'spatial checklist' provides an additional source of insight and illumination, of problem identification and problem-solving. I want to go a step further, to hope that adding the spatial perspective to increased international professional dialogue will expose the connectedness and comparability among the issues with which school leaders in markedly different contexts are dealing, with synergizing outcomes. This chapter proceeds by introducing spatial terms, which are revisited in later chapters at relevant points; and then applying spatial considerations to a critique of policies to address educational achievement in challenging urban environments in London.

Places

Places are physical locations. They have their own qualities and convey messages about themselves. Spaces, by contrast, are places *as perceived and experienced* by individuals using them. Spaces can take conceptual as well as physical form.

Yi-Fu Tuan (1996) observed that the two different meanings of 'place', referring either to a spatial location *or* to a position in society, are actually connected, because often one's spatial location derives from one's position in society. Tuan also considered that places have personality: they evoke awe or affection (or other emotions). Places may range from 'public symbols' to 'fields of care'. Tuan conceived 'sense of place' as being visual and experiential, and considered that to gain it fully, one must leave the place and think about it from a distance.

Can the 'personality' of a place, as understood by Yi-Fu Tuan, exist only in human perceptions of the place? Could the physical landscape alone have 'personality' as distinct from evoking human responses? Insofar as the personality of a place reflects its human footprints, is this an element of the culture of the place? Could a place be said to have a culture which is different from the sum total of the cultural spaces occupied by the people in the place? These questions help to illustrate the layers of meaning, and kinds of responses evoked, in the phrase 'sense of place'.

Places where learning happens include locations both on and off educational campuses, indoors and outdoors, and in both formal and informal settings. Learning places are hierarchically nested inside each other, spanning individual workstations; classrooms; specialized rooms such as laboratories or art and craft areas; communal spaces such as a hall, or a library/learning resource centre; the whole campus site; and the world beyond the campus.

Spaces

Murdoch's (2006) view of 'places' and 'spaces' provides a starting point to consider 'learning spaces'. 'Spaces' are not hierarchically nested: 'global city' and 'local neighbourhood' are different networks, not different locations. Spaces are not inert boxes within which actions take place, but the loci of relationships between people, ideas, associations and intentions. Spaces are defined and experienced subjectively and reflexively; they are different for each individual. Spaces are nodes in the networks of the individuals who use them, where topography meets topology (Murdoch 2006 pp 19–23).

Applying these thoughts to education, it is clear that teacher and pupils may be in the same room, but they are not necessarily in the same space. The spaces in which young people live both reflect and influence their identity. In that regard, spaces that do not exist for people may be as significant as those that do.

One of the problems for education is that for a proportion of young people, a gulf exists between the subjectively experienced spaces in which they spend their lives, and official perceptions of the spaces intended to be their learning spaces. Some young people move only between hostile spaces. Another problem for education is the variability in community engagement and community capacity, and how different types of networks generate 'spaces of prescription' or 'spaces of negotiation' (Murdoch 1998, Law and Mol 2002).

Students' perceptions of spaces are taken into account in the design of school buildings and campuses. Research with students may be used to 'design out' negative features and enhance the positive. In new school buildings, this may mean that the external features of school sites are designed to lessen bullying and increase positive engagement; that the location and supervision of toilet and washroom facilities are similarly 'engineered', and that eating areas are designed to form a positive element of school ethos. Student voice and student leadership projects often result in areas of the school acquiring a greater sense of ownership by the students.

Spaces exist in places: physical context, climate, landscape, townscape, local economy and human geography always matter, and cannot be set aside from the way in which individuals experience the spaces they occupy. In the worked example which follows, the context of London as a place has material bearing on the issues discussed.

Mobilities

Urry explained that mobilities are best understood in relation to the concept of 'moorings', which represent the fixed points between which movements take place (Urry 2007). For example, a person's first moorings may be their family home, their village or their primary school. Movement may then take place to a new situation which develops into a new mooring, which perhaps might be a secondary school in a town. Urry stressed that mobility to a new mooring makes the person look back at their previous mooring in a new way: they see new things about it and understand it differently from their new perspective. They may undertake further mobility, perhaps to a university in a city, or perhaps to a new country, and again they look back at their previous moorings in a new way. This process continues through life (Urry 2007).

Mobility is more than movement. As Cresswell (2006) observed, meaningful mobility has symbolic significance to the actor, and contexts are part of that significance. This is different from an abstract notion of 'movement'. A range of different power relationships may be associated with particular drivers of mobility: for example, compare the different connotations between student and teacher; pilgrim and missionary; migrant worker and entrepreneur, regarding the power relationships between the person moving and those they will be joining.

Educational mobility has both spatial and developmental dimensions. Spatial mobility includes movements of people, ideas and information, while developmental mobility includes the educational 'journey' from one point of development to the next. The making of that journey affects other people, not just the person doing the learning: this is Martin's (2011) 'process of encounter'. Thus learning spaces are in a continually dynamic state in relation to place, culture and the mobilities of people, ideas and information. The relevance of this for relationships between a school and its community is picked up in Chapter 5.

In challenging urban settings, the ethnic, cultural, linguistic and socio-economic profile of localities is strongly influenced by patterns of mobility in the form of inward migration. On the other hand, some of the educational issues that have to be addressed are the consequence of a *lack* of mobility away from contexts of multiple deprivation.

Stay-at-home mobility

The exponential growth of British international schools illustrates two phenomena. One, from the point of view of the British expatriate community, is the reproduction of moorings in a distant location. The other, from the viewpoint of host country nationals who might want to educate their children in Britain, is how these schools offer some of the benefit of that education mobility while staying at home. An example is a certain group of British international schools in China. These schools are associated in name and character with a distinguished English public (i.e. independent) school. They serve the needs of British ex-patriot families working in China, although a significant proportion of their students are of other nationalities including Chinese.

These schools are a direct product of the mobility of the British workforce which provides the fundamental justification for their existence; they in turn stimulate the mobility of the international teachers (partly but by no means wholly British) who work in the schools. The British teachers who work in international schools are often doing so because they see the benefits and lifestyle as more attractive than working in the UK. For parents of children of other nationalities attending the schools, they offer the prospect of mobility including progression to a UK university.

There is a clear collective mooring for these schools, which is the 'mother school' in England, and this is manifest in the places which are created, which represent not only little patches of England in China, but also the England of a previous genteel age. Typically these schools, although newly built, will incorporate architectural references to nineteenth-century gothic red-brick, fronted with a cricket pitch, and inside resplendent with oak-panelled hallway, honours boards and trophy cabinets: the look, feel and smell of elite English education.

These places will be experienced as spaces conveying different meanings according to the positions people occupy and the nature of their affiliation. Power relations are evident in the hierarchies and statuses of traditional schooling, and also between ethnic groups. Locally employed staff are on different (much lower) salary scales and are managed separately by a Chinese headteacher. Inevitably, these features convey a somewhat neocolonial flavour to the enterprise, although also serving the agenda of Chinese internationalization.

As a footnote to this example, it is interesting that Whitworth (2013), writing in *The Times*, reports the case of a Chinese company building a new school in Guangzhou modelled on British public schools.

Time

Although chronological time is important, many developments in education tend to ignore it. For example, students learn at different speeds, but also schools and education systems develop at different speeds and from different starting points: 'iron age' and 'space age' may exist side by side. In a typical city, some schools will be ten years ahead of the average in their way of thinking, and some will be ten years behind. A complicating factor is the way in which modern technology, especially ICT, enables schools to jump over (i.e. miss out) conventional stages of development. Mobility has its effect on the temporal dimension. The aspect of educational mobility that includes the movement of people, ideas and information across national systems has tended to intensify and complicate the temporal dimension. Individuals move to and fro not only between cultures but between different time periods, and between places where change is rapid and places where it is slow.

Learning spaces in their dynamic condition, as they are becoming through the mobility (movement) of people, ideas and information, are developing at different speeds, and in different directions, reflecting differences in the intensity and nature of those mobilities. In this way, mobilities (part of the spatial dimension) can speed up the pace of development (part of the time dimension). This way of understanding the time-space relationship offers one of the keys to making sense of the complex dynamic of current educational change.

Speed merchants: 0–60 by tomorrow

On the same point, through Anglo-centric eyes, and with vast first-hand knowledge of schools in England, it is sometimes hard, when looking at other education systems, not to make comparisons of the form: 'the classroom practices here, and approaches to school administration, are similar to where the English system was in the 1970s (or 1950s, or 1980s)'. I have seen contexts where the classroom, resources and style of teaching are remarkably similar to the nineteenth-century schoolhouse, and other international contexts where facilities and methods are globally leading-edge. More common are schools and systems exhibiting the practices, and showing concern for the issues, that were current in the English system between the mid-1960s and mid-1980s.

Some of these systems are striving, and politically committed, to bringing about a scale of change, within perhaps five years, which took between thirty and fifty years to achieve in England. If, as a young teacher in the 1970s, I had been confronted by a change agent with the mindset and expectations of the present day, I would have thought they were from another planet. While attitudinal change may take a generation, the pace of learning and adaptation among young professionals worldwide is remarkable.

Power

The remaining dimension to consider in this conceptual framework is power relations. Nye (2011) has drawn attention to the global shift of power away from national governments to others such as multinational companies, international organizations and social networks; and to the reduced reliance on 'hard power' and increasing influence of 'soft power'. Nye refers to 'smart power' which is the right combination of hard and soft power, together with strategies and leadership, to produce outcomes in specific contexts. Here, 'power' means the ability to alter people's behaviour to produce preferred outcomes. Thus relational power operates at three levels: commanding change through coercion; controlling agendas in ways which limit debates and choices; and thirdly through co-option, in which people are steered towards adopting the desired preferences, and may be unaware that they have been so influenced (Nye 2011).

Modern governments have become adept at influencing the news and hence public debate: for example, in England, governments have defined and talked-up various 'crises' happening in education that appear to justify the extreme and controversial policies they wish to pursue. Neither the popular media nor the serious daily papers seem to want to question the reality of these 'crises', so there is no debate about the issues and what counts as 'solutions' to them; no significant alternative suggestion regarding the priorities that might be better addressed. With such control of the terms of debate by government and other nebulous corporate and media interests, many teachers have come to accept and half-believe the onslaught on their competence and judgement, while others live with a sense of resentment of the gap between their own beliefs and values, and those that seem to prevail in their workplace.

In the case of education in London, the previous government, through its London Challenge suite of policies, used all three forms of power. Most central was the setting and controlling of the agenda of what counted as 'success' and what routes to that success were permissible. This agenda-setting was supported by coercive hard power in the forms of financial support with strings attached, and high-stakes testing with accountability. The strength of these forms of power applied over a period inevitably led to 'co-option', i.e. the acceptance and internalization of this agenda by many of those involved.

Learning spaces in the city: Urban education policy in London

Students in London's schools have come to achieve examination results higher than the rest of England, following a century in which attainment in London was consistently below the national average. The pace at which schools have improved in London is also faster than the national average. These gains are partly the effects of the previous government's London Challenge programme, summarized in the booklet DCSF (2008). Later I critique that programme's institutional focus, but start by acknowledging that where it produced improved attainment for individual students, that was a real and lasting benefit for those individuals. London's school system is, therefore, at a strong point in its history, but meanwhile its educational needs and challenges continue to grow. A summary profile of London education was provided in DCSF (2008 p 7), and a series of essays about aspects of education in London contemporary to this policy phase was provided by Brighouse and Fullick (2007).

London offers some advantages for school education, including the rich
cultural and linguistic diversity of its population, and proximity to national
institutions and learning resources, and a range of specialized services that are
less readily available away from the capital. It also presents some enduring
challenges, and these are not distributed evenly across the Greater London
area. Some Londoners, perhaps because of their occupations, interests and
lifestyles, are strongly conscious of London's status as a global city: as
something they are aware of on a daily basis, including perhaps a sense of
connection to other global cities. Others live their lives in one of London's
dozens of towns and villages; in one of its hundreds of neighbourhoods with
their particular characteristics and issues. For them, 'real life' is local, not
global. These different perspectives reflect different patterns of movement,
communication and networking, and hence different perceptions of identity
and belonging. For many Londoners, and for many London schools,
neighbourhood factors are both significant and inescapable.

In some localities, the school-age population includes many transient
young people presenting acute educational and welfare needs. In others,
some schools draw most of their pupils from communities experiencing
chronic and multiple socio-economic disadvantages. In parts of London, the
proportion of students who cross a borough boundary between home and
school is sufficiently high to be a complicating factor in the planning of school
places. Shortages of sites suitable for new school buildings limit the range of
options available for school reorganizations. In parts of London, extremes of
wealth and poverty are found side by side, and this can heighten the impact
of 'market forces' as schools compete with each other for the best staff and
most motivated students. In London, it is more complex and challenging to
arrange collaborations among groups of schools and colleges than it is in
some other areas, because of the complexities of administrative boundaries,
travel patterns to institutions and traditions of institutional independence.

Definition of 'problem' determines
what will count as a 'solution'

Pacione (2001) cited a range of models of urban deprivation which had been
published in the 1975 report of the Community Development Project. The
models differed in how they located the 'problem'. The 'culture of poverty'
model assumed problems arose from the internal pathology of deviant groups,
locating the problem with deviant behaviour. By contrast, the 'institutional
malfunctioning' model saw problems arising from failures of planning,
management or administration, locating the problem with the relationship
between the disadvantaged and the bureaucracy (Pacione 2001 p 290). He
went further, locating the 'problem' with policy-makers rather than with
disadvantaged communities: 'In the UK, most of the disadvantaged live in

cities, large areas of which have been economically and socially devastated by...ineffective urban policies' (Pacione 2001 p 289).

Policies for addressing problems of urban education in London have improved institutional performance measures but have done little to reduce the most persistent attainment gaps. The previous government's own assessment acknowledged this (DCSF 2008), noting in particular the wide local variations hidden within average statistics for London. Earlier, the Association of London Government's Commission on Race and Education had identified a similarly mixed picture, with patches of significant underachievement by specific ethnic groups in specific localities (Association of London Government 2003). Sergeant's (2009) study 'Wasted' depicts the bleak realities for some urban youths, of life dominated by a street culture of crime, drugs and gangs. She reports the example of a fifteen-year-old boy, part of a gang, proud of his aggression, who earns £200 per day running errands for the older drug dealers who are his only role models (Sergeant 2009 pp 1–2). Sergeant comments:

> A lack of social mobility goes together with a lack of aspiration. Boys from disadvantaged backgrounds do not aspire to a different life because they cannot imagine it. They lead isolated lives confined to a few streets or an estate.
>
> (Sergeant 2009 p 16)

The successes reported in DCSF (2008) had been achieved in relation to carefully defined political objectives. These focused on institutional success, in which schools were judged by their inspection rating category and by their overall pupil attainment outcomes. For example, an aim was not having any schools below certain specified floor targets of academic attainment. This approach to measuring the success of single institutions de-coupled them both from the successes of individual students and from the success of groups of schools in relation to the attainment of young people in a particular locality. School reorganizations of one form or another formed a significant strategy for delivering 'success'. So, there might be a school where many pupils failed to attain at the 'required' level because of multiple disadvantages. This school might be closed, and the pupils redistributed among surrounding schools, which had higher average levels of attainment. These schools absorbed their share of the poorly attaining pupils without that affecting their status of having results above floor targets. In this example, the government's objective of not having schools whose attainment level was below floor targets could be achieved, without any individual's attainment improving in any way. The disadvantaged pupils from the school which closed might then have had further to travel, to a school with which their home community had no relationship.

If the question is whether, by a combination of pressure, support and school reorganizations, it is possible for government to produce a school system in which the schools are judged highly by the government inspectorate, and achieve well in government-prescribed tests, the answer almost certainly has to be 'yes'.

A different question is whether those policies were supporting schooling in challenging urban areas in a way that met the statutory requirements encapsulated and re-affirmed in Education Acts from 1944 to the present day. These require that education be 'appropriate to the age, ability and aptitude' of each child; that subject to the avoidance of unreasonable public expenditure, children are to be educated in accordance with their parents' wishes; and that the education provided 'promotes the spiritual, moral, mental and physical development of pupils at school, and of society'. When these requirements are considered in relation to communities in specific geographical localities of urban challenge, the answer to this second question almost certainly has to be 'no'.

Alma Harris argued that in challenging areas, top-down initiatives rarely have lasting impact, so new locally generated solutions are needed that harness community capacity (Harris 2009). This is similar to Daniels' view of top-down urban management:

> Urban politics is not and cannot be monolithic – directed from the top down. Any attempt completely to control the apparent disorder and chaos of urban life through planning and careful 'administration' is ultimately doomed to failure.
>
> (Daniels et al. 2001 p 125)

This point was echoed by Murdoch:

> Difference is now more significant than unity…. In the wake of the shift from structuralism to post-structuralism, any effort to corral the multitude must be seen as either exclusionary or coercive or both. Following the deconstruction of the single narrative, diversity and multiplicity must, indeed, should reign.
>
> (Murdoch 2006 p 9)

The problem arising from Harris's observation above is what to do where community capacity is lacking, without reverting to initiatives. The answer may be to reconfigure learning spaces integrally with living spaces in ways that are mutually strengthening, as discussed further in Chapter 5.

How spatial considerations re-frame 'problem' and 'solution'

Gulson (2005) provided a spatial analysis of urban education policy in London through a case study of an Excellence in Cities mini-Education

Action Zone. This identified the deficit model underlying the policy; its reliance on physical proximity to visible wealth (at Canary Wharf) to promote selected middle-class values and aspirations; and the tension between such aspirations and the realities of students' everyday lives (Gulson 2005). Gulson contextualized the case study within its field as follows:

> As Massey (1993) argues, space is socially constituted, and the social is spatially constituted. This occurs across a multitude of geographical scales as a 'multi-scale re-articulation of space' (Perry and Hardman 2002). Consequently, and importantly for the study of urban areas and educational policy change, this position also permits the reconfiguration of the relationship between global processes and local mediations. Thus, I follow Smith (2001) in holding a key analytical predicate that 'cities, local states and community formations are not bounded self-contained entities'. Rather, the local, national and transnational are mutually constitutive.
>
> (Gulson 2005 p 142)

Gulson identified Excellence in Cities as a spatial policy that positioned disadvantaged urban areas as deficient in educational standards. The following comment reflects Gulson's observation that this community had visible proximity to wealth, but no access to it.

> This strategy uses Canary Wharf as an enabling focus for Mondale students' aspirations. I see this as … appropriating a physical location and positioning it in discourses of educational achievement and the life aspirations of students. I also identify some disabling elements of this appropriation.
>
> (Gulson 2005 p 144)

Thus Excellence in Cities aimed to enable individuals to consume education so as to escape their circumstances by participating in a competitive meritocracy. There was no focus on the development of the community. These policies were set against three layers of disadvantaging factors which limited their possibilities for success:

- The dynamics of urban processes reinforce the challenges for disadvantaged communities.

- The market mechanisms artificially introduced into schooling by the UK Conservative government of 1979–1997 unnecessarily magnify these effects.

- Definitions of 'success' and 'appropriate education' are poorly meshed with the actual needs and circumstances of disadvantaged communities, so they are further condemned to 'fail' against those criteria.

Regarding the first assertion above, Soja (2000), summarizing other writings, commented on the polarizing and socially restructuring effects of urban processes:

> Underlying these indicative themes is one of the most important and challenging findings arising from all of the discourses on the postmetropolis, that inherent in the new urbanisation process has been an intensification of socio-economic inequalities.
>
> (Soja 2000 p 265)

Regarding the second and third assertions above, I was personally present as a lobbyist through the committee stage debates during the parliamentary passage of what became the Education Reform Act 1988. The flavour of the debate through which the government of the day (whose support came mainly from advantaged rather than disadvantaged areas) introduced market mechanisms to schooling was openly partisan rather than purporting to offer 'one nation'-style general benefits. The market mechanisms, enabling schools in advantaged areas to become more advantaged, would create 'winners' and 'losers'. Government spokespersons seemed comfortable with advancing a policy which they knew would create 'loser' schools in disadvantaged areas, and I heard phrases such as 'not our problem' from government backbenchers.

When the Labour government came to power in 1997, it expressed the intention (I believe sincerely) to govern in the interests of the whole nation, and in particular to address educational disadvantage. For political reasons, however, it did not feel able to undo the market mechanisms, but instead overlaid on these its programmes of centralized intervention such as the National Literacy Strategy. While there have been many initiatives seeking to close attainment gaps, some of which, such as Surestart early years provision, have been seen generally as positive, the overall flavour of government policy appeared to ascribe most value to traditional and academic forms of schooling that are most closely matched to the needs and interests of the aspiring middle classes.

Gulson's (2005) analysis of Excellence in Cities raises a number of issues: Whose education? For what? Whose standards? The area is defined as deficient against certain externally imposed forms of educational achievement. The 'solution' offered by the system is for young people in that community to become upwardly and outwardly mobile, by subscribing to the norms of that externally imposed culture, which is offered as an escape route to a superior form of civilization. This 'ladder of meritocracy' argument seems little advanced on that of the opportunities offered in the 1930s for a small proportion of working class boys to enter white-collar occupations. This approach to education policy has parallels with some approaches to colonialism, in which the best route to improving one's circumstances was to adopt the ways of the colonizer, and to give them priority over one's own culture and identity. While acknowledging other strands of policy targeting disadvantaged areas such as economic regeneration, where was the hope for community and neighbourhood, if education policies seemed to be saying that the only way 'up' was 'out'?

A contrasting approach to urban education policies would progress from 'community engagement' to 'community building', and would negotiate the development of 'learning spaces' that mesh more closely with the community's perceptions of space. Communities need to be enabled to take ownership of places, and to become included in discourses of educational achievement, so as to enable the community to redefine its places as being about learning and achievement.

Knox and Pinch (2000 pp 60–61) explored the relationships between space, power and culture, and noted that 'public spaces' are not necessarily welcoming of all sections of the public: often some groups are excluded by formal or informal means. They noted that spaces 'reinforce cultures because the patterns of behaviour expected within them reflect particular cultural values'. This created 'spaces of exclusion': 'power is expressed through the monopolization of spaces by some groups and the exclusion of certain weaker groups to other spaces'. Applying this to education in challenging urban areas, often the culture of the formal education system will monopolize most of the spaces of the school site, while the culture of 'the street' will predominate beyond its boundaries. 'Success' in educating young people in challenging urban areas involves the two-way permeation of this division.

Negotiating learning spaces and networks

Examples of successful practices in meeting urban educational needs generally involve positive boundary crossing between school and community. Each party is able to enter the other's space to the extent that there is significant co-creation of shared spaces which cross the boundaries of the school site, as commended by Gulson:

> This approach allows for educational policy change to involve processes and places; a perspective particularly useful in envisioning schools as multiple and contradictory sites with porous borders. A policy analysis that is explicitly spatial takes note of elements outside the school gates, part of the place in which policy is 'done', as well as inside schools.
>
> (Gulson 2005 p 143)

The previous UK government's London Challenge strategy for 2008–2011 (DCSF 2008) spoke of 'going the extra mile to tackle deprivation'. It summarized (p 22) features of schools which had been particularly successful in overcoming barriers to attainment in disadvantaged communities. These included engaging local role models; a culture of mutual respect; providing cultural opportunities beyond the budget of local families; being socially attuned, with new teachers spending time getting to know the locality, and empathizing with local values; providing rewards and incentives, praising positive behaviour; teachers working hard to earn pupils' respect; and doing more outreach work than most schools (DCSF 2008 pp 22–23).

Knox and Pinch (2000) explored the temporal and spatial dimensions of social life, and the notion of 'structuration': the way in which everyday social practices are structured across space and time. 'Structures include the long term, deep-seated social practices which govern daily life, such as law and the family. Institutions represent the phenomenal forms of structures' (p 262).

Knox and Pinch cited Moos and Dear's model of the structuration of urban space, showing various inputs of control, leading to forms of signification, domination and legitimation, producing intended and unintended consequences, finally producing a feedback loop (Moos and Dear 1986, cited in Knox and Pinch p 263).

The schools referred to above used the processes of institutional signification, and 'structuration' of space, to 'stand for' and promulgate characteristics and values which were engaging of the local community, rather than representing a culture which would have been alien to them. All of the positive qualities listed have major implications for the characteristics of the spaces as occupied and experienced, in school and in neighbourhood, by all of the main actors: school staff, pupils, parents and community.

Mulberry School for Girls, in Tower Hamlets, achieved remarkable results despite 96 per cent of its intake coming from Bangladeshi families, many of whom were recent immigrants, and many of whom experienced high levels of poverty (Hofkins 2009). The school emphasized personal development, making opportunities that enabled the girls to 'work in the same space as professionals', both by bringing high status organizations and individuals into the school, and by enabling the students to travel, for example to perform or to take part in conferences. These approaches enhanced the students' experiences of the places and spaces they were able to occupy.

Generally, good examples of schools succeeding against the odds in challenging urban settings owe much to the visions and values of their headteachers and leadership teams. These are policy entrepreneurs whose courage, conviction and energy result in exceptional outcomes. While government is happy to praise these outcomes and to hold them up as good examples, it does not claim them as directly attributable to national policies. At best, the policy context might be seen as neutral or enabling of such initiatives; the view could equally be taken that these schools achieve exceptionally despite, rather than because of, the policy context.

In the good examples discussed above, certain kinds of spaces were generated. In many schools, they are not. It would be interesting to speculate why not; perhaps the following comment is relevant.

Equally, some attention must be paid to spaces that do not emerge; to the sets of relations that fail to gain any kind of spatial coherence. Relations between relations therefore become important. The shape of space can be seen as the 'expression' of 'underlying' relations; but it can also be seen as the suppression of all those other relations that might have gained some amount of permanence.

(Murdoch 2006 p 20)

The way in which learning spaces are generated and experienced is a key factor in understanding the dynamics of education change. In any particular locality this is why some schools are more effective than others that appear superficially similar. It is also how some schools contribute to the capacity building of communities, both locally and far away. The example of urban London illustrates unhelpful constraints and wasted potential that, in comparable ways, can be found in a wide range of contexts globally.

Michael Fielding (2009) argued a case for inclusive public spaces in schools, linked to support for democracy, which 'concerns the nurturing of a vibrant public realm within schools, that is to say, public space where staff and students can reflect on and make meaning of their work together and develop shared commitments' (Fielding 2009 p 498).

Fielding defined 'public space' as 'not dominated by the state and separate from the arena of market relations, in which people can come together to reflect as equals on matters of mutual importance'. He identified strands within this thinking, including a presumption of agency; the communal contexts of identity formation; the importance of enabling difference; and the development of an inclusive solidarity (pp 499–501).

Community connection and institutional scale

Could a different approach to institutional structures enable schools to contribute more to community building in urban areas? The issue involves finding the best balance between two factors which pull in different directions. The first is the distance (physical, social and cultural) between a student's home and their place of education. The second is the scale required to make effective educational provision of various kinds. It is accepted that the education and care of young preschool children is normally best organized near to children's homes, on a small scale. Expectations are that as children grow older, their education will involve longer journeys and larger institutions. Tradition and convenience say that eleven- to sixteen-year-olds must be schooled in large institutions, where there can be specialized teaching and facilities, and which to be utilized fully and hence cost-effectively require large numbers of students.

On the other hand, the best of private tutoring, some home schooling, some out-of-school provision, some small special schools and other small independent schools tell a different story: they show that good education for eleven- to sixteen-year-olds can be given in small groups retaining close parental involvement. In these cases the small-scale ('human scale': Kumar 2005) operation is justified by students' special needs, or challenging behaviour, or wealth. Yet modern learning technologies mean that there are diminishing technical reasons why all phases of schooling could not be offered partly in local neighbourhoods. On a selection board of choice and diversity, the opportunities for highly personalized forms of education that are currently available to toddlers, delinquents, the very rich and those with special needs could perhaps be extended to marginalized communities in areas of urban challenge.

For example, a dispersed secondary school (or secondary phase of an all-through school) could operate through a series of local learning hubs each with very strong community engagement ('the whole village educating the child'), supported by a core. This would bridge the physical, social and cultural distance between learning and home and also have benefits for the vibrancy and economy of the locality: a territory of becoming, through interaction with the mini-school on the street corner.

> Space and place [are] territories of becoming that produce new potentials. Such potentials derive from the openness of space and place, from the way social relations and spatial relations intersect and combine: space is practised and performed in the same way that social identity and belonging are practised and performed.
>
> It would be better if geographers could approach space as a verb rather than a noun. To space … Spacing is an action, an event, a way of being.
>
> (Murdoch 2006 pp 17–18)

Spaces of prescription or negotiation

The dynamic aspect of space-making can also be understood as an outcome of the ways in which networks operate. In some networks, the enrolling entity (the 'centre') can speak for the entire network because its elements, while varied, are aligned and the network as a whole is stable. Murdoch refers to these networks as producing 'spaces of prescription'. In other networks, links are provisional, norms are not established, and components of the network continually negotiate with one another; its shape keeps changing so there is no clear centre. These networks produce 'spaces of negotiation' (Murdoch 2006 p 79). Perhaps the creation of urban learning spaces needs to become less prescriptive and more negotiated, allowing, on occasion, the 'centre' of the network to emerge in community-owned spaces.

McEwan (2009) observed that cultural identity and power relations affect how spaces are experienced. They may be spaces of exclusion and disconnection: how and by whom are these created? What patterns of intercultural relations and power relations engender these perceptions? She noted that some global perspectives erase the specificity of places and spaces, and questioned whose cultural identities prevail (McEwan 2009).

There is another aspect of networking. Daniels et al. (2001) summarizing the views of other writers including Massey (1999), Castells (1996) and Amin and Graham (1999), drew attention to how cities are linked to wider networks of economic and political relationships, making them 'intersections of multiple narratives'. While some sections of the city population are connected into these networks, others are disconnected and excluded: 'physical proximity increasingly co-exists with relational difference…the connected live alongside the disconnected' (Daniels p 118).

Recent policies for urban education in the UK may be interpreted as aiming to help some of the 'disconnected' to become connected to the economic and political networks that are seen as desirable by government and by 'middle England'. Perhaps, as well as supporting that agenda, one of the functions of schooling is to enable 'disconnected' communities to develop their own connectedness into different networks which are relevant and efficacious to them.

Paul Clarke (2010) emphasizes the interdependence of community and learning, and argues for a shift of focus from 'building schools for the future' to 'renaissance of community for the future'. He sees learning as arising at the intersection of place, connection and action, and views the formal institutions of the education system, especially insofar as they present education as a commodity rather than as an activity, as undermining the confidence of communities to pursue learning independently. Perhaps some communities would do better with forms of education provision which appear less 'institutionalised'. Thus there is a case for reconsidering conventional approaches to school organization in challenging urban areas, to take greater account of the community's perceptions and experiences of networks and spaces.

Leadership needs space

The spatial perspectives relevant to this line of argument go even further than the formally designated 'learning spaces' of educational campuses, and informal local community contexts in which learning and living are intertwined. Another element is the idea of 'leadership space'. This applies to 'power' the same subjectivity and reflexivity that distinguishes 'space' from 'place'. Leadership space concerns perceptions of autonomy and efficacy, and of threats and opportunities. It also concerns subjective, personalized appreciation of context, overview, direction of travel, degree of choice and resonance with personal beliefs and values. While leadership spaces can be created by institutions as well as individuals, they are always experienced at the individual level, although the characteristics of colleagues, teams or organization may heavily influence individuals' subjective perceptions. Leadership spaces include the spaces that ministries of education and international agencies carve out for themselves, within which they and the individuals they employ are able to cultivate particular mindsets. Leadership spaces also include the spaces that school leaders develop for themselves, not only within the confines of their formal role but also beyond the immediate demands of their work: spaces in which they can flourish as thinking moral individuals. Their networks and mobilities shape these spaces.

If one of the functions of a school leader is to create effective spaces for learning, then a prerequisite will be how they themselves create effective leadership space. Three factors concerning this active making of learning spaces and leadership spaces will help school leaders to counterbalance the globally pervasive second and third forms of power: agenda setting and subtle co-option. These are reflective practice, the strength of school as community and international networks.

Reflective practice is an effective means of surfacing and balancing the second and third forms of power. It does so by its combination of critical professional reading, school-based enquiry leading to the independent generation of data, and active interest in published research findings. These generate confidence in challenging prevailing orthodoxies, and creating learning spaces that reflect their users' educational beliefs and values. This theme is developed in Chapter 7. Martin's (2011) definition of education as 'encounter' highlights the significance of the interface between the school, its local community and its host culture. This will be discussed further in Chapter 5. The power and potential of international professional networks as a form of leadership development will be discussed in Chapter 9.

CHAPTER THREE

International Perspectives and Global Reach

Various factors motivate school leaders to take an interest in global educational developments. One is the recognition that in societies with many cultures, much movement and communication, leading the learning process benefits from understanding and respecting other people's spaces and networks. Another is the recognition that through international school-to-school links, interactions at international conferences and interactions through professional networks, school leaders can on an individual basis contribute to dialogue and have influence across continents, and collectively through professional bodies, can have global reach.

Understanding change within a global context

What does it mean to understand the global context? Three different kinds of perceived realities need to be distinguished: espoused stances and intentions; actual happenings; and perceptions and interpretations both of the intentions and of the actualities. National governments and supra-national bodies espouse policies, ranging from high-sounding statements of principle and aspiration, to legislation intended to have practical consequences. What happens on the ground is another matter. Some policies are for political public relations rather than for actual implementation. In some jurisdictions governments have a tight grip on their people; in other places, such as rural Yemen or the North Western Frontier Province of Pakistan, what national government purports to be doing has less impact on local people. The role of legislation varies between different constitutions: Rizvi and Lingard (2010) suggest, for example, that in the USA and China, legislation invariably has significance in the authorization and implementation of policy, whereas in the UK and Australia, the position is more mixed. Meanwhile, academic commentators conceptualize and interpret these developments through their own culturally positioned standpoints and analytical lenses, which might range from Marxist to neoliberal. This processing provides the bread-and-butter of professional reading material: thus a school leader in Ghana might gain their knowledge of education in South East Asia through the viewpoint of a left-leaning North American.

Perspectives on policy

Rizvi and Lingard (2010) re-appraise 'policy' as an aspect of the globalization of education. As well as formal texts, 'policy' embraces school principals and practitioners as policy players because they interpret and mediate policy through the process of implementation. Rizvi and Lingard (2010) follow Luke and Hogan (2006) in emphasizing policy as a process rather than as text:

> We define educational policy making as the prescriptive regulation of flows of human resources, discourses and capital across educational systems towards normative, economic and cultural ends.
>
> (Luke and Hogan 2006 p 171, cited in Rizvi and Lingard 2010)

They draw attention to the spatial dimension of education policy, and the need to consider:

> The extended multi-layering of policy, recognising the simultaneous plays of the local, national and global as spatial relations in the education policy cycle. The geography of policy discourses and processes is today not simply territorial.
>
> (Rizvi and Lingard 2010 p 15)

Rizvi and Lingard see policies as responses to perceived problems. The nature of these problems is not self-evident but constructed from a viewpoint, with the presentation of the policy 'solution' often forming part of the process of problem construction (Rizvi and Lingard 2010). In Chapter 6, I offer a model of problem identification, based on different paces of change among normative, institutional and environmental factors. Policies are also a way of dealing (or seeming to be dealing) with competing demands:

> Policy texts often seek to suture together, and over, competing interests and values … [and] represent their desired or imagined future as being in the public interest: … they often mask whose interest they actually represent.
>
> (Rizvi and Lingard 2010 p 6)

Rizvi and Lingard (2010) distinguish between symbolic and material policies, and between incremental and rational policies. Symbolic policies are the ones espoused for managing public opinion, and the arts of politics, rather than with serious intention to bring about change. For the federal government of Pakistan to pass the Right to Education Act shortly before devolving education responsibilities to the provincial governments, without additional resources, might be seen as an example of such a policy.

Rizvi and Lingard note that most policy development is disjointed ('incremental'), with 'politics and trade-offs involved' (p 10), and that implementation is mediated through the values and organizational realities of individuals at various points in the system. Rational policies involve major new developments, and incorporate within the policy itself a prescription of the logical steps that must be taken by particular parties to effect its implementation.

Rizvi and Lingard (2010) identify three changes to the nature of the education policy process which have run concurrently with the development of globalization. First, a shift from redistributive to distributive policies: that is to say, a reduction in the extent to which governments actively use positive discrimination to offset disadvantage. Secondly, a reduction in the extent to which the exercise of power is specifically linked to legitimate authority: modern methods through which power is exercised obviate the need for such legitimation. Thirdly, Rizvi and Lingard note the move 'from government to governance', reflecting both extensive devolution of power, and extensive private-sector involvement, which have required the development of new forms of accountability.

Globally there is marked growth of for-profit schools, and 'world class' schools which aim, among other things, to enable their students to progress to high-status Western universities. At the same time, the governments of an increasing number of countries are actively encouraging the growth of low-fee, community-based private schools as the only realistic route for approaching universal primary education. In a number of systems, school autonomy is being increased; this goes hand in hand with improvements in the use of ICT for school monitoring. Increased school autonomy does not necessarily mean less state control: there are plenty of places where national governments are growing, not shrinking, their powers. In both India and Pakistan this includes significant new state regulation of the large independent school sectors of those countries. More governments are entering the PISA international comparison of student attainment and prioritizing measures to improve their ranking. Meanwhile, international aid aims to improve literacy, progression to secondary and tertiary education, and female participation rates.

Western policies towards, and practices in, school improvement, school leadership development, assessment of student attainment and interactive pedagogy are spreading into other national and cultural contexts. These movements of thinking and practice are underpinned by movements of individuals, information and funding. Sometimes these developments are 'pushed' by the World Bank and by donor governments; sometimes they are 'pulled' by the governments of the countries concerned. Many developing countries are stratified, with Western educated elites providing the 'pull' both for the import of Western ideas and for the opening up of markets in school provision, notwithstanding that in-country educational differentials may become even wider.

The standardizing tendencies of globalization and the growth of international comparisons of student attainment are being counterbalanced by the resurgence of regionalism and nationalism, as countries and cultures assert their identities through their approaches to education reforms.

Globalization and internationalism affect how education is developing. These have been studied through a number of disciplines and from various positioned stances. This chapter has to be selective, and focuses on three themes: the scope for pro-activity or agency of school leaders at the local level; the complex relationship between school education and cultural identity, illustrated in contexts of ethnic conflict; and the need for professional educators to be alert to uses of power which treat opposition as pathological.

There are some 'isms' for navigating different perspectives. Cosmopolitanism in education emphasizes interest in the world as well as in one's own nation. Cosmopolitanism can sit alongside patriotism. It involves developing a sense of moral obligation to the rest of the world, which in turn leads to the idea of global citizenship. Multiculturalism emphasizes the culturally diverse nature of society. It involves learning about other cultures in order to promote tolerance. Inter-culturalism emphasizes the dynamic and evolving relationships between cultural groups. It involves dialogue between cultural groups leading to mutual understanding and mutual respect. This summary of perspectives is based on McMahon (2011).

School leadership is cosmopolitan and inter-culturalistic

Joel Spring (2009) sees dynamic conditions in which the major players are (by implication, in addition to national governments):

- Intergovernmental organizations
- Global and local school leaders and citizens
- Media and popular culture
- International non-governmental organizations
- Multinational learning, publishing and testing corporations

'Global and local school leaders and citizens' represents quite a wide group, and highlights the role for leaders of schools and school systems as part of influencers and shapers of civil society. Spring (2009) ascribes the complexity of these dynamic conditions to radical school agendas; religions; mass migrations; and the ways in which nations and local communities 'can change and adapt educational ideas in the global flow' (p 206).

For school leaders, the nature of the relationship between school education and globalization works on two dimensions. First, are school systems, and the directions in which they are developing, to be regarded as part of the effect of globalization, or as part of its cause? The answer has to be 'both', so this dimension is not a linear scale. Some developments in some school systems at particular points will seem to be very much the effects of systemic globalization, such as the adoption of English as the medium of instruction for science and mathematics teaching in government secondary schools in Punjab. Other developments, such as the growth of high-status private schools offering traditional British education in South East Asia look more like an active contribution to the process of globalization, although such entrepreneurialism is only possible because it is permitted by the policies of the host national governments.

Secondly, to what extent is the relationship between school systems and globalization consciously perceived by school leaders, and is it a matter of willing choice or resentful endurance? There are two specific issues for leadership and leadership development here. Part of the leadership role includes understanding the environment and horizon-scanning, as inputs to visioning and choice of strategic direction, so a rational case may be made for conscious and informed awareness of global context as a desirable attribute for school leaders. Also, insofar as school education has influence on the shaping of future society, there arises the normative, rather than rational, question of what school leaders ought to do with that influence. That question needs refining. Within their role as a professional educator, leading an educational institution within a particular set of accountabilities, what is it right and proper for a school leader to *want* to do with the influence the school may have, and what are the right and proper ways, within that professional role, to act on that desire?

The last chapter focused on education in challenging neighbourhoods of London. Some of the issues from that analysis apply, in principle, to other geographical scales. The largest unit for spatial analysis within the field of education is of course the whole world. How might the issues of place, space, culture, power and mobility that seemed to be relevant within a metropolis throw light on education issues at the global scale? In London, the key power relationship was between national government and marginalized neighbourhoods. Globally, the equivalent power relations are between Western governments, aid agencies and the international community, on the one hand, and developing countries on the other, with new economic giants including China and India becoming a significant third force.

The parallels include questions about the relevance and efficacy of the standardized agendas of the power-holders to the diverse contexts of the less powerful; the use of deficit models to diagnose how others ought to be changed; and the provision of 'ladders to advancement' that place restrictions and conditions on the forms of mobility offered. Similar also is a set of questions about whether, how and to what extent other people's cultures should be recognized, understood and respected. This is a question of values, and the stance taken here, on both normative and pragmatic grounds, is that school leaders in the modern world should be both cosmopolitan and inter-culturalistic in outlook. That is to say, they should be interested in, concerned for, knowledgeable about and respectful of other countries and cultures, both *in situ* and in migration. Moreover, school leaders need to remember the evolving relations among cultures, in which their own culture is one among many, in an ongoing state of negotiation and adjustment. Leaders of schools and school systems need an informed view of the cultural dynamics of their context at a range of nested levels, including their own personal spaces, their immediate surroundings, the organization they work in, their city or rural district, their country (of residence and of origin if they are different), their global region and the world.

Internationalism and globalism

Internationalism sees as significant the relationships between different nation states and their peoples. This is reflected in a curriculum that includes links with schools in other countries, and encourages students to learn about and appreciate other nations and cultures. Cultural and national identities are important. Globalism, on the other hand, as a viewpoint which foregrounds globalization, sees the significance of developments and processes on a larger scale than that of countries or even regions. Inevitably global forces tend both to lessen the significance of nation states in the modern world, and to give momentum to global standardization in relation to matters that are particularly impinged upon by global forces. While in some respects internationalism and globalism roll forward in parallel, like two sides of the same coin, and may be mutually reinforcing, internationalism may also be seen as a counterbalancing force against the standardizing tendency of globalization. This tension between (inter)nationalism and globalization presents choices regarding the assertion of national and cultural identities. At the same time, choices have to be made, or, more accurately, stances adopted, towards continental regionalism, localism and individualism. These choices are exercised by governments and by non-governmental bodies ranging from aid agencies to proprietors of chains of schools which spread across national boundaries.

The concept of internationalism in education usually embraces such factors as the 'footprint' of Nation 1 in Nation 2 (for example, a British school in China); bi-national and multinational projects; encouraging understanding of other nations; and preparing young people to visit, live and work in other nations. The profile of internationalism within a school often manifests itself in school culture, ethos and educational philosophy; the degree of diversity of nationalities and ethnicities among the student and staff populations; the choice of curriculum and assessment systems; the extent to which the pattern of external relations and communications includes an international element; and whether the forms of professional development provided include international experience.

Whereas internationalism concerns interactions between nations, the concept of globalization represents an additional layer of affiliation, communication and engagement taking place at a supra-national level. Usually its core components are economic, technological and cultural globalization. Some of the literature explores the relationship between globalization and neocolonialism, while educational practitioners highlight global issues and global citizenship, and through their own interactions demonstrate the globalization of knowledge and professional communities.

Globalization may be seen as either an independent variable, or as a dependent variable. As an independent variable, it is a global trend that is moving under its own momentum – the 'march of history' – over which people have no control because it is too big and powerful. In this viewpoint, the only choice for people and institutions is to try to anticipate developments, and adapt and respond so as to be able to survive. If, alternatively, globalization is seen as a dependent variable, then it becomes a global effect that is the cumulative consequence of many decisions and choices made by individuals and institutions around the world. From this viewpoint, individuals and societies have a degree of choice in engaging selectively with the 'opportunities' of globalization. For example, globalized technologies have enabled greater assertion of local identities. The extent to which individuals and societies perceive themselves as having control over their future reflects their ability to see the big picture and to make strategic choices.

Rigg (2007), summarizing the work of others, comments on the apparent contradiction 'between a world worn flat by … globalisation, and a world where localities and localism are gaining in significance' (Rigg 2007 p 11). He considers that 'globalisation has not erased the local and the everyday but, often, re-energised it' (p 11). Thus globalization can strengthen local groups and cultures. Rigg observes that globalization operates at all scales, that local and global are nested, that globalization is uneven in its effects, and that globalization leads to multiple modernities, contradictory outcomes and parallel re-localizations (Rigg 2007 pp 11–12).

Networks are important to 'globalisation from below': to globalization as a dependent variable affected by many individual decisions. Rigg comments that this is 'composed of networks that operate across scales … the network (is) more important than scale, whether that is global, regional, national or local' (Rigg 2007 p 20). Rigg cites Amin's non-scalar interpretation, which challenges the assumption that 'the local [is] near, everyday and "ours", while the global [is] distant, institutionalized and "theirs" ' (Amin 2002, cited in Rigg 2007 p 20). This means that, despite the pervasiveness of global processes, the global scale is not rising in importance at the expense of the local scale. It is not possible to look at local things without also seeing whatever effects may be present from global processes. But nor is it possible in any literal way to 'see' globalization other than in localities, because the whole world consists of localities. The importance of localities is a reminder that even in highly networked contexts, place remains of central significance to individuals' identities and their interpretations of their daily lives. Schools remain highly localized, and this recognition that the world is made up of localities emphasizes that school leaders have agency notwithstanding a globalized context.

Development and deficit

Chapter 2 referred to the deficit model which underlay the policies for dealing with districts of acute urban challenge in London. Shifting the scale and focus somewhat, in the preface to his book *An Everyday Geography of the Global South*, Rigg (2007) explained:

> I felt there was no ... textbook that focused on the Global South ... without taking 'development' as its point of departure. I wanted to extract the Global South from the tyranny of the development discourse ... I wanted the focus to be on individuals, households and communities, rather than on governments, corporations and international organisations, ... [to] privilege the local, the everyday and the personal.
>
> (Rigg 2007, preface)

It is not in fact practical to escape the 'development discourse' for long, but central to Rigg's work is gaining understanding of the livelihoods, issues and outlooks of 'real' people. This implies adopting the mindset of the ethnographer: to see the world through the other person's eyes and to try to understand the meanings which they attribute to the phenomena they describe. In the field of school leadership, whether the focus of attention is a conventional mainstream school anywhere in the world, or the alternative education in the UK examined by Kraftl (2013), or make-shift village schooling in a developing country, or education provision in the context of emergencies, it is equally beneficial to understand before judging. That is to say, to look at what there is, and what that might be in the process of becoming, including from the viewpoints of those involved, before straightaway deciding what there is not, and what there ought to be. In many situations, social justice and equity will still point to the need for an agenda of development, but with more likelihood that this will be supportive and empowering, rather than dismissive and disempowering.

Avoiding stereotypes and determinism

In this book I try to take approaches to analysis and argument which describe and explore phenomena in ways that do not include cultural or national stereotyping, nor deterministic hypotheses or predictions in which culture, ethnicity, nationhood or geographical environment are treated as independent variables in causal relationships. I do not underestimate the significance of cultural characteristics as a factor in cross-cultural developments. For example, Shaw (2005) presented an analysis that drew on Hofstede's seminal typologies (including individualism-collectivism, power distance and uncertainty avoidance), which have some insight and explanatory value. In Chapter 6, I offer an approach to understanding problem identification across different cultures, which, like Shaw's, includes cultural factors while also keeping them in perspective. Classifications of cultural characteristics may, at a generalized level, tell descriptive truths which are relevant to the design and planning of cross-cultural education development work. There are, however, two limitations to such mapping. First, school leadership involves real individuals, groups and specific contemporary organizational contexts which tend not to conform to the generalizations expected of them. On that point, Rigg (2007), commenting on his earlier study of everyday livelihoods in rural Laos, noted that:

> Reviewing the 55 case studies, and looking through the notes from the key informant interviews and group discussions, one of the most striking features was how far it was normal for households to buck the trend and deviate from the expected state of affairs.
>
> (Rigg 2007 p 28)

Secondly, many of the factors that affect education slide across the changing meanings and usages that have been given to 'culture' over time, making the term 'culture' itself too loose to have much depth of explanatory value without further unpacking and defining.

Where does 'culture' begin and end?

At the heart of its traditional usage, 'culture' concerned means of survival and livelihood, and in particular the relationship between human societies and their natural environments. The term embraced patterns and forms of settlements, technologies and social structures. Thus 'culture' included the modern fields of economics and politics. Later, from the seventeenth-century

Enlightenment onwards, 'culture' foregrounded the intellectual and aesthetic products of human societies, including knowledge, beliefs and self-expression. In modern educational usage, for example, in relation to 'multi-cultural education', 'culture' might typically include ethnicity, religion, language, literature and the arts. It might include place, or place of heritage in the case of migrated communities. On special occasions it includes dress, textiles, food and music. These factors may or may not coincide with a national identity, according to how, when and by whom national boundaries were drawn.

Religion is near the heart of cultural identity for many people. Spring (2009) believes in the importance of the links between education, culture and religion, and in particular, that religion has been overlooked in the discourse of educational globalization from two specific standpoints. For world culture theorists, national leaders utilize techno-rational processes in planning school systems, and for them religious considerations are unimportant for educational planning, whereas for post-colonialists, religion 'is often treated as another instrument of domination' (p 203), or as an obstacle to progress. Hart (2011) noted that religious faith paid a particularly important part of the coping strategies and resilience of Palestinian students living in the occupied territories, but that this did not mesh well with the universalistic human rights values of peace education programmes intended for their benefit.

For understanding the global dynamics of school leadership, a case can be made for keeping to the tighter definition of 'culture', and calling other factors by their own proper names. Culture, as narrowly defined, has a strong interrelationship with beliefs about what education is or should be. Among some cultural groups, a lack of value accorded to girls' education is an enormously significant example of a direct relationship between culture and educational opportunity. Ethnicity is part of culture and, as will be amplified later, conflicts related to ethnicity and/or religion are, worldwide, remarkably significant to school provision.

With those two major exceptions, the amount and kind of education people actually experience seems to be much more strongly influenced by factors other than culture, including parents' socio-economic status, parents' own level of education and the range of choices permitted by the political regime under which people live. To these might be added mastery of a global language, and access to electronic communications. These factors appear to operate worldwide. In parts of the world, problems of health and general security impact on access to education, and may be seen as sub-sets of socio-economic status, because they tend to impact most on the poor and powerless. So at the level of individuals, while culture (essentially ethnicity, religion and language) is linked in important ways to education, it is, overall, a minor factor in determining the amount and nature of education that people receive.

It is unhelpful to regard factors that are essentially economic and political as if they were dimensions of culture. Cultural identity is 'owned', or even where it is rejected, the individual is choosing to distance themselves from an inherited birth-right. That is quite different from living under grinding poverty, chronic ill-health and fearful coercion, which are not chosen and ought not to be inherited. Social justice, and countering determinism, both require resistance to accreting imposed conditions onto 'culture' in ways that imply 'that is just how they are': instead, and particularly in relation to education, 'agency' must be assumed in people's relationship with their environment.

School leaders, as a professional group, exhibit great diversity in how, and to what extent, cultural identity impacts on their approach to their school leadership role. This reflects the extent of their mobility from the 'moorings' of cultural roots to new 'moorings' in the professional education community. It is likely also to reflect whether their work serves a distinct and homogeneous local geographical community; whether they work in the government or private sector; the extent of their own education; and the extent of their social networks. It will also be affected by the policies of the organization and system they work in: a private-sector international school will cultivate a more cosmopolitan cultural climate than a government school in a system where curriculum is tightly controlled and linked to the government's view of 'national identity'.

Regional cultures and national geographies

Cultural identities are conventionally associated with major global regions, such as the Arab world of the Middle East and South East Asia. In both cases, important variations within the region in how school systems are developing seem to reflect geographical features of nation states. In the Middle East, there are undoubtedly strong, distinctive commonalities among schools and school systems within Arab societies, including government policies and reform agendas. When it comes to implementation, however, there are contrasts, in particular between Saudi Arabia and the small Gulf states of Qatar and the United Arab Emirates, especially Abu Dhabi. Key geographical features of the latter are their small native populations and geographical compactness; their positions as major trading ports; and high numbers of expatriate residents. By contrast Saudi Arabia covers vast territory, much hardly inhabited; its controlled tourism is almost entirely for pilgrimage; and its traffic with the outside world, while significant economically, does not to the same extent involve interaction between foreigners and the general population. Saudi Arabia's protective insularity is not unrelated to the challenges of government arising from its size and pattern of population distribution. In Yemen, underdevelopment and political instability born of historic internal rivalries impede education reform. It is difficult not to conclude that within the regional culture, the sizes, locations, economies and demographies of different Arab states have a bearing on their different approaches to school system reform.

In the Far East, similar contrasts might be made between approaches to school leadership in mainland China on the one hand, and in Singapore, Taiwan and Thailand, or (notwithstanding the complication of colonial legacy) in Hong Kong, on the other hand. Again, in the latter examples, smaller size and intensity of international interaction correlate with a different appetite for, and flavour of, school system reform, in contrast to that found across the geographical vastness of mainland China.

In South America, educationists display, in debate, something distinctive in their educational philosophy, style and approach, which reflects regional culture. On the other hand, issues in the school systems of the individual countries are affected by national geographical and demographic factors, including the varying extents to which ethnic groups have remained distinctive. The inaccessible terrain of much of inland Colombia, and consequential grip on local populations exercised by criminal gangs, has affected that country's choice of approach to school reform.

Ethnicity, conflict and education

If school leadership is to be inter-culturalistic in outlook, then it is necessary to take serious and realistic notice of the scale of adverse circumstances that are related to ethnicity, religion or culture. Ansell (2005 p 193) cited figures estimating that thirty million children have been displaced by conflict (by implication, this is cumulatively since the 1980s and the lower figure cited below refers to a more recent period). El-Ojeili and Hayden (2006), drawing on other sources, noted that between 1955 and 1996, 239 wars, regime changes or genocides took place arising from ethnic conflict; and between 1980 and 1996, sixty distinct ethnic or religious minorities were victims of wars or genocides. They reported that in the late 1990s, nearly one fifth of the world's population, comprising 275 groups in 116 countries, lived with the threat or actuality of one of the following three conditions: violent repression from their national government; initiating open rebellion against a national government controlled by a different ethnic group; or engaging in violent collective action against other groups. They also estimated that in the year 2000, one-third of the population of Africa and the Middle East, and one-quarter of the population of Latin America, were at risk of openly ethnic conflict, and they also list thirty-five ethnic conflicts between 1990 and 2002 (El Ojeili and Hayden 2006 p 161).

Ansell (2005) summarized the effects of armed conflict on children as including deaths from a range of direct effects, and a much larger number of deaths from indirect effects including disruptions to medical, agricultural and food distribution services and water supply. Among other effects, a million children have been orphaned in recent conflicts, and twelve million have been displaced, of whom 420,000 were unaccompanied. There are 250,000 child soldiers. A wide range of psychosocial impacts of war on children have been analysed. Children's resilience is generally high, and factors affecting its extent include social networks, economic resources, critical thinking capability, temperament, previous experience, age and gender (young girls and older boys being more resilient) (Ansell 2005 pp 195–197).

Armed conflict is of course profoundly disruptive of formal schooling. In 2010 I saw how little educational infrastructure remained functional in South Sudan at the end of its war of independence. Dealing with education in emergencies is a specialized field of activity both within educational administration: organizing forms of education as part of emergency relief activity, and within professional practice: developing educational therapies for children working through particular experiences and challenges.

Hart (2011) critiques what he refers to as this dominant discourse on children and armed conflict. Hart considers that it has been dominated by the three fields of mental health, human rights, and international security. It emphasizes global statistics and overgeneralized classifications of children's experiences, such as 'trauma' and 'separated'. These generalizations feed the process of cross-national policy-making, and the application of standardized approaches to different contexts. Hart considers these apply also in the educational field, where the methods used assume common experiences among children in conflict zones and displacement camps in different parts of the world, including the tendency to regard young people as either trauma victims or resilient survivors (Hart 2011 pp 13–15). Hart worked in the Occupied Palestinian Territories, on which experience he commented:

> Peace education materials [were] precooked. The inappropriateness of some of the advocated approaches has produced bewilderment and even antagonism among young participants.
>
> (Hart 2011 p 12)

Hart (2011) quotes a World Bank publication as typifying generalized assumptions:

> In a context where families and communities are often divided or dispersed by the upheaval of conflict, schools are seen as key institutions that will play the major role in rebuilding core values, in instilling new democratic principles, and in helping children recover lost childhood.
>
> (Buckland 2005 p 16, cited in Hart 2011 p 14)

In fact, as will be illustrated below, the role of schools is much less straightforward than this quote assumes. Hart writes as an anthropologist, and echoes Rigg (2007) in advocating much more attention to the actual daily lives of young people, including their motivations and political positioning, and their social and economic roles and responsibilities (Hart 2011 p 15).

Given the enduring significance of ethnicity as a cause of armed conflict, a question for mainstream school leaders is how best to assist young people, through an educational process, to form their own answers to the questions 'Who am I?' and 'Who are we?', where 'we' refers both to the individual's own group of affiliation, and to the many groups that exist in close proximity. If schools are constitutive, and if educators and students all have some measure of agency, then working with that latter question must be part of a school leader's responsibility. The answers to those questions must resonate credibly with a third question in the minds of students: 'How will engaging in this educational process help me to improve my situation?'

These question are not easy, and answers that may seem obvious can be counter-productive. The next chapter focuses on activist agendas in education, and how school leaders can be part of them, and Chapter 5 explores the relationships between schools and their communities. Later chapters emphasize the potential of international professional networks of school leaders as a force of influence and mutual support.

Chapter 1 explained that this book is in part a response to the challenge posed by Brock (2011) in the flagship volume of the *Education as a Humanitarian Response* series of books. One in that series is *Education and Reconciliation*, a collection edited by Paulson (2011) in which she also makes substantive contributions. It contains insights relevant to understanding the global school scene in ways that keep in focus real children in real localities. It deals with educational reconciliation initiatives in a range of situations, from Rwanda and Bosnia-Herzegovina to Northern Ireland and the USA. The value of these studies to mainstream school leaders is that the issues apply, in less acute form, in other situations, and, systemically, must be seen as part of the business of school systems. Three themes from Paulson's (2011) collection fit into this chapter's discussion, and all three are expressed as negatives in relation to the three questions posed above. The answers to those questions do not include making the school system part of the problem, as occurred in Peru; nor replacing education with indoctrination, nor assuming that a curriculum can be a substitute for addressing the real issues in people's lives: the two latter strategies are common to numerous examples. The following commentaries illustrate these points.

Conflict and education in Peru

In Peru, a Truth and Reconciliation Commission (CVR in its Spanish acronym) examined a violent conflict that lasted from 1980 to 2000, between a Maoist group called Shining Path, and the Peruvian security forces. Its relevance to this chapter's exploration of inter-cultural issues in education is that the area most affected by the conflict coincided with concentrations of indigenous population, and that education was identified both as a cause of the conflict and as a means of reconciliation. CVR was active from 2001 to 2003 and published its nine-volume report in August 2003. Paulson (2011) reports the research she conducted in 2008 on the role of education in the reconciliation process.

Paulson (2011) records that low investment in, and low quality of state schools since the middle of the twentieth century resulted in the failure of mass state education to register upward social mobility to the indigenous population, and to other groups such as the urban poor. The entry of Peru into the OECD's PISA comparison put the spotlight on the need for school improvement, and generated Ministry of Education policies in 2004–2006 which coincided with the proposals of the CVR (Paulson 2011 p 129).

Paulson records that while the conflict was a factor in the poor standard of education, it was also the view of the CVR that the education system was itself a factor in sparking and sustaining violent conflict. The Shining Path subversive group was considered to feed off the education system. This group was based in a public university in a poor highland area, influencing students and extending that influence to other state universities. Shining Path controlled several teacher training institutions and had a presence in the teachers' union, and through these means gained followers among state school teachers, and among young people (Paulson 2011 pp 129–130). In a statement that says much about shortcomings in teaching and learning, Paulson, summarizing several sources, comments:

> It helped that Shining Path indoctrination mirrored the authoritarian, didactic and unquestionable pedagogic style that had long characterised teaching and learning in Peru's state schools.
>
> (Paulson 2011 p 130)

The CVR recorded that considerable force had been used by the security forces against teachers and students generally because of suspicions that they were linked with terrorism. The CVR criticized the Peruvian state 'for its equation of education and students with terrorism, for its neglect of the education system, and for its failure to ensure that education enabled the aspirations of the young people within it' (Paulson 2011 p 131).

Part of this well-deserved rebuke was that schools in the affected areas became indiscriminately associated, in the government's mind, with revolutionary activity, with profoundly damaging consequences. In a less extreme fashion, members of governments in the UK have from time to time sought to portray teachers' unions, teacher trainers, universities and the entire 'educational establishment' as being united in not caring about children, and in being spokespersons for left-wing standpoints. Politicians can make statements which from others might be considered defamatory, and there may be little that school leaders can do to curb that tendency. School leaders have to find a balance between a necessary measure of solidarity with the community they serve, and visibly maintaining in their work the impartiality associated with members of an expert profession. That did not happen in Peru.

The CVR made a series of educational recommendations, some of which were specific to the conflict zone, such as scholarships for orphans and victims of political violence, and a special project with children in regions affected by violence to promote a culture of peace. Others were of a more generic nature, such as professional development for teachers, and educational decentralization, and these were closely aligned with the National Education Project being developed at the same time, as part of wider reforms concerning Peru's return to democratic government. Paulson documents in detail how the CVR's educational recommendations were in effect absorbed into plans which the Ministry of Education had already made, and that these in turn were not implemented.

The political background is significant. The corrupt, militaristic regime of President Fujimori (1990–2000) collapsed at the same time as the end of the conflict with Shining Path, and both the setting up of the Truth and Reconciliation Commission (CVR), and the development of new national policies for education were the work of the new regime, led transitionally by President Paniagua and subsequently by the populist president Alejandro Toledo, the first Amerindian head of state, elected in 2001. Both the government and CVR were comfortable criticizing the previous regime for its reprehensible conduct. By the time of Paulson's research, power had changed again as President Garcia had regained power in 2006: he had been president between 1985 and 1990, when human rights violations had taken place which CVR had criticized. So it was unlikely that this new government would show much commitment towards CVR's educational recommendations, because of their association with the previous regime.

Paulson's interest was particularly focused on the effects of the Truth and Reconciliation Commission, having also researched a similar commission in Sierra Leone, whose recommendations gave impetus to a World Bank programme of reform (Paulson 2006). From that perspective, Paulson sees as negative the absorption of CVR's recommendations into general government policy, believing that this mutual reinforcement did not help the implementation of either agenda. I do not find that argument convincing. Straightforward high-quality teaching, which students find engaging and motivating, in a school where they feel known and cared about, is the answer to most educational problems. The schools mentioned in Chapter 2, which succeed against the odds in difficult districts of London, could be cited as examples of good practice in many different specialisms: inclusive education; multicultural education; ethnic minority education; educating speakers of English as a second language; and special needs education, working with students with behavioural difficulties, with refugees and with vulnerable, marginalized, homeless or disaffected young people. These are all important specialisms, but they relate to categorizations rather than to individuals, and it is actually more accurate to say that these schools are simply good at educating children and young people. In the same way, in school system development, it can sometimes be the case that the best way to bring about long-term, sustainable improvement in education for specific targeted groups is to improve the quality of the school system generally. It is not obvious that had CVR recommended an agenda different and separate from the national policy agenda, it would have had greater chance of implementation.

From Paulson's account, the Government of Peru lacked capacity to manage change. Paulson's sources described weak institutions within which ministers and their close advisers made policies, often in response to personal views and agendas. Small units in the ministry worked on specific issues without a holistic approach. Bold aspirational policy statements were made for political public relations, not backed by practical action plans (Paulson 2011). This description would equally fit a number of developing countries, and this lack of capacity is what World Bank–funded programmes are structured to address.

The CVR had recommended a process of reconciliation that required acknowledging and dealing with the inequalities which had been at the root of the conflict, and that required, in educational programmes, 'every Peruvian (to) reflect upon and take responsibility for the armed conflict' (Paulson 2011 p 143). When the ministry eventually distributed CVR-based materials, this was only to schools serving poor, indigenous and rural areas selected on the basis that these were the likely sites of future political violence. This policy reverted to previous stereotyping: these groups, who had suffered much of the violence in the conflict, were to accept responsibility for keeping the peace in future. It was not something that students in mainstream Peru needed to think about.

Discontent treated as pathological

One day at the Institute of Education, my colleagues and I received a high-level delegation from a small state, not in Latin America, which was currently experiencing civil unrest, in which the religious majority of the population were protesting against what they saw as repression by the religious minority in power. The delegation wanted advice about citizenship education, and expressed interest in our sending experts to work with some groups. Innocently we outlined our thinking and approaches to such work. Gradually it became apparent that words were being used in different ways. By 'citizenship education', our visitors meant a programme just for the groups who were protesting, to 'teach' them that they must stop protesting: the ruling regime had nothing it wished to learn about or reflect upon, and no need to be engaged in this process of 'education'. Of course the discussion was not pursued.

Hart (2011) describes how, in the area of al-Tuwani in the West Bank, part of Palestine occupied by Israel, Palestinian children are routinely attacked by settlers on their way to and from school (p 17). He includes the account of one student whose journey is much prolonged by delays at Israeli check-points, which would sometimes be closed on school- days on which the students needed to pass through in order to sit examinations. Hart juxtaposes that daily experience with a published Israeli viewpoint that 'a reworking of the textbook teachings should be mandated as a condition of any upcoming peace process'. This must include 'prolonged in-depth re-education to peace and reconciliation with the state of Israel' (Burdman 2003, cited by Hart 2011 p 19).

This is an instance of what Hart describes as 'the underlying assumption that the disposition of young people is informed to a decisive extent by curriculum' (Hart 2011 p 19). When children and young people live with the daily experience of humiliation and hostility from occupying forces, Hart argues that it is unrealistic to expect that their disposition towards the 'enemy' is going to be changed fundamentally by a school curriculum until their actual daily experiences change also. A contrasting attitude to Burdman's is illustrated by an initiative by the Institute for the Advancement of Shared Citizenship in Israel, to deploy Arab-Israeli teachers in Jewish-Israeli schools, as reported by Ward (2013).

Hart makes the additional point that while it is common for people speaking from the standpoint of one side in a conflict to deplore the indoctrinating propaganda with which the 'enemy' seeks to condition young people's thinking, 'peace education' can itself fall into the danger of meriting similar criticisms for seeking to inculcate a different set of beliefs in equally partisan fashion. This is not unrelated to the psychosocial approach which treats the emotions of anger and frustration as pathological, which 'transforms political subjects into humanitarian objects in need of healing' (Hart 2011 p 20). Thus political matters are re-classified as security matters, and security is maintained by classifying dissidents as either criminal or sick. This is part of the mosaic of contexts within which school leaders aspiring towards professional standards need to negotiate morally and pedagogically defensible processes of learning.

Similar indoctrinatory intentions marked the attempt researched by Kearney (2011) to achieve ethnic reconciliation in Rwanda through Ingando Peace and Solidarity Camps: a scheme in which the UN and DfID had invested 11 million US$. In 2008, Kearney spent three months at the Rwandan government's flagship Ingando camp at Nkumba, where he observed the provision, interviewed 900 students and gathered survey data (Kearney 2011).

The camp was used to 'educate' groups of between 500 and 900 pre-university students through a one-month residential programme in leadership, peace studies, civic education and history. The scheme was justified on the grounds that it would imbue this potential elite with leadership qualities and the capacity to think critically. The government strongly discouraged any mention in Rwanda of the ethnic identities involved in that country's notorious genocide. At the camp, groups of students mixed both by ethnicity and gender received instruction in a new version of history which imagined a shared, amicable culture in Rwanda prior to the arrival of European colonial powers (Kearney 2011).

The camp was run on military lines, with students wearing military uniforms. The day began with roughly six hours of hard military training, in which collective punishment often involved rod-whippings. This was followed by between two and four hours of formal lecturing, in which there was limited interaction and the students were generally exhausted and compliant. There was no development of critical thinking, no open discussion, and no exposure to any alternative version of Rwanda's history.

Kearney (2011) concluded that solidarity and belief were being promoted at the expense of judgement and reasoning; 'unity' was being confused with reconciliation; and a top-down insistence on the erosion of identities was not conducive to sustainable cohesion or stability. That would require an open debate about ethnicity and the past (Kearney 2011 pp 172–174). Whatever description might reasonably be applied to what was taking place at Nkumba, it was certainly not education.

Educational terms such as 'internationalism' and 'multiculturalism' have positive and benign connotations, but beneath the superficial lie complex educational questions and choices. In most schools in most of the big cities of the world, it is likely that there will be students whose extended families have known experiences of the world's less benign character. What can school leaders, wherever they are globally, do about the many and varied problems that affect the context of schooling, and hence affect the states of mind that students bring with them into the classroom? that affect students' senses of identities, affiliations and aspirations? What should they do within their role as education professionals? The next chapter explores that question.

CHAPTER FOUR

Pedagogies of Access and Inclusion

School leadership addresses humanitarian needs

The last chapter suggested that school leadership benefits from a cosmopolitan and inter-culturalistic disposition, taking an interest in understanding and respecting the spaces occupied by others. A further step is the proposition that school leadership is concerned with addressing humanitarian needs, insofar as this is possible within the broad function of school education. In many countries, this is intrinsic to the legal responsibilities of teachers and state school systems.

Humanitarian needs relate to people's well-being as 'whole persons', including not only the basics of safety, shelter, food and health, but also sense of worth, dignity, peace of mind and fulfilment. While school leaders, collectively, are as involved as most occupational groups in contributing to the relief of human suffering in its broadest sense, their focus as professionals is on how education can contribute to well-being.

There are two distinct levels to 'education as a humanitarian response', to use Brock's (2011) terminology. First is the intrinsic value of education. Like being healthy, nourished, safe and at liberty, being engaged in education is good in itself as an aspect of human well-being. That is separate from the purposes which might be enabled by any of that list of benefits. Involving children, young people and adults in education who would not otherwise have it, and thereby turning spaces of exclusion and disconnection into spaces of meaningful and relevant learning, is a good end in itself that requires no further justification.

Learner agency and freedom to choose

The second level of education's benefit grows from the first. This is the connection between an individual's learning and their ability to address the issues in their lives. Consciousness of this connection is what marks Ranson's 'Learning Society' (which is also, incidentally, marked by the ability of different cultures to share the same spaces in contexts where there are no longer majorities, but only numerous minorities) (Ranson 1994). This combination of consciousness and agency suggests that the core purposes of education must:

- Improve the quality of the learner's life now

- Widen the options for the learner's future

- Enable the learner to make informed choices about their life both now and in the future

- All of the above involve individual learners, groups of learners and the learners' communities, and have regard to beneficial outcomes for groups and communities as well as for individuals.

These purposes are fundamental. They provide a threshold measure of worth of educational developments, and help to differentiate genuinely educational agendas from other agendas that involve schools. Education has both intrinsic and instrumental justifications. It is, however, important to differentiate between internally and externally driven instrumentalities. When an individual uses education to address the issues in their lives, and to pursue their ambitions, that is internally driven learner agency. That is different from the kind of instrumentality evident when politicians emphasize that schools must produce a competitive labour force.

Wherever writings about pedagogy start off, a high proportion of them end up talking about relationships, power and democracy, and cite Freire (1970), a monumentally influential figure who, by helping to spread literacy, applied liberation theology to education. Thus mainstream explorations of pedagogy have been overshadowed by critical pedagogy.

Shotton (2002) explored how pedagogic change could contribute to the quality of education in low-income countries. He noted, from first-hand observation, the very formal, strict, one-way, fact-giving, rote-learning experience offered to 'the poor and weakest sections of society ... in typical primary classrooms in low-income countries' (p 415). Drawing on the ideas of Freire, Dewey and Stenhouse, he argued for greater learner engagement, including in the design of their learning, greater respect for learners, for learners to be assertive and for teachers to engage in research. Although Shotton would be well aware of the contexts he described, this particular contribution did not acknowledge that the barrier in the way of such a change is that teachers have very low levels of education, professional preparation, support or materials. That notwithstanding, Shotton (2002) exemplifies the connection of pedagogy with learner-centredness, educative empowerment, enquiry and mutual respect.

Presenting a view of 'critical urban pedagogy', Pratt-Adams, Maguire and Burn (2010) urge urban teachers to enable students 'to recognise and challenge unjust hierarchies of class, race and gender' (p 99). They describe various projects which apply the thinking of Freire and other critical writers, including Burn's experiences of teaching maths, which make an interesting comparison with those of Gutstein (2012), below.

Youdell (2011) similarly draws upon the 'critical pedagogy' movement, presenting case studies of 'everyday political pedagogies'. She develops the notion of 'pedagogies of becoming', which, if I correctly interpret quite a deep exposition, change subjectivities in ways which bring about increased consciousness and inclination to be assertive in edging in a desirable direction.

Coates (2010), by contrast, presents a 'pedagogy for community empowerment' which, while admitting to be 'subversive' (p 48), and having resonance with agendas of activist reform, does not mention or rely upon the left-wing paradigm of the examples above. Coates proposes to address the dual problem experienced by communities in some localities: low socio-economic status and low aspirations; and schools which, however energetically they believe they are interacting with the community, are not *owned* by the community. Coates proposes the use of a coaching model (in contrast to a teaching model) to enable local residents to progress to paid employment in school, in significant numbers, to the point where the community feels that it owns the school; the school has permeable boundaries, and the knowledge and perspectives brought in from the community have significant effect on the school's approach to teaching and learning.

The purposes of education summarized in the four bullet points above include enabling people to make up their own minds. Part of this process is developing beliefs and values. Popper's 'Open Society' is marked not only by the capacity of individuals to make such choices, but also by their acceptance that they are confronted with a moral responsibility to exercise that choice (Popper 1966, Vol 1, p 173). There is complete consistency between cultivating the Open Society and the intrinsic purposes of education. At the heart of the latter is the development of criticality and the ability to engage with a range of viewpoints, leading to an informed personal standpoint. While individual educators, in their capacity as citizens, must be free to hold whatever political views they like, there seems to be a real tension between the development of true criticality and fashioning a pedagogy within such a strong political paradigm as Marxism. Indeed, left-leaning writings have adopted the word 'critical', so that instead of referring to true criticality, it now refers to ways of thinking that are critical of the establishment, right-wing or neoliberal positions.

Every individual and organization takes a position, whether consciously or not, and whether extreme or middle-of-the-road, and it is difficult to draw lines beyond which education begins to turn into indoctrination. There are faith schools across the whole continuum from mainstream to divisively extreme, and schools whose overall political ethos may be at any point on a wide spectrum. Schools can become part of society's problem, rather than solution, at any point on that spectrum. At the extremes, they promulgate attitudes that lead to confrontation. At the mid-point, they may stand for nothing at all, and promulgate a dangerous complacency.

Ireson, Mortimore and Hallam (1999) emphasized clarity of goals in the design of pedagogy, also fitness for purpose and connecting the learning that takes place in the different contexts of the learner's life. Considered globally, embracing vastly different circumstances, those elements of pedagogic design must also include regard for modes and means: how, when, where and with what resources the learning is to be enabled. A pedagogic response to what I have referred to as 'Brock's (2011) challenge' will include the two important goals of extending access to education to groups currently excluded, and developing the complementarity of learning in formal, informal and community-based settings. That is about goals. Turning next to means, this new pedagogy must generate solutions to the problems regarding the practical resourcing of conditions for teaching and learning.

Ways and means

The goals can only be met if solutions are found to the massive problem of funding. Given population growth and the state of the world's economies, it is inconceivable that the levels of public state funding for school systems that are found in the 'best' systems could be extended universally. What solutions could viably and sustainably ameliorate disparities to an acceptable level? Certainly it is necessary to reject the equation of learning that is 'fit for purpose' to the amount spent per learner.

Education leaders are driven by a complex web of motivations as varied as the individuals involved. In the case of for-profit independent schools, growth of turnover and reach are ascribed organizational value for their own sake. The new philanthropic sector includes a wide range of organizations. In some, the core philanthropic purpose seems to be accompanied both with growing political influence, and with associated opportunities for commercial activity.

Patterns of resourcing include how school education is paid for in different contexts; absolute levels of spending; conditions and expectations attached to particular forms of funding; how people interpret 'value for money', and the extent to which that value is actually being achieved.

Globally, the most obvious (oversimplified) pattern is that in the most economically developed countries there are mature education systems that offer their citizens reasonably standard levels of state school provision in which, by global standards, the levels of resources and facilities range from quite good to very good. In those Western systems where there is a flourishing independent sector, parents who prefer to use it can match their budget to levels of resourcing and facilities that are likely to range from somewhat below to markedly above the level that would be found in the state sector. The striking feature in much of the rest of the world is the greater diversity of levels of school resourcing and facilities found in the same country. This diversity often reflects much wider differentials between socio-economic strata, and hence between the kinds of schools available to children from different strata. In many countries it also reflects marked disparities between the quality of government-provided schools in major cities and in remote rural areas. For these reasons, schools in many countries range in level of resourcing from the most basic facilities (not necessarily including any form of school building) to facilities equal or superior to those of the finest English 'public' schools (i.e. elite independent schools).

Globally, activities relevant to the resourcing of education include officially funded projects to address strategic or humanitarian development needs; the growth of independent (private) school provision on a cost-recovery or for-profit basis; the rise of philanthropic provision and public-private partnerships; and local devolution of school resourcing decisions including moves towards school autonomy. In developing countries, the distinction between sustainable and time-limited project-specific funding significantly affects strategic planning.

The opportunities for effective leadership in the fields of resource generation, procurement and deployment will be found in different mixes at different levels according to the structure of the system and the pattern of financial delegation. In the UK and other Anglo-Saxon countries high levels of school autonomy give state school headteachers significant resource leadership responsibilities, so that they may see themselves with some justification as 'chief executives running a business'. It is certainly a substantial business with high turnover and complexity, although in the state sector the scope for real decision-making is curtailed, and institutions do not have to worry about cash flow and working capital. In the independent sector there are no such limitations, and large chains of schools can represent very big business indeed. In this sector there are wide variations in the extent to which headteachers lead business management as well as the educational programme. In state systems without much financial and management autonomy at school level, the headteacher's leadership of resource deployment focuses mainly on getting the best outcomes from the staff, students and facilities they are given to work with, and the scope for adding value by doing so is considerable. In these systems, the locus of decision-making in relation to other and wider aspects of budget allocation and resource deployment is usually found in a unit of local government such as a district.

The relationship between resource inputs and educational outcomes is complex and contested. There are three levels of resourcing decision-making: budget allocation, which decides the amount of money available; procurement, which decides what goods and services are bought; and deployment of the resources procured. Budget allocation attracts the most attention, but procurement and deployment decisions have the greatest effect on outcomes. A staffing budget is not effective if the wrong people are employed and are then mismanaged.

The main factors that affect educational outcomes and, in particular, account for differential outcomes among similar schools, are the quality of classroom teaching, the quality of leadership, and the quality of relationships within school and between school and community. Among similarly resourced schools, variations in these factors rarely show up in accounts as input differences, so the cost of quality is often the cost of the short-term development necessary to turn mediocre performance into sustainable improved performance: to get more operating like the best.

Giving

In a world where different communities are at different stages of economic development, and hence where there are extremes of material well-being, much education provision has depended on resources flowing from 'haves' to 'have-nots', within and between countries. Alongside self-help, private enterprise and, lately, state education systems paid for through taxation, philanthropic support for education is as old as civilization. Education is one of the classic 'charitable purposes'. The resources involved in the non-mandatory support of education may be various: money, expertise, volunteering, information and the use of facilities. Different forms of support include charity, philanthropy, aid by donor countries and major organizations (which tends to adopt top-down approaches), and activism which is usually associated with locally driven 'grass-roots' initiatives. Some of these elements form part of what Karpinska (2012) terms the 'humanitarian aid industry'; all come within 'education as a humanitarian response' as defined by Brock (2011); and all are relevant both to school leadership as a global profession, and to the curriculum.

How should school leaders relate to and engage with the structures, mindsets and politics of donor agencies (which, like formal schooling, can be both part of the solution and part of the problem), especially for the purpose of making strategic choices about the school's discretionary, philanthropic outreach activity? How should they relate to, manage and indeed engage in the growing tide of activism, which is becoming more significant in the dynamics of addressing educational issues?

Disparate patterns of global economic development and material well-being pose many issues for the leaders of schools and school systems. How school leaders, individually and collectively, view issues of educational disparity matters. This issue is important to how school leaders can best be prepared for their role. As an occupational group, school leaders have immense influence and capacity. Their attitudes will determine how and to what extent the relationship between formal schooling, the community, and the educational needs of groups in specific challenging circumstances might be set to change. In a context of greater institutional autonomy, and increased global communication, a larger canvas is offered to school leaders, upon which they may choose to paint a new educational landscape.

In a number of jurisdictions, neoliberal policies are being pursued, including more devolution of responsibility to school principals, more recourse to market forces and more involvement of private-sector organizations in school provision. At the same time, international organizations are impacting on school systems from two different directions. Some of their activity strongly supports the agenda of globalization and market forces. Other programmes and organizations are working on a contrasting agenda of education as a humanitarian response. Governments, the international community and aid agencies are becoming even more active and organized than previously in their work on these issues. These organizations are also changing the landscape in ways which reflect particular policies and philosophies of international development and humanitarian relief. This means that school leaders may need to review their understanding of, and response to international educational needs, in order to navigate their way through a more complex political environment.

The range of responses to global educational issues involving disparities and adverse circumstances may include giving, volunteering and campaigning, and using international links for communicating and for learning about education development issues in different contexts.

Some major programmes such as World Bank–funded projects are resourced through loans (on favourable terms) rather than grants. In my work I have encountered resentment, on the part of individuals speaking for recipient governments, of the attitude of agencies delivering the implementation of these projects. They dislike what they see as patronizing and overbearing attitudes built into project design, and also the high proportion of project funding that goes back to Western-based consultancies and project management companies. 'It is only a loan, this is our own money', they emphasize to me. These mixed feelings on the part of recipients may be one of the reasons why ministries of education like to establish separate 'project implementation units' to deal with donor-supported programmes. Such structures give the visible project management that donors expect to see, while keeping the activity at arm's length from the day to day business of government and administration. This can exacerbate the lack of integration of donor-supported programmes into mainstream activity; the fall-out when short-term funded projects come to an end; and the passive perception that any development beyond the most basic operational maintenance activity must 'wait for a donor'.

In the case of school-to-school partnerships, the resources may take any combination of forms, including money, expertise, volunteering, information, the interests and energies of students, and the use of facilities. The flow of benefit is certainly not all one-way: well-resourced schools involved in international partnerships will often gain in two main ways. The curriculum (in the broadest sense) is likely to be enriched, and international links contribute also to the professional development of school staff. Present and evolving conditions are raising the potential of these school-to-school links in respect of their reach, the accuracy of the perceptions on which they are based, the level of interaction with the community surrounding each school and the effectiveness of the actions taken. This is mainly reflective of improved networking.

Space-making through networking

To elaborate the point above, and as noted in Chapter 2, headteachers manage certain kinds of spaces, and impact on or interact with other spaces. The headteacher manages the spaces they occupy, physically and mentally, as an individual human being, as a professional, as a person with values and commitments, and as a repository of their own knowledge, resources, energies and motivations. At the next level of spatial scale, headteachers manage a school, or perhaps a group of schools, embracing all of the formal and informal learning spaces and ambiences that make up the campus. Thirdly, they in their individual capacity, or the school in its institutional capacity, interact with a diverse range of spaces within communities: from the students' homes to community groups, to businesses which have links to the school, to other schools with which the school may have various kinds of partnership.

If one of the schools in the latter group is an international link, that is, a school in another country, it may be assumed that the headteacher of that school has an equivalent network of spaces with which they interact. The nature of that network may be different, but the idea is the same. When the two networks become joined through an international link, the range of potential linkages across the combined networks is multiplied. An important part of the energy and potential capacity of each part of the linked network is the students themselves. The overall effect of the combined network is the potential for considerable synergy. The movement of resources around the network does not have to be a zero sum gain, but instead could generate new resources and capacities in three ways. Where the partnership involves a flow of material resources from a high-cost to a low-cost environment, there is the benefit of greatly increased purchasing power. Secondly, insofar as international partnerships aimed at addressing educational problems have a developmental effect on the individuals involved, that increase in individual capacities means that the same number of people are able to achieve bigger impact. Thirdly, well-managed partnerships should be designed to achieve leverage by stimulating and co-opting other local sources of support. These multiplier effects give the school leaders of the future the potential, in an increasingly networked world, and acting through professional collaborations, to make a far bigger impact on global educational issues than in the past.

From charity to activism

Organizations which are constituted as 'charities' do a wide range of work: for example, from long-term research and development, to the teaching of degree courses. In this chapter, the word 'charity' is used in its popular and narrower sense, to describe acts of kindness and mercy to relieve acute suffering. That suffering may be by individuals or by large groups as in cases of natural disasters and emergencies. Of course 'charity' also includes ongoing support for 'good causes'. It is, however, in the nature of much charitable giving that it is a moral and emotional response to visible acute suffering. Words other than 'charity', such as political campaigning, social reform or activism, might more naturally come to mind to describe activity directed to dealing with underlying causes, structural change and sustainability.

Activism and charity are on the same spectrum but differ in their emphases. Activism tends to be less detached, more partisan, and more focused on addressing the causes of problems rather than merely the symptoms. Both may include similar processes such as volunteering and campaigning.

School leaders need to strike a balance in how their institutions respond to issues. Activist writers can imply a negative view of charity, but short-term practical assistance continues to be necessary. It is impossible to predict one's sentiments in extreme situations, but I suspect that if I were very hungry I would value a bag of rice more highly than a lorry-load of protest. Willingness to be concerned, to do something practical, to be generous with money and time when made aware of the acute suffering of other people, are entirely laudable dispositions which school leaders will wish to encourage among students, and, preferably, model in their own leadership behaviours.

The question for school leaders is not 'is activism relevant to school leadership?' since in reality encounters with activism of one kind or another are unavoidable. A more practical series of questions for school leaders is, 'How do I recognize and navigate the activist agendas being pursued in my context?' 'What kinds of activism should I permit and support within the life of the school I am leading?' and 'As a leading individual, to what forms and agendas of activism should I direct my personal authority and influence?'

In exploring these questions, it may be helpful to ask of any particular project:

- Does it offer a viable solution or merely fuel discontent by attracting attention to a problem?

- Will it become self-sustaining or does it perpetuate dependency?

- Does it promote divisiveness and confrontation, or community cohesion?

- Does it encourage people to think negatively or positively about their situations?

- If it forms part of an educational curriculum, does it aim to give learners a fair and balanced understanding of different viewpoints?

School leadership is a professional activity: this assertion provides a foundational perspective for the majority of people working in education. It is within the context of undertaking a professional role as an educator that school leaders choose their priorities and strategies for interacting with the educational opportunities around them. This would be a different book if it were written mainly for politicians and community activists. On the other hand, it is important to recognize that individuals bring with them into their work their own values, motivations and beliefs, including political beliefs. Sometimes these will have a significant bearing on the ends they pursue and the causes they support. In Wilkins (2011, Chapter 8) I argued that much educational research is positioned in relation to particular viewpoints and agendas, and explored the implications of this for school leaders who are keen to encourage practitioner research and to use published educational research. Here, by contrast, my focus is on the leadership role itself. It is important to recognize the politically positioned nature of many education initiatives pursued directly by governments, by other organizations with government backing and by international agencies, but it is equally important to recognize that similar positioning applies to the actions of individual school leaders.

De-coupling activism from its Marxist roots

A striking political positioning is also found in the literature of educational activism, some of which is written from a Marxist perspective which sees the world through the lenses of oppression and struggle. Writing from this viewpoint draws attention to the adverse circumstances of particular communities and groups, and then ascribes cause and solution in an argument that takes the following form: 'This group is suffering, *therefore* they are the victims of oppression, *therefore* they should rise up against their oppressor'. Worldwide, some eminent educators have supported that viewpoint. Many education leaders would, however, reject all three steps in this argument. First, not all suffering is due to oppression; secondly, people in adverse circumstances can exercise a range of roles much wider than those of victim and revolutionary; and thirdly, problems can be addressed through strategies that are collaborative rather than confrontational.

It would be a pity if those reasonable objections (which I share) to adopting a Marxist perspective cause education leaders to ignore or reject the substantive issues within that literature. Notwithstanding its fixations with 'oppression and struggle', it has something to say about the relationship between schools and their host cultures; and about curriculum development to make learning engaging for vulnerable, marginalized young people. Some of the processes of issue identification and problem-solving reported in the activist literature could be applied to more mainstream school development agendas. It is, nevertheless, essential to de-couple the stance and practice of activism from its Marxist roots. In the modern world, much education activism is applying problem-solving to humanitarian concerns in ways that could be consistent with a range of political motivations, including such capitalist aims as economic development, developing human capital and creating markets.

The activist curriculum also connects more generally with what Joel Spring (2009) identifies as a 'Progressive Education World Model', which values the following beliefs:

- Teacher professionalism and autonomy
- Learning based on students' interests and participation
- Active learning
- Protection of local languages
- Education for ensuring social justice
- Education for active participation in determining social and political change

(Spring 2009 p 126)

Spring (2009) traces the progressive education movement from John Dewey's lecture tour of China in 1921 and its influence on the educational thinking of Mao Zedong: 'Dewey and Mao Zedong's pedagogies both stressed linking theory with practice, and teaching students the social origins of knowledge' (Spring 2009 p 128). This line of thought in China influenced Latin American revolutionary movements, including especially the educational ideas of Fidel Castro, and exposure to these movements led Paulo Freire to develop the ideas published in 1968 in his seminal work *Pedagogy of the Oppressed* (Spring 2009 pp 127–130).

Activism occurs at every scale, including at classroom level, where it may be led by individual practitioners. Exploring the concept of 'leading learning for public value', Mongon and Leadbeater (2012) cite Bennington's definition of 'public value', as including:

- Ecological value: promoting sustainability

- Political value: democratic dialogue, public and civic engagement

- Economic value: generating enterprise and employment

- Social and cultural value: social capital, community cohesion, cultural identity, well-being.
                    (Bennington 2009, quoted in Mongon and Leadbeater 2012)

This statement offsets the usually dominant economic justification of schooling with three other important domains. This list is similar to the concerns addressed through activism within the curriculum, which typically focuses on advocacy, environmental sustainability, problem-solving, cultural enrichment or enterprise. The inclusion of community activism projects within the curriculum raises a range of potential concerns for school leaders. The educational value of the activity must be ensured. The school may have to manage accusations of engaging inappropriately in political campaigning. The processes of the project need to recognize and cater for a range of viewpoints among students (and their parents). On the other hand, such projects may offer a range of potential benefits. These include motivating and engaging students who are marginalized, giving them a stronger affiliation with school and with learning, and increasing their self-esteem. Projects may teach a range of skills including analysis, advocacy and teamwork. Experience of community activism may strengthen students' preparation for active citizenship and cultivate their disposition towards social responsibility.

Gutstein's critical mathematics

The extent to which these and other benefits are realized depends on the form the activism takes, especially in relation to the 'checklist' of questions I suggested earlier. This can be illustrated by what I regard as a bad example, because from the information reported it does not score highly against that checklist. This example of activism is Gutstein's (2012) account of a project he had led in Chicago, titled 'Using critical mathematics to understand the conditions of our lives'.

The setting of Gutstein's study is an area of Chicago troubled by a gang culture of youth-on-youth violence. Official policy aimed to close neighbourhood schools and replace them with charter or 'contract' schools, which are similar to charter schools. These 'turnaround' schools would have staff changes involving current staff in re-applying for positions, and changes to admissions which would alter their 'neighbourhood school' character. Gutstein (2012) recounts how the community resisted these changes, warning that the closure of neighbourhood schools would cause an increase (a 'spike') in youth violence. He does not acknowledge that perhaps the quality of education being provided was poor, that the 'territories' reinforced by the neighbourhood school system were part of the problem, and that, whether misguidedly or not, the new policy was intended to bring about school improvement. Instead, he declares a position:

> The sooner marginalised and excluded youths understand who their real enemy is, the sooner they will stop killing each other.
>
> (Gutstein 2012 p 183)

Who is 'the real enemy'?

> The enemy … [is] … systems of oppression: institutionalised and structural racism, economic exploitation, stratified labour and educational systems, gendered exclusion and sexism, environmental devastation, poverty and more – all of which are integral parts of the larger system of global capitalism. The righteous rage that many Chicago youth of colour bring into the classroom is based on their position at the bottom of US society.
>
> (Gutstein 2012 pp183–184)

The fact that many of them are illegal immigrants is portrayed simply as a further manifestation of oppression. Gutstein records that he and the mathematics department collectively decided to teach maths to a twelfth-grade class entirely through a study of the students' 'social reality'. This involved making up sums to show, for example, that the median income locally was insufficient to pay for housing; and that people who underpay mortgage payments by $90 every month for thirty years end up owing a lot of money and paying a lot of interest. Every example cited is equally negative. The students made a final presentation of what they had learnt. One is cited as saying:

> The reason why some people act so aggressively is not because that's how we are, but because that's how we are meant to be because of what's happening to us. So, like all the … shootings … it's just that that was led by something else
>
> (Gutstein 2012 p 191)

Gutstein portrays this as a laudable educational outcome, because the students came to realize 'who were their real enemies'. The unit of work as presented raises serious ethical considerations. Every example cited was negative, and seemed designed to make the students see themselves as victims, and to fuel their sense of grievance and anger. It offered neither constructive solutions, nor sense of responsibility. Surely examples could be found of households finding ways to cope with adversity, or of positive community role models, or of how the students might themselves have collaborated to help solve some of the community's problems?

Contrasting examples

A different example of a community activism project in the curriculum concerned Tar Creek, led by Rebecca Jim and reported by Celia Oyler (Oyler 2012). Tar Creek was a site in Oklahoma, USA, of about forty square miles, in an area still heavily populated by indigenous North Americans. The project involved some of the young people of this community who were often in trouble, and this was considered to arise partly from issues of identity: 'they don't know who they are' (Oyler 2012). These young people's grandparents used to fish in the creek, but it became heavily polluted. The area also contained abandoned mines, which had collapsed, generating sink holes. The tips from these mines emitted poisonous dust. The young people were enabled to lead a project to generate understanding of the issues, and to raise funds for environmental improvement. Care was taken to ensure that the project achieved a balanced understanding of issues and viewpoints (Oyler 2012).

At Ringstabekk School in Norway, a form of thematic learning is used (Bolstad 2012). The students work in a cross-curricular manner using methods such as project work, storyline and enterprise. The school is divided into large classes with team teaching, and the learning is organized into blocks of activity that are five or six weeks long. The students are involved with the teachers in planning the activity and they are part of a steering group for each theme (Bolstad 2012). The students are systematically trained in the project method as part of their preparation for later life. Each project is problem-orientated, product (i.e. outcome)-orientated, has collective leadership, and, significantly, includes high-quality subject teaching within the interdisciplinary approach. The projects include simulation exercises and enterprises. Topics (i.e. 'problems') cover a range of cultural, environmental and civic concerns. Outcomes include, for example, a film, an exhibition or a public performance.

Oyler's activist pedagogy

Celia Oyler (2012) researched projects involving community action as curriculum, of which the Tar Creek example above was one. Her introduction to these accounts frames them within positive educational purposes. 'School can prepare students to engage in authentic problem solving', involving understanding, analysis, and 'joining together with others to create solutions' (Oyler 2012 p 2).

Quoting Kirschner, Oyler draws the distinction between charity and activism: 'People enter the democratic fray in order to solve a problem that affects their lives or the lives of community members. In contrast, when social action is framed as charity or service, it is often apolitical and can reinforce a deficit view of the community' (Kirschner 2008, quoted in Oyler 2012).

Oyler was interested in finding out about advocacy projects focused on community improvement, involving some form of creative connection to other people. Plurality was important: plurality of stakeholders, viewpoints and issues in the substantive matter and plurality of opinions among the students working on the issue. Thus the projects would give students experience of 'taking up matters of the common good, ... collaboratively and co-operatively with others, ... designed to foster engaged civic agency rather than passivity or self-interest' (Oyler 2012 pp 3–4).

These criteria imply an agenda including balance and criticality, which is educational rather than merely political. This is confirmed in the questions Oyler used to frame her data analysis, which included how the students' activities were structured for learning; the role of 'public good' as motivator; and how students were able to engage with multiple viewpoints (Oyler 2012 p 8). In summary, Oyler offers the following as some principles of activist pedagogy:

- The teacher overtly values justice, equity and the common good

- The teacher designs instruction for student voice and decision-making

- The teacher helps students to situate problems, gain content knowledge and conceptual understanding

- The teacher makes room for multiple viewpoints

- The teacher enables students to learn skills of community organizing outreach and advocacy

- The teacher creates opportunities for students to reflect and to evaluate both process and outcomes. (Summarized from Oyler 2012)

These principles may be helpful in addressing some of the questions that arise for school leaders regarding community activism within the curriculum. How is the quality of the learning process and learning outcomes understood and evaluated? Does the involvement of students in community activism support or distract from their academic attainment? Often teachers involved will say that they see a positive impact although it is hard to prove. Where the activist project is intended to include or support subject teaching, it can be a complex task to design the subject specific elements in ways that will present the steps of subject conceptual development in the right order, at the right levels, to offer a coherent learning journey.

Teaching to agendas

Moving upwards in scale from projects within the curriculum is the notion of the whole school pursuing a mission which ties it to an activist agenda. In 2011 I visited the City Montessori School (CMS), Lucknow (www.cmseducation.org), to speak at a conference which the school was hosting. This claims to be the largest school in the world, with over 40,000 students, although what a visitor will see is a chain of schools under common management, spread across the city of Lucknow, on a similar model to many chains of independent schools in South Asia. A visitor will also find an institution which takes promotion of itself and its founder to an art form. Enormous screens, some facing the street, project a positive spin on the school's activity. Students appear to devote much time and energy to elaborate stage performances which provide footage. There is nothing wrong with this, of course, because most schools do this to some extent, and anything which inculcates pride in achievement among the students is likely to benefit their attitude to learning. The two distinctive features of the school's mission are a strongly multi-faith religious ethos, and a commitment to campaigning for world peace. The latter is built into the curriculum, for example giving students the real experience of international lobbying of prominent individuals, some of whom have had high-profile interactions with the school. It was not clear to what extent the many and complex issues getting in the way of world peace are examined, or students enabled to form their own views, but I have no reason to assume that they were not.

Laudable though these aims may be, and despite statements such as 'the children are asking world leaders to give them a peaceful future', this agenda is set by the proprietors rather than by the students, although their parents must be happy enough with it to choose the school for their children. How far should a school leader impose their own viewpoint on the organization they lead, and is it ethical to enrol children in their campaigns? Are the proprietors of CMS Lucknow, who are personally committed to the Baha'i religion, doing anything different in kind from the distinctive ethos offered by Roman Catholic schools in England? The principle, which is found in many cultures, that children are to be educated in accordance with their parents' wishes, may raise issues for some about the rights of the child, but practical alternatives to that principle are elusive.

An activist partnership for professional development: TAKE

In 2010 the Institute of Education was invited to enter a partnership, in the spirit of a joint venture (i.e. sharing the financial risks) with a new body which became TAKE (Trust for the Advancement of Knowledge and Education: www.take.pk). The leading policy entrepreneur has throughout been Taymur Mirza, an IOE alumnus and the founding headteacher of The International School, Karachi. TAKE was established as a separate charitable body in the summer of 2010 specifically to develop infrastructures for enabling IOE to support teachers' professional development in Pakistan, and, moreover, to do so through a 'capacity-building' partnership rather than a 'colonial' approach. Two key strategic decisions were agreed between IOE and TAKE: first, for financial necessity, to work in the first instance with the high-fee-charging independent school sector in order to develop and showcase practice which might then attract sponsorship for spreading to other sectors; secondly to commit to a long-term, step-by-step approach.

In November 2010 I spent a few days in Karachi to understand the context. Features of the Pakistani context included sparse local provision of quality continuing professional development (CPD) and no widespread tradition of serious investment in it, and also dynamic political circumstances and high levels of actual and planned donor country involvement in educational development, mainly directed to the government school sector. The school system is stratified: independent schools are popular and span a wide range of provision to cater for different levels of parental spending power; at the top level they are world-class. There is also a very low-fee philanthropic sector often working with children in areas of acute social need; and the government schools (i.e. free state education) which vary in effectiveness and are often regarded as the least desirable form of provision. Urdu is the medium of instruction in government schools and many independent schools, while elite schools are English medium. Recently, however, Punjab Province started a transition to English medium teaching of maths, science and ICT in the secondary phase in government schools, using teaching materials developed with the support of donor countries. Often international schools and elite independent schools will have Westernized approaches to professional development which are similar to English practice, while national lower-fee and government schools will be more variable with many relying on ultra-traditional styles of teaching and management.

I saw a range of schools, including some very-low-fee philanthropic schools provided by The Citizens' Foundation, one of which served the population of an illegal shanty settlement. I listened to the views of parents, teachers and headteachers; met a range of prominent individuals; and planned with TAKE the first steps towards provision. The outcome was a set of four short courses presented by IOE facilitators in March 2011: one each on teaching and assessment, and school leadership, in Karachi and in Lahore. These were successful in attracting participants, in achievement of learning objectives and in levels of satisfaction; they were also important for relationship building. While mainly in conventional interactive short course format, these events emphasized reflection and follow-up, and a significant number of participants subsequently sent in action plans of developments they were implementing connected with the courses.

Both partners (IOE and TAKE) wrestled with how best to build on this beginning. TAKE established a consultative forum called TAKE Advice involving a large group of education stakeholders, and we appointed a number of Karachi-based experts as IOE Associates. I returned to Karachi in November 2011 to do more planning, and to conduct a two-day workshop called 'Making it stick: embedding a learning culture into professional school life'. This included sessions on critical professional reading, professional writing, developing a coaching culture and developing professional learning communities. To begin to reach beyond the high-fee sector, the partners provided scholarships (i.e. free places) to enable a batch of delegates from the philanthropic sector to participate. To move on from the expectations surrounding 'visiting experts' I began the workshop not with a keynote, but by interviewing participants, enabling them to share the stories of the developments they were working on, through a multi-layered, analytical interview structure.

The workshop emphasized the aim of generating an ongoing network for professional learning, and set as the post-workshop task a piece of professional writing. One example was a paper produced by Kiran Asad Javed at The International School, reporting a small research project on teachers' perceptions of the professional growth arising from 'international exposure' associated with working with the curricula of the International Baccalaureate and Cambridge International Examinations.

A locally owned conference

This workshop confirmed the partners' intentions to commit to a twice-yearly three-day event, called TAKE Time Out, conceived as a conference rather than a course, designed to support professional networking, reflection and the sharing of practice. The first in this series took place in March 2012 and represented a breakthrough in a number of respects. It attracted sponsorship from the British Council, so the well-attended event embraced, in addition to the high-fee sector, not only the philanthropic sector but also some participants from government schools. Participants came from Bangladesh and Sri Lanka as well as from Pakistan. Much of the design and all of the arrangements were led from Pakistan rather than from England, with the two IOE personnel being visiting facilitators contributing to a locally owned event. The programme included two sessions led by Pakistani visiting speakers and two devoted to presentations of participants' papers. TAKE Time Out also included Executive Challenge tasks through which the participants worked in groups to find and present solutions to local priority issues which had been identified through the TAKE Advice forum.

Further conferences in this format took place in October 2012, March 2013 and October 2013, with the prospect that this will continue to grow into an effective and self-sustaining conference for reflective practitioners in

South Asia. An objective is to support the local generation of practitioner contributions to professional literature, and a locally produced journal is planned. The key point of this story is, however, the decision of Kiran Asad Javed, introduced above, to cascade a similar model of professional development, in Urdu, which is described below.

ILM Ka Safar

ILM Ka Safar is a twice-yearly teacher training programme provided in Karachi for teachers at underprivileged schools, for the affordable fee of 5 US Dollars which covers three days of intensive training, including meals. The training is provided on a voluntary basis by experienced teachers from privileged (high-fee) schools. At the first three-day course in December 2012, ninety-two teachers from ten schools attended. This course was on child development and effective teaching with limited resources. In June 2013, sixty teachers from twelve schools attended the course, which was on classroom management and teaching languages. The December 2013 course, on the assessment and motivation of students, enrolled 100 participants from fourteen schools.

'ILM' stands for 'Independent Learning Mentors'; 'ilm' is also an Urdu word meaning knowledge, and 'safar' is a journey. ILM Ka Safar was founded and is led by Kiran Asad Javed, a teacher of Economics at The International School, Karachi, which is the headquarters of the TAKE initiative described above. Having been an active participant in TAKE events, Kiran decided to reproduce an equivalent professional development experience for teachers who could not afford to pay for such provision. Kiran linked up with Dr Salima Ahmed, President of the Pakistan Federation of Business and Professional Women's Organisation (PFBPWO) to establish the scheme, which aimed to support quality education at grass roots level by giving professional development to teachers at underprivileged schools.

In addition to running ILM Ka Safar, and her 'day job' as a teacher, Kiran also lectures on a BSc (London School of Economics External Programme) course, and in some more of her 'spare' time, she is School Director of BPW Quality School, which is run by PFBPWO for 600 underprivileged students. She is an example of the energetic, entrepreneurial, philanthropically minded young professionals who are making a difference in Pakistan. This is what I mean when I write about international professional networking triggering the release of local energies and leverages.

Save the Children's global strategy

Webley (2012) describes Save the Children's 'Rewrite the Future' campaign, which aimed to increase access to education for three million children;

improve the quality of education for eight million children; demonstrate the protective role of education; and increase the financing of education for children in countries affected by conflict (Webley 2012 p 81). There are Save the Children organizations in twenty-nine countries, working in 120 countries, and with UNICEF it jointly leads the education cluster of aid agencies. Webley's study is an insider account of the strategic internal process which took place between 2003 and 2010 to pull the global organization together and give it a sharper strategic focus in order to make greater impact. She presents a good example of the shift from charity to activism within a major organization, and adopts an interesting definition of leadership:

> It is not enough...to develop a theory of change in terms of a vision and objectives. A leader – whether individual or institutional – must also be able to negotiate agreement between disparate institutions and their representatives, as well as to mobilise action.
>
> (Webley 2012 pp 71–72)

The transition to co-ordinated focus and impact undertaken by Save the Children has parallels in other organizations and also in relevant departments of donor governments, such as the UK's Department for International Development (DfID).

Global-scale activism

An example of an international organization working for education as a humanitarian response is INEE, the International Network for Education in Emergencies (www.ineesite.org/en/strategic-plan) INEE is composed of over 5,000 individuals working with a range of organizations in over 130 countries (INEE 2013). INEE's aim is that the 'provision of quality, safe and relevant education for all is strengthened in crisis and crisis-prone contexts through prevention, preparedness, response and recovery'. The introduction to INEE's Strategic Plan (2011–2013) provides a clear example of a shift from charity to activism:

> INEE has identified five key strategic directions, integrated throughout the plan, that articulate a new phase for INEE. The first of these, a shift from primarily a response mandate to consistently addressing prevention, preparedness and recovery as well, is the most salient, and reflects developments in humanitarian and development contexts.
>
> (INEE 2013)

Other elements of INEE's Strategic Plan illustrate the purposeful approach of an activist organization. It will enhance capacity and knowledge, by expanding the evidence base. INEE plans to influence policy-makers and other stakeholders; to increase visibility, awareness and resources; and to facilitate policy dialogue and policy development (INEE 2013).

A central plank in Brock's argument is that harmful disconnections exists between the formal institutions of the school system, and informal community-based learning, and the organizational responses to educational needs in contexts of extreme challenge or crisis (Brock 2011). It is noteworthy that the eight women and one man who make up INEE's Secretariat include, from their Internet profiles, only one person who has worked in formal education (not at leadership level): they are all career professionals in the aid and emergency industries. This is not a criticism, because the organizations that make up this network must operationalize their missions in whatever ways make most sense in their own organizational contexts. It may be that some of these organizations have arrangements to draw experienced headteachers into aspects of their work. Or it may be an example of how individual organizations pursue directions of development which have cumulative effects which were not intended and which may exacerbate wider problems.

Perhaps if the personnel involved in education as a humanitarian response included more people with experience of the leadership of schools and school systems, this would be an easy way to cut through some of the gulfs and barriers between these fields of activity. Equally, in the same way that the professional development opportunities for headteachers have included short secondments to industry (to enable them to see life in the 'real world'), so in the future it might be equally developmental to have some such short secondments to organizations working to enable education in challenging and emergency situations.

CHAPTER FIVE

Leading Communities as Educational Infrastructures

School leadership creates infrastructures for building capacity

Leading change includes impacting on educational problems and needs well beyond the leader's own institution. Context will determine what kind of infrastructural development will be relevant and achievable. In developed systems, where institutions are well established, infrastructural development may include changing the dynamics and functionality of networks, developing new organizational structures and business models, and new forms of data usage and communication. It may involve making spaces for new ideas and approaches within old-fashioned buildings and campuses. It may also include seeking a much more far-reaching, higher-leveraged return on the investment represented by the inherited structures.

In contexts which are both underdeveloped and sparsely populated, educational infrastructures may be almost non-existent. These are the contexts where the processes of map-making have impacted least, both on perceptions of place by their inhabitants, and on the physical manifestations of places. These 'regions of difficulty' (Fleure 1919), where there is the educational equivalent of subsistence farming, not only pose obvious challenges for twenty-first-century notions of school leadership, but also offer blank-sheet opportunities to design new infrastructures for newly understood purposes, without being fettered by a historical legacy. The question of what infrastructural developments are most helpful in specific and very different contexts is central to problem identification and problem-solving. Related questions are whether and to what extent reducing inequality and exclusion must be assumed to require the reduction of diversity in forms of educational provision, and to require standardized role distributions between formal educational institutions and the communities they serve. It might be that reviewing traditional assumptions on these matters is the way to break out of the impasse which sees the 'necessary' solutions as being increasingly unaffordable.

'Infrastructure' includes sites and buildings, organizational structures and communications. It also includes issues of access and interface: how and by whom these are used, and how they sit in relation to the other organs of civil society. Infrastructural development involves decisions about investment and resource deployment. In many parts of the world, achieving an adequate level of physical facilities – sites and buildings – continues to be a challenge and obstacle to school system development. Elsewhere the challenge is how to modernize existing facilities and/or to use them more effectively. Forms of organization are also changing, although the traditional institutional organization of schools remains remarkably enduring. 'Post-modernist' organizations have fluid shapes and boundaries, and the range of business models underpinning schools as organizations has also become more complex.

Transport to and between educational sites can be challenging. In the rural areas of Punjab Province, Pakistan, for example, there are on paper quite well developed arrangements for school support and supervision at district level, but in practice this is limited by shortages of functional motorcycles, and because the staff find it hard to buy petrol. The real infrastructural 'game-changer', however, is the impact of ICT on the range and forms of communication, both for educational administration and for teaching and learning. In Punjab, government schools are connected to an impressive performance data monitoring system. Notwithstanding difficulties visiting schools, provincial headquarters staff can see which teachers in a school are letting down the achievement of the half-termly targets.

It is possible now for a skilled educator, equipped with a laptop computer and occasional access to electricity and Internet, to engage in leading-edge teaching while sitting with pupils under trees. In some areas where almost every other form of modern infrastructure is missing, mobile phone usage is widespread. This has opened up possibilities for mobile phones to support both learning and school administration: for example, for reporting absences of students and staff.

'Building capacity' also has several meanings according to how the purposes of school systems are perceived, both at official level and by the individuals engaged with them. 'Capacity', that is to say, what people, individually and collectively, can do, how much of it they can do and to what effect, is a function of motivation; knowledge, skills and dispositions; and efficacy. The ends to which these are directed receive differing emphases between standpoints. Capacity to contribute to the generation of wealth is the dominant paradigm, while other perspectives emphasize cultural, social and political capacities. As in other areas of leadership, what school leaders are able to achieve in relation to building infrastructures reflects the range and nature of the forms of power at their disposal, and how they choose to use them.

Local communities

The discussion of space and place started in Chapter 2 is relevant to local communities. Robertson (2009) applies spatial lenses to two educational topics: grouping, tracking or streaming – an example of spatial stratification; and decentralization and the introduction of market forces, which is an example of spatial governance. Robertson uses Lefebvre's (1991) threefold distinctions between spatial practice, representations of space and spaces of representation, which she summarizes as, respectively, spaces as perceived (in the sense of seen objectively), conceived and lived. She combines these with David Harvey's different threefold distinction between absolute space, relative space and relational space (Harvey 2006, cited in Robertson 2009) to give a three-by-three matrix of nine cells.

Rigg (2007), also drawing on Lefebvre (1991), saw space becoming both network and process: both place and flow. Rigg considered that for Lefebvre, space is a product of social and political action: this space is not abstract but is both mental and material. All spaces have histories and are continually reconstituted by social and political actions (Rigg 2007 p 15). 'Spatial practice' is the activities and actions that structure everyday life, consisting of networks, flows, patterns and routes. Rigg suggests as an example the participation of individuals in community activities and projects. I understand 'spatial practice' as what is actually going on, regardless of what anyone intended, or what anyone thinks about it. 'Representations of space' refer to the spaces of planners, experts and analysts. Although this space can be measured it is essentially abstract because it is a construct of dominant knowledge. Rigg's examples include decentralization policies, and the policy of hukou in China that classifies people as rural or urban. 'Representations of space' usually seem to involve someone in authority classifying things and ascribing intended characteristics to them. The third category, 'representational space' is the space of everyday life and experience: the actual spaces people occupy, that planners and technocrats try to influence, which in Rigg's view might include 'spaces of resistance' (Rigg 2007 p 17). It is confusing that in Lefebvre's model the word 'representation' features in both of these categories: I understand 'representational space' as what spaces represent to those who occupy them – space as perceived and experienced.

Robertson's first worked example concerned the spatial stratification associated with grouping, tracking or streaming processes (Robertson 2009). Here, representations of space include student groupings, school types and designations; ascribed student characteristics including abilities and aptitudes;

official definitions of success and failure including through inspection reports; and the rationale of 'meritocracy'. Spaces of representation, 'as lived', might include perceptions of worth or worthlessness, belonging or alternatively, withdrawal, resistance and rebellion; aspirations and expectations including expectations of failure; and the rejection of schooling as 'un-cool'. Spatial practice might include particular curricula and pedagogies offered to students in different tracks, different levels of student development, the social and cultural mix found in each track, and school as a system reproducing social stratifications over time (Robertson 2009 p 12).

Robertson's second example is decentralization and market forces affecting the spatial governance of schooling. Here, representations of space feature discourses of choice, markets, self-management, entrepreneurialism and neoliberal politics; local visioning, sub-contracting, outsourcing and development planning; partnerships including public-private and third-sector, social capital and community expertise. Spaces of representation could include consumerism, anxieties about responsibility for one's future, different feelings of involvement, feelings of organizational responsibility without the necessary powers, performativity and surveillance. Spatial practice might include movements of responsibilities to new nodes, different geometries of governance, and competitiveness (Robertson 2009 p 13).

Using these worked examples as a stimulus, what might be some of the factors relevant to thinking about the local community (i.e. the combination of formal and informal institutions in a locality) as an infrastructure for learning?

Representations of space designate formal institutions as the sites where learning happens which is officially sanctioned, recognized and valid. Schools have, to varying extents, spaces equipped with physical resources to support learning, but access to these is both regulated, being almost entirely for registered students, and also heavily conditional on conformity to the school's methods. According to the type of school, the physical ambience of the school may convey privilege and a cultural ethos superior to home culture. Knowledge which comes from the community is represented as being of lower status than the formal curriculum. Informal learning which takes place in the home or in community organizations may be regarded as amateurish and of no real significance. If students do not make good progress with the school curriculum, a significant part of the responsibility for this is seen to rest on the student and their parents.

Spaces of representation will vary according to the degree of 'cultural fit' between the student and the school they attend. This will often reflect socio-economic status and the level of the parents' education; also the strength of parental aspiration to use the school system for their children's advancement. According to that level of fit, school spaces may be affirming, enriching and enjoyable; alternatively they may be hostile environments in which students and their families are made aware of their inadequacies. Pennac (2011) represented from personal experience the tribulations of school for students who do not find easy the forms of learning which schools value.

Spatial practice often includes various forms of underutilization. Specialized school facilities may be used for only a fraction of the day and year. The resources, knowledge and goodwill of the community are not fully drawn upon to support the learning process. Sometimes, young people may not achieve to the extent they might because of inadequacies in communication between home and school, and in connections between school learning and discretionary learning.

Brock's (2011) challenge as discussed in Chapter 1, the disjuncture between formal and informal learning, is much the same issue as the disjuncture between, in Lefebvre's terminology, representations of learning spaces, and representational learning spaces, that is, between learning spaces as planned and denoted, and learning spaces as actually experienced by those who use them. One way to lessen that disjuncture is if there is greater overlap between these two groups: those who do the denoting, and those who do the experiencing. The combination of greater school autonomy and more professionally assertive school leadership provides an opportunity to increase that connection.

The community's readiness to be connected will vary. Volansky (2006), looking at education leadership in Israel's pluralistic societies, found that solutions were linked to the devolution of decision-making to the local level. By contrast, in Indonesia, Parker and Raihani (2011) found that the policy of democratizing Indonesia through community participation in Islamic schooling had limited impact because parents were reluctant to get involved in the governance of madrasahs.

Devolution and capacity

A feature of context concerns the extent to which school systems practise centralized detailed operational management. This goes beyond the issue of 'school autonomy' as that term is understood in Anglo-Saxon countries, where centrally managed systems had never been complete. In the UK, in the decades before 'local management of schools' (the precursor of school autonomy) was introduced, state schools had in practice considerable freedom to manage their internal affairs. There was no prescribed curriculum. The state was not involved in the approval, printing and distribution of textbooks. Examination boards were at that period predominantly run by universities, independently of government. As school autonomy increased and Local Education Authorities lost operational functions and gained an increased emphasis on strategic leadership, this change was for most authorities a change of degree and emphasis rather than a fundamental change. There are some who say that had the English Local Education

Authorities been more energetic in embracing strategic governance, then perhaps we might still have rather more local democratic accountability for public education in England. That is not the point.

The point is that it is easy for Western commentators to underestimate the extent to which the apparent leadership capacity in some systems: Ministries and central agencies, regional or district offices – apparently well-staffed infrastructures – are in fact deployed on heavy burdens of basic operational administration. This may include the commissioning, production and distribution of textbooks; setting and administration of school examinations; detailed personnel management of teaching staff; liaison with homes and families such as distributing vouchers for early education; the supply and distribution of school furniture, and functions such as organising the means for district level staff to travel to the schools they are supposed to be supporting. The construction, maintenance and funding of schools may also be major operational undertakings in some systems. In these contexts, an apparently well-staffed system may have very little developed strategic leadership capability.

Agency and livelihoods

Rigg (2007) drew attention to the distinction between agency-oriented perspectives, which emphasize the degree to which individuals have control over their lives, and structurally oriented perspectives which emphasize the constraints on people's actions arising from contextual ('structural') factors such as their location, social status, ethnicity, gender and limited freedom. Rigg (2007) observed that within geographical analyses, structurally oriented approaches shifted their focus on environmental factors to a focus on political factors during the twentieth century.

Rigg (2007) saw the growth of interest in 'livelihoods' as a means to reconcile debate between what I might summarize as the victimhood of structure and the personal responsibility of agency. Thus a focus on livelihoods, as expanded below, resonates with the (non-Marxist) activist agendas advocated in Chapter 4. Livelihoods are the assets, access and activities that together determine how an individual or household gain a living. Sustainable livelihoods cope with and recover from stresses and shocks.

The aim of understanding livelihoods through a focus on people and localities has influenced approaches to several fields, as Rigg (2007 p 29) summarized. In research, it is reflected in participatory methods; in politics, in decentralization and attempts to empower communities; in economics, in community management of resources; and in epistemology, in accepting local communities as sources of knowledge. The core elements of sustainable livelihoods analysis are:

A focus on people and communities rather than on structures and national context; a concern with seeing livelihoods in holistic terms crossing sectors, spaces, actors and institutions; and a commitment to identifying the salient macro-micro linkages.

(Rigg 2007 p 32)

The UK's Department for International Development produced a model of sustainable livelihoods (DFID 1999) which defined livelihood outcomes as including more income, increased well-being, reduced vulnerability, improved food security and more sustainable use of resources. Livelihood assets are made up of forms of capital, including financial, human, natural, material and social. These assets are brought into a relationship of access to and influence upon, and influence by, a series of 'transforming structures and processes' which may include laws, policies, culture and institutions, the latter including levels of government, and the private sector. This set of factors affect both the livelihood strategies that individuals adopt in pursuit of their livelihood outcomes, and the 'vulnerability context' factors which might include, for example, shocks, trends and seasonality (DFID 1999).

While this model was clearly designed with developing countries in mind, with small modifications, such as replacing 'food security' with 'professional job satisfaction' in livelihood outcomes, and 'seasonality' with 'inspection' in vulnerability context, it might equally apply to how headteachers in England earn their livelihood. This is another illustration of how professional educators engaged in supporting community-based learning in widely different global contexts can talk a common language about their work when they are connected to each other through international professional networks.

School and society

Both of education's trajectories: as commercial commodification, and as humanitarian response, are encouraged by donor agencies and they do not have to be mutually exclusive. In the longer term, education leaders will need to explore how the capacity and infrastructure developed through the commercial provision of education can also be used to assist education's humanitarian function.

Many countries are experiencing a changing balance between the three legs on which school systems rest: education as a function of civil society, that is, as an extension of family and community life; education as a universal public service provided by governments on the basis of need; and education as a commodity provided in accordance with market forces. In some Western countries, the public service model has been dominant for a long time; marketization has grown but more in rhetoric than reality; and there have been lukewarm, tokenistic gestures towards restoring ownership of education to families and communities. In some developing countries, family and community-based education continues to be very significant; public service provision struggles, falls well short of universality and looks increasingly unaffordable; and the private sector is increasing dramatically. The interrelationship of state and private sectors in education has become and will continue to become more complex. This advance is not always necessarily accompanied by proportionate extensions of market choice, nor by a procurement 'client side' developing in sophistication.

The local community is part of the infrastructure of schooling. In the 'developing country' example above, three kinds of resources, networks and efficacies will be evident. Families will be collaborating with traditional self-help: 'the whole village educating the child'; they may be users, and potentially proactive partners, of state-provided schools; and they may be buyers of various forms of private schooling, including very low-fee community-based provision. The way in which these choices are exercised, and roles played, impacts on livelihoods. The same factors apply in fully developed mature school systems, but may be less obvious, and uneven, with many parents happy to pass responsibility for their children's schooling to the state.

For a century, some school system leaders have seen the march of history proceeding towards universal provision of education by state school systems. From that perspective, home education and private schools are enemies to be eradicated. Now, a different perspective is needed, in which school leaders and school system leaders ask themselves how, in their role as senior professional educators, they can best support and enhance the quality of learning in all of these settings, and strengthen the coherence between them.

The history of school institutions makes a strong connection between 'school' as a community of learners, and 'school' as the site and buildings which house that community, to the point where in popular usage, they mean the same thing. When looking strategically at infrastructures, it is necessary to de-couple these concepts. There are places, such as in rural Yemen, where state schools function without any school buildings. It is more important to get people engaged in worthwhile learning than to get them sitting in a certain type of building. Similarly, where school buildings exist or are to be developed, there is a case on the grounds both of economy and coherence, for those facilities to support both the formal school organization and learning initiated and owned by the community.

Perceived purposes of schools and schooling

Political rhetoric, and actual policy decisions (across a broad field of government policy) imply purposes for the school system and its contribution to society. These rarely focus on the intrinsic value of education. Generally they foreground its instrumental purposes. Sometimes these assumptions invite challenge because they are imbalanced; sometimes because they are contradictory; and sometimes perhaps because they are so entirely conventional.

In England, politicians speak as if they regard schools as a useful tool to serve the needs of different areas of policy. So, for education ministers, schools are the tool for producing workers who can compete in a global economy. For the Home Office, they are a tool supporting law and order: for reporting suspected illegal immigrants, helping to prosecute parents and as a way of fighting crime and anti-social behaviour, maintaining a kind of vigilante responsibility for their students' conduct outside school hours. Some sections of government want schools to be driven by market forces, competing against each other for the most desirable 'consumers'. Other sections of government want schools to be an extension of social services, supporting the health and welfare of the community. This aim reached its peak, in theory if not actually in practice, in policies for 'full service schools' which were to have provided extensive community services and facilities on their campuses, encouraged by the New Labour government (1997–2010) but abandoned subsequently.

That schools seem required to deal with expectations that are not all compatible will surprise no one and is unlikely to change. Just as individuals balance competing demands and obligations in their lives, so do institutions, sectors of the economy and public services. Negotiating the right balances for specific contexts is part of leadership. The model introduced in Chapter 6 for analysing problems can be used to understand the dynamics of these competing pressures. It is necessary to look below the sound bites. It is natural that educational institutions will struggle to keep up in contemporary harmony with the changing needs and demands of their context. That must be distinguished from the entirely manufactured miss-matches between school and society that are 'stoked up' by political rhetoric, which are actually attempts to change what is valued, while pretending to be 'necessary' responses to changes in the environmental context.

Education for human capital

The economic justification for investing in education, especially the concept of human capital, is dominant. Woodhall (1997) summarized how the concept of human capital had dominated the economics of education since the 1960s. At its core is the notion that 'human beings invest in themselves, by means of education...which raises their future income' (Woodhall 1997 p 219). Attempts to measure the rate of return have been controversial. The rate of return on the investment, and its cost-benefits, apply differently and separately to individuals and to society. To some extent in some situations, educational accreditations serve as a convenient screening device, as a proxy-measure of innate ability, and to that extent it is not correct to attribute to education the full cause of the increased earnings that correlate with such accreditations. Overall, that argument is weak, because the big picture is one showing a correlation between skills acquisition and improved earnings (Woodhall 1997).

Woodhall's reference to people 'investing in themselves' perhaps does not sufficiently differentiate the systemic perspective associated with human capital theory from the notion of education as a consumer product, which is dealt with below. Spring (2009) sees education for human capital as being popular with national elites, and being essentially concerned with educating workers for competition in the global economy. Spring (2009) criticizes this perspective for its emphasis on educating for acceptance and compliance, and failing to educate for active citizenship of the kind that would assist societal reform.

Woodhall (1997) cited the findings of a study of forty-four countries by Psacharopoulos (1981) which had shown four overall patterns:

- Primary education yields the highest return on investment.

- Private returns exceed social returns, especially in relation to investment in education at university level.

- All rates of return exceed the normal yardsticks for justifying capital investment.

- Less developed countries get relatively higher returns on investment in education.

(Psacharopoulos 1981, cited in Woodhall 1997)

Spring (2009) cites and adapts Anderson-Levitt (2003) to summarize the education policies associated with the human capital perspective as including the following: standardized curriculum, mandated textbooks and scripted lessons; standardized testing of students and evaluation of teaching based on the outcomes of those tests; and the teaching of world languages, especially English (Spring 2009 p 16).

The relationship between the investment made in the pursuit of these policies, and the economic return achieved, is complex and highly problematical, largely because of the number of uncontrollable variables. This does not stop experts from making confident predictions.

Andreas Schleicher is Deputy Director of Education and Special Adviser to the Secretary General on education policy at the Organisation for Economic Cooperation and Development (OECD). He is responsible for the Programme for International Student Assessment (PISA). Writing in TES on 16 November 2012, Schleicher (2012a) claimed to be able to put a cost on the failure of the school system in the UK to learn from other countries which have been more successful in the PISA league tables. He estimated that the generation born in UK in 2012 is likely to lose £4.5 trillion in economic output over their lifetimes because of this factor.

He cited the examples of South Korea, Poland and Germany as countries where school performance has moved up the league table: reducing the variability between schools and lessening the impact of social background on student attainment, whereas in the UK:

> expenditure per student has increased by 68 per cent over the past decade and yet the PISA results have remained flat. More generally, spending per student explains less than a fifth of the performance differences between countries. The image of a world divided neatly into rich, well-educated countries and poor, badly-educated countries is out of date.
>
> (Schleicher 2012a p 44)

I agree with the last comment, but not with the calculation that preceded it. So many factors affect what will happen to a country's economy and what a person will do with their life. There are plenty of people who did not shine at school who make wealth. It is not credible to make a precise projection of economic output for the next seventy years on the basis of PISA results, especially as Schleicher's projection relates not to the students who took the tests, but to the cohort of babies born that year. Yet economic justifications for investment in education are characterized by such assumptions.

Education as technology

A theme in school leadership literature, and in some policy debate, treats the school system as a 'technology' which has become outdated. It is a matter of fact that in many respects the fundamental design features of the school system have changed little from those of the nineteenth-century schoolhouse. There is a line of argument which takes the following form. A relevant comparison is between the nineteenth-century schoolhouse and the factories of the same period. In most industries, the factories have been replaced by completely new ways of doing things, through the development and application of new technologies. Schools are outdated because they have not gone through the same kind of metamorphosis, but they could do so because of the potential of ICT as a learning tool.

Projects with names such as 'Schools of (or 'for') the Future' tend to incline towards this view, although their reality may be somewhat more incremental. Looking back a decade or so provides a useful perspective on such developments. The project of that name introduced in the State of Victoria, Australia, in the early 1990s, described by Caldwell and Hayward (1998), certainly sought to maximize the utilization of new technology, although the thrust of the reform also involved a high level of delegation to schools, many school closures and staff cuts, an imposed curriculum and a strong framework of school accountability to the State. Supposedly strong accountability to the community was represented by an annual opportunity to attend a meeting at school at which questions could be asked about the school's (already finalized) annual report to the state. Townsend (1997) considered this project one of the 'sharp transformations' that occur in society only once every few centuries. It is difficult to see why. By investing in an educational satellite TV channel, giving schools access to the Internet, providing computers and laptops for teachers, and professional development in ICT, Victoria may possibly have been a few years ahead of the global pack, but this was incremental modernization, not transformation.

Caldwell (1997a) examined the 'megatrends' in school education and considered that these primarily concerned the increased application of technology, changes in building design and school workforce remodelling. He quoted D. Hargreaves' (1994) comparison of schools to nineteenth-century factories and his suggestion that they should change to be more like hospitals. Hargreaves appeared to believe that factories had largely disappeared, that hospitals had been transformed, and that schools had, by comparison, stayed largely the same. This is a viewpoint that invited challenge at the time, and certainly in retrospect, and even Caldwell noted that 'not all will warm to Hargreaves' image of the school as a hospital' (p 251).

These predictions of the school of the future assumed schooling to be primarily a 'technology'. Caldwell noted that the trends he projected would require changes in the role of parents and communities but appeared to see these as external to the school's business. He identified as 'unresolved issues' the governance of education, and how schools are funded (and left them unresolved). By implication, the effect of these megatrends would leave in the hands of the providers of education (i.e. government officials, headteachers and, perhaps, teachers) the job of deciding what counts as 'a good education'. The question must be asked, 'Technology for what?' Schooling might be seen as the 'technology' for developing mainly vocational skills to produce a competitive workforce. Or it might be seen as the 'technology' for helping families to socialize children and young people into adult roles within the community. These perspectives carry contrasting implications for curriculum, learning processes and governance.

Whitty (2002) noted the view that high-tech developments such as the Edison Project will diminish the physical aspect of going to school, through new methods of study which will also bring far more egalitarian relationships between students and their teachers. Whitty observed that on the latter point, the evidence in Britain was to the contrary: often, schools at the leading edge had become more formal and more authoritarian than they used to be, in their pursuit of a favourable public image.

Education as a commodity

Another way of looking at education is to see it as a consumer product. This viewpoint came to prominence in England in the 1980s with the application of 'market forces' to education by the Thatcher government, and by similarly neoliberal governments elsewhere. In England that thinking has been continued by all subsequent governments, although the New Labour government of 1997–2010 also had a parallel set of contradictory policies designed to mitigate its worst effects.

In the context of the UK this viewpoint has, to date, been less relevant in practice than in political symbolism. The highly regulated provision of a universal state system of compulsory education does not display any of the essential features of a real 'market'. State schools cannot decide whether, where and on what scale they will operate, nor can they develop different products at different prices. Parents' entitlement to 'express a preference' on two occasions in their child's life hardly amounts to any real capacity to 'shop around'.

In the UK, the policies pursued in the name of promoting market forces made life significantly harder for schools serving localities of socio-economic disadvantage. Whereas public spending and human resource deployment conventionally reflected different levels of need, a contrary policy became evident during the 1980s. Schools facing the greatest problems were disadvantaged financially through loss of pupil numbers, and by the effects of this on the recruitment of able staff, while schools which were already successful and faced few problems were 'rewarded' by becoming magnets for parents who cared most about their children's education, and through ability to attract and appoint the most able staff. Policies to reward schools financially for developing 'specialisms' (supposedly to increase 'choice'), in the main, merely widened the disparities between schools which largely reflected the socio-economic profile of their pupil intakes. The current UK coalition government's introduction of the 'pupil premium' as an element within additional funding for schools which is linked to specific socially disadvantaged children, has significantly ameliorated the previous fall-out from the emphasis on market forces.

Proponents of market forces in education will argue, quite reasonably, that the notion has never been properly tested in developed systems such as the UK, as this would require the wholesale deregulation of schooling: the privatization of provision, the freedom of schools to offer widely differing curricula, and to charge differential fees. No British government in the foreseeable future would do that because of the loss of control it would involve.

The position is different in countries whose school systems are still developing, where there is in effect almost a pincer movement between two quite separate drivers of the commodification of education. Top-down, some businesses provide for-profit schools while others have service provision contracts with governments. Bottom-up, there is public demand for low-fee, community-based independent schools. Together these factors make private-sector education in many countries much more significant than it is in the UK.

William Stewart, writing in TES, reported on the Global Education and Skills Forum held in Dubai, at which governments had acknowledged their dependence on the private sector (Stewart 2013a). Stewart noted that in 2000, all 193 UN nations pledged to achieve universal primary education by 2015, but a UN progress report published in 2010 had reported that although the primary school enrolment rate had risen from 82 per cent to 90 per cent since 1999, a closer look at the data revealed that

> nearly all of this growth occurred between 1999 and 2004, and that progress in reducing the number of out-of-school children slowed considerably after 2004.
>
> (Stewart 2013a, p 25)

The Forum in Dubai recorded that many governments lack the means to provide schooling for everyone, and accepted that the private sector should fill the gap. The article cites an example in Accra, Ghana, where in the Agbogbloshie slum, Queensland School provides low cost private education for four- to eleven-year-olds. It reported:

> The IDP Foundation's research shows that the private school sector in West Africa grew by 26% between 2006 and 2009, by which time 6000 low-cost institutions were open. Similar schools exist to serve poor communities in Pakistan, Nigeria, Kenya and India, where up to 70% of children in Delhi attend them.

It also quoted Michael Barber (who has worked extensively in Pakistan):

> So many poor parents have voted with their feet that it is no longer possible to solve the problem of universal primary education without taking the low cost private sector into account.
>
> (Stewart 2013a p 25)

Meanwhile Uganda is actively developing public private partnerships (PPP), and Uganda's minister of finance is quoted as saying:

> Private providers are playing an increasingly important role in education in Uganda. Education remains a largely public good but high quality education requires innovative programmes and initiatives in addition to public resources. This is where the private sector comes in with its innate agility and innovative thinking.
>
> (Stewart 2013a p 26)

Total global education spending is expected to rise from £2.9 trillion in 2012 to £4.1 trillion in 2017, according to a market analysis from US firm GSV Edu. Within this, the for-profit sector is expected to more than double from £379.8 billion in 2012 to £838.9 billion in 2017. As well as spending on education by individual consumers, there is a growing market in selling education services to governments, such as in Abu Dhabi and Kazakhstan. Typically these cover contracts for teacher training, curriculum and assessment (Stewart 2013a).

For the rich, there is a global market in purchasing elite school education. Writing in *The Times (Times 2 Section)*, Whitworth (2013) reported on organized tours that bring wealthy Chinese parents to Britain to choose public schools (i.e. elite, long-established private schools) in which to enrol their children. The article reports that there are 25,000 international students in British private schools, whose parents live abroad, and of these, there are 4,000 students from mainland China making them the second largest group after students from Hong Kong (Whitworth 2013). Parents are quoted as saying:

> The Chinese system is too formalised, too narrow in its perspective. The British system offers independent learning and leadership skills, creativity and problem-solving, and public speaking.
>
> We have a lot of homework and tests from 3 years old to 23. It is very stressful. We want him to go round the world and learn, not just in China.
>
> Politically the environment in China is not so good. So I send the children to a well-developed country to open their eyes to the world.
>
> The standard of British teaching is really brilliant and hard to find elsewhere. The children are well educated but in a fun way. In China it is more strict because there are too many people ... I want my son to receive a rounded education ... I would like to find a school that encourages the children to get involved in more activities.
>
> (Whitworth 2013 pp 2–3)

The examples given above show that school education is a market commodity, although of course it must be other things as well. The important point is that communities, and entrepreneurs within communities, show themselves to be capable of getting on with finding their own solutions to shortages of suitable education. Clearly, in their global professional networking, British teachers will encounter a dynamic between the private and state sectors of education which is different from that in the UK.

Education as an aspect of civil society

The idea, mentioned earlier, that the correct 'technological' comparison for schools is with nineteenth-century factories or with modern large scale industrial processes is highly questionable. School development in the nineteenth century was significant because of population growth and migration from rural to urban areas. School building took place on a large scale as part of urban infrastructure, and most nineteenth-century urban schoolhouses were integrated into the residential neighbourhoods constructed at the same time. The massive expansion of state schooling in Britain between 1870 (when government adopted the aim of universal provision) and 1902 (when school attendance was made compulsory) used concepts of 'school' that were already well established. The rationale for the expansion of schooling at that period was social and economic, and was not occasioned by any notable leap forward in the 'technology' of teaching and learning.

While technological change has transformed some sectors of the economy, it has not fundamentally affected others. Market stallholders, hairdressers, orchestral musicians, painters, actors, carers, caterers, hoteliers, athletes, courtroom lawyers and judges, and MPs debating in the House of Commons, all continue to ply their trades in essence much as they might have done in ancient times. Perhaps schooling is better compared with these more people-focused sectors of the economy than with industrial processes.

One of the functions performed by schools is an extension of the function of parents: supporting parents in the upbringing and education of their children. The law of England still requires that subject to certain provisos, children are to be educated in accordance with their parents' wishes. Governments appear to believe, in their apparent cavalier disregard for this law, that what all parents really want is education reflecting the latest political fixations. The common law status of teachers as being *in loco parentis* also encapsulates this function of schooling. Some schools developed as a kind of outsourcing of the aspects of parenting that might otherwise have been delegated to nanny and governess. This quasi-parental function is inevitably most evident in early years settings, where education is combined with care, where parental involvement is encouraged, and where education, social services and health professionals increasingly work together to support parents in bringing up their children. That was the rationale for the previous UK government's development and planned expansion of the Surestart programme.

The basics of being a parent have not changed much over time. Just as birds have not moved on from the technology of nest-building, the kinds of support that infants need from their parents or parent-substitutes have continued over the centuries. In their role as part-time parent-substitutes, schools are in the business of bringing up children, introducing them to the workings and norms of society, supporting them in coping with life and enabling them to realize their potential. This very personal, caring, human aspect of schooling is understated by those whose aim is the technological re-engineering of the school system.

Early years education and childcare typically takes place very close to the child's home: it tends to be small scale and local. With the youngest children, parents' choices of which provider to use, and whether and for how long to leave their children there, may often reflect their judgements about whether the provision 'feels right', and their degree of affinity with the characters and attitudes of the staff. This sense of ownership of provision which is local and is genuinely responsive to parents' wishes declines as children grow older. That may be one of the reasons why interest in home schooling, and collaborative developments based on the model of home schooling, appears to be expanding.

Views of the school of the future which emphasize the acquisition of (largely vocational) skills through e-learning underestimate the importance of school as a place for social interaction, and leave a question mark over how the custodial and 'parenting' functions of schooling would be carried out.

In another chapter of the book quoted earlier, Caldwell (1997b) reviewed other, contrasting views of the future of schooling, notably those of Drucker. The key issues for Drucker arose from the rise of knowledge as a resource and as the principal factor of production in the modern economy:

> As knowledge becomes the source of post-capitalist society, the social position of the school as 'producer' and 'distributive channel' of knowledge, and its monopoly, are both bound to be challenged.
>
> (Drucker 1993)

Drucker (1995) contended that

- We must redefine what it means to be an 'educated person'.

- We must resist sterile credentialism, an overvaluing of immediately usable knowledge and an underrating of fundamentals, and wisdom itself.

- Schools lie at society's centre in a context where other social structures have weakened.

Nearly twenty years later, these still seem to be topical concerns. Drucker's first two contentions reflect the fact that as the education of a child moves further away from the heart of the family, the state and its agencies increasingly determine the nature and purpose of education. That is natural enough in a modern nation state, but governments' views of the purposes of education can appear somewhat muddled.

The means that schools use to achieve individual and social development have changed over the years and centuries. Modern education in mature systems treats children with care, respect and dignity, in contrast to the intimidation and physical violence that typified 'education' in previous ages. A trend has been a shift from transmitting information to developing learning and investigative skills. Concerns for developing emotional intelligence, thinking skills and for differentiating activity to take account of different learning styles are examples of how schooling moves forward. The use of formative assessment combined with individual target setting has become a major means for supporting the achievement of each individual. Schools have developed greatly in their approaches to continuing professional development, and in their cultivation of a whole-school culture of learning.

The basic 'technology' of schoolhouses with classrooms in which lessons are conducted by teachers may be centuries old, but, in mature systems, within those classrooms, revolutions have been taking place in the educational experiences offered to children.

McKenzie (2001) questioned whether the weight and volume of knowledge and skills that the majority of the school population are expected to acquire has become unreasonable, needlessly branding people as failures. Needlessly, because she also questioned whether that kind of education will benefit the economy in the ways supposed. She wondered whether social cohesion might be better supported by education aiming to develop wider intellectual and creative capacities. One of McKenzie's scenarios for education is more emphasis on reflexive knowledge:

> It is simply not possible, or humane, to insist that all students internalise the mass of information available today...Looking afresh at what we mean by 'knowledge'... means encouraging an opening of minds through education so that individuals can appreciate the ephemeral nature of knowledge and engage in genuine creativity.
>
> (McKenzie 2001 p 315)

This kind of learning requires personal interaction, and sensitive guidance and stimulation; it requires teachers who know their students very well. While students may access information and some technical skills through fleeting electronic interactions, or impersonal e-learning materials, their *education* requires sustained relationships within a learning community.

Lawton and Gordon (2002) illuminated the tensions and inconsistencies within official systems and policies:

> One important method...is 'unmasking', that is, exposing the contradictions between the public goals, values and mission statements of institutions and what happens in reality. For example, it is claimed that markets are 'free' when they are really manipulated or rigged; or it is claimed that bureaucracies operate 'rationally' when their real practices are often lacking in reason and fairness, frequently disobeying their own rules.
>
> (Lawton and Gordon 2002 p 230)

Lawton and Gordon suggested asking, 'Whose interests are served by this?' They posed as supplementaries the questions identified by Habermas (1976) as expressing the 'legitimation crisis': 'Why accept this authority?' 'Why bother to participate?' and 'Who am I, where do I belong?'

I can understand why some students and their parents, and some teachers, would ask these questions of the education service, if technicist thinking were to take schools too far away from their traditional role within society. In addition to the home-schooling movement, mentioned earlier, there are localities in some English cities where some sectors of the community, including particular ethnic or religious communities, no longer believe that the local state schools are capable of educating their children in accordance with their parental wishes. The 'Saturday School' movement has been one response to this lack of a sense of ownership of schools by their communities. Recent policies open the door to the establishment of new, small schools by groups of parents. For example 'Free Schools' are similar to certain of the schools created by the Charter Schools movement in the USA. In Britain the result could be an increase in segregated schooling in inner cities, motivated by a desire to reclaim schooling as an extension of family and community.

The problem with the more extreme technological projections of 'schools of the future' is that they either portray 'modernisation' as an end in its own right, or assume a narrow purpose such as imparting skills required, short-term, in certain kinds of workplaces. If a consensus were to be reached for a broader and more realistic understanding of the purpose of schooling within society, then 'blue skies' thinking about the structure and form of the school system might produce ideas fitter for purpose.

Local support for formal and informal learning

What are the implications of different views of schooling for the kind of local infrastructure needed? The view that the processes of learning supported by schools could or should be 're-engineered' technologically implies a step towards 'de-schooling', at least partially shedding schools' custodial role. Proponents of this scenario would probably agree that in the first instance it would have most to offer to students age 14 plus rather than to children at earlier stages. I have talked with able and visionary headteachers who advocate this development, not because they especially wish to shed their custodial responsibility, but in order to design education around modern knowledge of the learning process. Education which is individualized, largely community based, and in which the school acts as a resource centre and meeting place, and as a base for a team of experts in learning (rather than in subjects) might be the twenty-first century's manifestation of the traditional notion that 'it takes the whole village to educate a child'.

If schools were to develop in a direction which returned them more towards being an extension of the family, this would require a different kind of local infrastructure, providing space and opportunity for the development of much more diverse and responsive forms of education to meet parents' wishes. If schooling continues to become more like a consumer product, the local infrastructure would need to support some sectors of the community to become effective and assertive consumers, while also stimulating the supply side to offer suitable choices. In each of these scenarios, the question, 'What would counts as a good, relevant, worthwhile education?' needs to be examined afresh, and in ways that support a stronger sense of ownership of schools by the communities they serve.

CHAPTER SIX

Innovation within Spatial Power Dynamics

Understanding innovation within contexts

Current international developments in education represent a mix of forward- and backward-looking stances driving educational change. Radical educational thinking is limited by the conservatism of parents, often including a predominant interest in test scores and exam passes, and by risk-averse governments. Parents, the media and some governments also love retrospective definitions of what is a 'good school', in which 'traditional' equals 'better'. On the other hand, some of the new private-sector providers of schools, philanthropic agencies, and activist individuals may be more ready to experiment with truly innovative schooling.

Most innovation is driven by the desire to solve problems that are not being addressed by conventional methods, so addressing the problem involves trying out new solutions. In this case, the problem is the starting point, and the solution as yet unknown. Some innovations, especially those involving the development and application of new technologies, may take the form of solutions looking for problems. Technology opens up new possibilities for doing things differently, and the process of innovation is in the development of applications for use in situations where the new way will be better. In this case, the solution is the starting point, and the extent of application as yet unknown, but worthwhile innovations of this latter kind can still be seen as problem-solving, even if the existence and nature of the 'problem' only become clear at the point when a better approach becomes available. Changing the names and governance arrangements of schools, an 'innovation' beloved of UK governments, may also be seen by some as a solution in search of a problem.

The trend towards internationalization of education is heightening the tensions that already exist in many systems between national prescription, often for the purposes of driving improvements in standards, and the acceptance of diversity to meet the diverse needs of particular local communities. These tensions play out in relation to regional differences within countries, and differences between urban and rural education, and between state and independent sectors. At whatever level a leader of schools or school systems may be working, and in whatever sector, it is often an open question how much room they are permitted within which to innovate. This will reflect how much subsidiarity is allowed by the structure of decision-making; and how much confidence the leader, their associates and local community have to push back boundaries and take possession of spaces. Innovation can also come top-down. While many governments are cautious and traditionally minded, some are prepared through the unilateral exercise of power to impose dramatic innovations on their school systems. Of those that do so, some are markedly more successful than others, reflecting differing levels of competence in managing change.

Innovation is necessary. It is also controversial because it applies untried experimental methods to children's once-only opportunities. The rationale for innovation is important. There is a blurred line between the genuinely visionary leader blazing a worthwhile new path, and the individual in a position of power who imposes their own pet whims and vanity projects on others. Then there is the confusing presence of the larger sector of leaders whose egos require that they label their work as innovative when it is not.

The word 'innovation' usually has positive connotations, hence its application to developments that are neither particularly original nor even necessarily beneficial, so it will be helpful to work towards a concept of worthwhile, responsible innovation.

Innovation and power

Jensen et al. (2012), in their examination of successful educational innovation in South East Asia, use the notion of 'push' and 'pull' factors. The 'push' factors propel, whereas 'pull' factors compel. Examples of 'push' are curriculum reform, and teacher development and support. Examples of 'pull' are accountability and testing. These authors maintain that the distinction between 'push' and 'pull' is not the same as between 'top down' and 'bottom up', because they may work horizontally, and because they focus on learning rather than governance (Jensen et al. 2012). This explanation is not entirely satisfactory, because, while these factors may not, strictly speaking, be about governance, they are, nevertheless, about the exercise of power. In all four examples, it is easy to see power relations at work. Testing and accountability are forms of coercive hard power; curriculum development may combine this with agenda-setting; and teacher support may be a strategy of co-option. Thus expressed, both the 'push' and 'pull' factors seem to be different types of top-down exercise of power.

Innovation is connected with power in two directions: permissively and generatively. An innovator must have sufficient power to implement their innovation. Where the innovator is a government, the less fettered their power, or the more adept they are at using 'smart power', the more radical can be the innovations they are able to impose should they choose to do so. Where the innovator is a philanthropist, their independence grants permission, and the amount of wealth they are prepared to put behind the innovation influences their power to achieve its implementation. Where the innovator is the leader of a mainstream state school in England, their power to innovate under current conditions often reflects their sense of job security, which is likely to be directly proportional to their Ofsted inspection ratings and the attainment of their students. As and when school leadership asserts greater recognition as a mature profession, the profession will itself generate frameworks of good practice and accountability which allow greater agency for innovation.

While innovators need power, they also gain power. Successfully carrying out a genuine and worthwhile innovation undoubtedly confers on the innovator the power that derives from enhanced recognition and influence. The innovator becomes an authority, perhaps even a 'guru'; they may achieve statuses, honours, higher salary and enhanced career prospects; and they gain around themselves an extra layer of protection from criticism.

Building schools for the future

An example of the complex interplay between innovation and power was the Building Schools for the Future (BSF) programme operated by the UK's New Labour government between 2003 until its termination by the incoming government in 2010, by which time the programme had run into deep trouble.

The government announced that it would rebuild or refurbish every secondary school in England in order to transform secondary education. Moreover, in line with the 'something for something' political motto of the time, measures would be taken to ensure that schools would not get a transformed building unless the education taking place in it would be transformed as well. Who could disagree with this laudable aim?

This policy was nested within the bigger trend of increasing central government's direct control of schools and reducing the role and influence of local government. Following the delegation of school management to schools, the last significant power left to local government politicians concerned the capital development of the school system: where new schools would be built, and which schools would get new buildings or be refurbished. At the stroke of a pen, with no constitutional debate, BSF transferred that power from local to central government.

A complicated delivery mechanism was set in place, involving the creation of an agency, Partnerships for Schools; and a series of frameworks for technical support which gave major roles to consultancy companies to help local authorities produce a vision statement, an outline business case, and a strategic business case, before any new buildings would be approved.

There were more conditions, all reinforcing central government political priorities. Central government wanted schools to vote to leave local government and become academies, supposedly independent but in reality managed by central government. It became clear that in practice, BSF plans would not be approved unless they included significant take-up of this option. Other compulsory elements included the outsourcing of support for school ICT systems to a 'managed service provider', regardless of the merits of current arrangements; the involvement of private finance for school building, and the creation of a private-sector 'Local Education Partner' to procure and project manage the entire building programme. Only at that stage would the actual architectural design of the new schools take place, usually involving a different architect from those who had provided indicative designs as part of the approval process. A further constraint was that the government's school building regulations, stipulating minimum and maximum floor areas for each type of accommodation within schools were not in any way relaxed to encourage creative design solutions.

From 2004 to 2006 I gave consultancy support to a number of London Boroughs as part of this process. This required detailed consultation at every school about how students' learning would be transformed by BSF. This had to tick all the boxes of the government's priorities, such as, how will the new building narrow the attainment gap, increase inclusion, reduce disaffection, increase 'personalized learning', enable community engagement, improve attendance and, above all, of course, raise examination results? While it is always easier to teach, and to promote a positive school ethos, in an inspiring new building with modern facilities, the design features of that new school building will rarely be the major enabler of the aspects of educational practice listed above, and the relevant aspects of design tend to be matters of detail which are resolved at a much later stage.

In England, school building design goes through fashions which make it easy to date when a school was built. Were the designs of BSF schools which finally resulted from this cumbersome and expensive process any different from those that would have resulted from the conventional collaboration between an architect and a school governing body? Not at all.

Did schools think differently as a result of the process? Yes, from my own experience, I believe so. Often in the workshops I conducted about how practice might be different in new buildings, participants would realize, 'actually, we could start doing that straight away without waiting for a new building'. The biggest change, however, was the one the government wanted all along: the mass shift of secondary schools to academy status, and greatly increased involvement of the private sector in the education support industries, in both cases at the expense of the power and role of local government. By sleight of hand, by heralding it as innovation in school building design, a desired innovation in school governance was achieved.

Innovation and activism

Innovation is also strongly connected to activist and philanthropic approaches to problem-solving. There are two reasons for this. Innovations are responses to problems, so they arise in places where there is a commitment to problem-solving, whether activist or not. Secondly, there is a tradition in education of new approaches and professional practices originating (not exclusively) outside the government sector. So in nineteenth-century England, philanthropists, social reformers and grass-roots 'movements' were prominent in championing new educational ideas. The examples of activism in Chapter 4 are either 'grass-roots' or philanthropic in their drive. Where governments pursue activist agendas through their international aid and development departments, they tend to do so with and through the agency of philanthropic organizations. There are, nonetheless, examples of governments which have behaved innovatively in education. There can be a tendency to overlook this in the literature, as the following example illustrates.

Leadbeater (2012) presents sixteen examples of educational innovation from around the world, that have received awards from the World Innovation Summit for Education (WISE), one of the projects of the Qatar Foundation, which has annually showcased six of the 'most innovative and promising education projects around the world…[to]…inspire original thinking and concerted action both at the grassroots level and among policy-makers' (Leadbeater 2012, Foreword, p 13). It is noteworthy that not one of the sixteen projects showcased was initiated by a governmental organization.

The sixteen projects present a snapshot of responses to issues. Three apply new technologies. Massachusetts Institute of Technology provides free worldwide access to the materials of over 2,000 courses. The (British) Open University has linked with twelve partner organizations to create the Teacher Education in Sub-Saharan Africa (TESSA) programme, which provides in-service training to more than 400,000 teachers annually. Thirdly, the Hole-in-the-Wall project, initiated in India, provides free self-directed access to computers in public places, mainly for children living in slums (Leadbeater 2012).

Four of the showcased projects support informal home- and community-based learning. The Mother Child Education Programme in Turkey trains mothers to become early educators; the Week-end School in the Netherlands supplements the learning of mainly immigrant children; We Love Reading, in Jordan, trains mothers to lead reading groups in community settings; and Aprendiz in Brazil promotes community-focused learning alongside school.

Three projects support individuals: the African Institute for Mathematical Sciences in South Africa provides 'talent-spotted' higher education; Nanhi Kali in India supports girls to help them stay in education; and Pathways to Education in Canada gives financial incentives and mentoring to support poor students at pre-college secondary stage (Leadbeater 2012).

Three of the projects provide schools. The Shafallah Centre is an all-age special school in Qatar. Rewrite the Future, a Save the Children campaign, has built or improved schools for millions of children in conflict zones, but its proponent admits that the focus should have been on learning outcomes rather than buildings, as the shortage of trained teachers was often a bigger problem (Leadbeater 2012 p 45). The Citizens Foundation provides a large number of very-low-fee independent schools for the children of poor communities in Pakistan.

Escuela Nueva in Colombia is a learning scheme for self-organized groups with printed materials, which enables a single teacher to support a large number of learners. The remaining two projects share the feature of income generation. In the Cristo Rey group of independent Catholic schools in the USA, the students work for part of their time to earn money to pay for their education. Finally, Fundacion Paraguaya, originally in Paraguay and spread more widely, provides secondary-phase farm schools where farm produce and tourism pays for the education (Leadbeater 2012).

Interesting and inspiring though this collection of projects may be, it is not at all clear that they help to define 'innovation', except through the circular definition that they have won awards in a scheme that has the word 'innovation' in its title.

There is very little in education that could be said to be truly 'new to the world'. If that is what is meant by 'innovation', then this is likely to be limited to technological breakthroughs. There is nothing new about the ideas of building schools for children who don't have one, or informal community-based learning, or a special school, or distance learning, or financial scholarships. Most of the examples showcased by Leadbeater (2012) apply practices that can be found in broadly similar form elsewhere to a context or to a group of people for whom they are new. It is problematical to look at these examples as 'innovations', if the connotation of that word is that the practice itself is distinctly breaking new ground. To do so might also be a distraction from their primary significance. Attitudes and dispositions can be innovative in their context. A person who acts on a belief that it is really important that a group previously excluded from education should now be included, is in that sense an innovator in their context.

The greater value of Leadbeater's examples as pointers towards the educational future is their status as activist responses to needs which would otherwise have remained unmet. That is more noteworthy than whether these projects use tried and tested methods or methods with no proven track record. Perhaps the significance of these developments is not so much that they are, as individual projects, 'innovations', but rather that collectively they represent the new power dynamics of educational change. Individuals and organizations have decided to take unilateral action to address perceived educational needs. Showcasing these projects, which are a sample of a wider number of similar projects, may convey the impression of a 'movement': a new way of working, a global wave of change. That impression would be misleading. In fact there is no evidence of connection between these projects. They grew independently in their own contexts, as many innovations do, and it is only the WISE recognition system that has 'joined up the dots' to make a picture. Because only non-governmental innovations received the WISE awards, that is not necessarily a balanced picture of what is new and exciting in the world of education.

Problem identification and problem-solving

Innovation is nested within the broader process of perceiving something as a problem to which solutions need to be found. The word 'perception' is important to understanding where problems come from, because what counts as a 'problem' is often connected with changing values and expectations.

In Wilkins (2010) I continued a long-term exploration (begun in juvenilia, for example Wilkins 1986) of asynchronous change as a method of understanding problem identification. This built loosely on the work of Brian Holmes (1981), although I reject Holmes's attempts to apply scientific analysis to human behaviour. Holmes (1981) identified three sets of factors, or 'patterns'. The *normative* pattern includes beliefs, expectations and aspirations relevant to education. The *environmental* pattern includes factors such as technology, economy and demography, which provide the contexts within which school systems function. The *institutional* pattern embraces all the formalized arrangements for educational provision, such as organizational structures, financial systems, curriculum, examination systems and school admission arrangements.

Laws span the normative and institutional patterns. Laws making statements of high principle and aspiration need to be treated as part of the normative pattern, while those regulating practical arrangements are part of the institutional pattern. It was Holmes's contention that the problems for education policy-makers and administrators arise from the fact that linked factors within these patterns change at different speeds. Change in itself is not a problem: the problems come from some factors changing, while other factors linked to them stay the same or change more slowly.

From my own observations it is clear that some factors in the normative and environmental patterns change very quickly. There is a time lag before institutional arrangements can 'catch up', if they ever can. Thus the school systems we have were, in the main, designed to match the expectations and contexts of a previous period. On the other hand, it is also the case that some elements of the normative pattern, such as highly traditional public expectations of what schools should be like, lag behind what the school system may be trying to achieve.

In Wilkins (2010) I elaborated this conceptual framework to show five pairings of factors which may be changing at different speeds, presenting problems for school system leaders. These pairings are of course simplified to illustrate the concept: in real life they overlap and there are always multiple factors. Normative to normative tensions (type 1) arise where there are conflicting aims, such as when governments want to promote both competition and collaboration, or where communities with liberal and deeply conservative beliefs exist side by side. Normative to institutional tensions (type 2) arise where current institutions and systems cannot meet current aims and expectations. A government may pass a law decreeing that school education is both free and compulsory, which is incapable of implementation in parts of its jurisdiction where there are insufficient schools of all kinds, and a high proportion of those present are private fee-charging schools. Normative to environmental tensions (type 3) arise where changing contextual conditions are at odds with stated beliefs and values. In the UK, a legal requirement on state schools to conduct a daily act of collective worship which is normally wholly or mainly of a broadly Christian character may lead to theological gymnastics in schools serving wholly Muslim student populations.

Institutional to institutional tensions (type 4) arise where different parts of the legal, regulatory or organizational systems no longer mesh well together. For example, in England, central governments have pursued their desire to curtail local government's education functions, not by constitutional change, but by the piecemeal removal of individual schools from local government overview. In areas where a large proportion of schools have left local government, local authorities are left with important legal duties and responsibilities which they no longer have the means to exercise, and which have not been picked up by anyone else. Finally, institutional to environmental tensions (type 5) arise where the school system cannot adequately respond to changing contextual conditions. An example would be where the school curriculum and examination system lags behind changes in the skills and aptitudes required in the labour market. More acute examples are school systems attempting to function in conditions of flood, epidemic or civil war.

Of these pairings, two seem particularly significant. In systems that are still at an early stage of development, most school system leadership activity is directed to putting 'roofs over heads' and making basic provision of teachers and textbooks. Aspirations are clear and simple: the drivers come from the environmental set of factors, such as population growth in a context of poverty and poor infrastructure. In these situations, the key asynchronous changes are between institutional and environmental patterns (type 5).

In fully mature school systems, the issues are different. There will still be pressing drivers for action arising from the environment, such as those associated with technological change, demographic changes caused by migration, and economic changes affecting labour market needs. That notwithstanding, in mature systems the normative pattern is more complex and tends to be much more prominent as an influence on what issues are regarded as the 'problems' that must be solved. The politics of education is more subtle and more elaborate, and the history of education casts a longer and darker shadow over current standpoints, loyalties and differences. The school system is pressurized to 'catch up' with changing expectations (type 2) – the difference here being that those expectations come not so much from the environmental context, but rather more from the political doctrines of national governments.

In systems that are developing, often decision-making is highly centralized and is focused on the minutiae of operational management. Sections of the ministry of education may be responsible for commissioning, producing and distributing textbooks; for setting and marking school examinations; and for ordering and distributing school furniture. In such systems, government is itself an integral and significant part of the institutional pattern at school level: at the point of service delivery.

In fully developed, mature systems, operational management may be delegated or devolved to an extent that government, while clearly being the major player in the institutional pattern at the level of policy and regulation, can distance itself from actual service delivery by schools. By doing so, government places itself more deliberately within the normative pattern, setting expectations and aspirations of which schools must take notice. In England, where blame culture is rife, governments talk up these expectations, piling pressure on schools, while often failing to acknowledge that the main obstacles preventing the desired development are laws and regulations that the government itself put in place. In such situations, the asynchronous changes generating problems are largely self-generated by governments that choose to set policy expectations that run far ahead of their own laws, regulations and administrative systems.

This way of looking at patterns of change gives insights into where the 'problems' come from, to which various developments are seen as the 'answers'. Of course a problem is only a problem when it is seen as such. What is problematized reflects not so much objective conditions, as changing perceptions of those conditions by different groups of people at different times. Expectations of articulate people and organizations are central to problematization. Many problems fall into two categories. Expressed simply, someone has an expectation that cannot be satisfied in current conditions, or someone has an expectation that is incompatible with someone else's expectation. A government that does not have to stand for election, and wants a quiet life, will not go out of its way to raise expectations unnecessarily. Some people I worked with in one country I visited felt sure that their government preferred large sections of the population to remain under-educated. The combined effects of historical colonialism and modern globalization complicate the interaction of different expectations, because Western expectations and perceptions of what is problematical have been widely exported.

The generation of problems happens at every scale, from micro-problems affecting small groups of individuals, to the global scale. The leaders of schools and school systems are positioned somewhere between these extremes. This means they are responsible for identifying and addressing problems arising from below, while being affected by and responsive to problems descending from above. School leaders are people of power and influence, so they also have the capacity to be part of the problem, by adopting stances and expectations supporting a pace of change that is either too slow or too fast to mesh with changes to linked factors.

The more that school leaders are able to undertake their own appraisal of the multi-layered, multifaceted 'problems' that people are perceiving and trying to solve, the better able they will be to exercise their own discretion in whatever spaces they have for innovation.

Leadership designs pragmatic solutions for specific contexts

Delineating those spaces involves striking balances among obligations coming from three directions. One set of obligations comes from the policies and expectations of government and society at large. A second set comes from the needs and aspirations of the local community served by the school. A third set of obligations comes from school leaders' professional knowledge. They will take account of what they believe to be good professional practice, as they respond to the needs of their student body, in ways that satisfy legal requirements and public expectations. In some situations, school leaders may have to make difficult choices as they strike these balances between national, local and professional perspectives.

Globalization impacts on each corner of this triangle. It is likely to impact on the community served by the school, perhaps affecting employment prospects, tastes in culture and media, aspirations and use of technology such as mobile phones; or perhaps changing the community through patterns of migration. The professional knowledge of education leaders is also being affected by the spread of information through professional networks, and the Internet. Globalization is also, of course, a significant influence on the policies and mindsets of national governments.

The importance of place is evident from the widespread acknowledgement that leadership is contextual. While undoubtedly there is a basic core, or threshold, of leadership competences that are needed in any situation where people's activity must be directed and their behaviour influenced, there are also cases where a headteacher has moved from one school to another and found that their practised and favourite approaches do not have the desired effect in their new situation.

Two of the many contextual factors that could be chosen for scrutiny are the ability and motivation of the students, and the level of resources and community support. These factors can be visualized graphically in the form of a 2×2 matrix comprising the following four circumstances. For the purposes of this exploration, 'ability' embraces prior attainment as well as aptitude on a scale from learning disability to giftedness.

Elite contexts are those with highly motivated and able students with high levels of resourcing and support. This situation is found in world-class, elite schools, where standards and expectations are high, and where the student may be seen as a discerning client. The headteacher has the task of sustaining continuing improvement: they are a pioneer of excellence, making 'excellent' even more excellent.

Specialized intervention contexts are those with students presenting challenges regarding their level of ability and/or motivation, in a context offering high resourcing and support. The clearest example of this context would be a special school in a well-developed system. Here, the student is a focus for intensive support. The headteacher has the task of designing an effective educational regime to meet the student's needs. The headteacher is a technician and expert problem-solver who knows how to construct the best combination of inputs from the resources and support available.

Low-resource, high-motivation contexts are those with highly motivated and able students in a context lacking resources and community support. This context may be found in a range of developing country situations where securing access to schooling is a priority and where this is being achieved with minimal resources. Here, the headteacher has to make a little go a long way. The main resource they have is the motivation and latent ability of the students, so the students are the builders of their learning environment, and the headteacher is the transformer who unlocks their potential and energy.

Low-resource, low-motivation contexts are those with students lacking motivation and ability in a context lacking resources and community support. This is the most extreme and challenging context. It may be found wherever educationists are working beyond the normal front line of schooling, without infrastructure or support, with children and young people for whom education is not a priority. It might be with disaffected under-classes in slums or shanties; or in refugee camps working with children displaced, suffering from natural disaster or traumatized by war. In these extreme situations, the students are victims of circumstances, and the headteacher is a humanitarian relief worker. They have to be an initiator, a creator of structures but also just as importantly a builder of hope.

These contexts require different leadership qualities, dispositions and behaviours. The kinds of innovation that will be possible and appropriate within each context will also vary. It follows, therefore, that leadership development must be differentiated. The contexts above are depicted as those that might apply to a single institution. This book argues, however, in favour of cross-context professional collaborations. So, for example, a leader in an elite context and one in a low resource, low motivation context may be collaborating to take forward innovation in both contexts, in the expectation that they will learn from each other. Pioneers of excellence, expert problem-solvers, transformers, and builders of hope, can, through professional networking, produce synergising permutations.

Circumstances that encourage innovation

In *Oceans of Innovation*, Barber, Donnelly and Rizvi (2012) explore how global leadership is transitioning from countries bordering the Atlantic to those bordering the Pacific Ocean, and what this might imply for the leadership of educational thinking. They propose that 'intergenerational dialogue is potentially highly productive in inspiring innovation, and ought to be consciously developed by organisations' (p 2). Leaders of schools have particularly good opportunities to do this.

Barber, Donnelly and Rizvi (2012) argue that economic growth follows innovative capacity (p 6); that innovation is necessary because dependence on gradual sustained improvement leads to downfall (p 20); and that innovation must be not just in science and technology, but in human relations and in 'subtle and subjective domains' (p 21). How can innovation be cultivated?

Drawing on a wide range of sources, Barber, Donnelly and Rizvi (2012) suggest that the right conditions include 'individuals with leadership responsibilities (who) are well-educated enough to make good decisions' (p 21); working in teams engaged in extensive interactions, and which are open to ideas and vigorous debate, and within which dissent and discomfort exist (p 22). The incidence of innovation correlates with a lack of censorship, international orientation, and cultural diversity (p 22). While a measure of order is necessary, 'innovation often results from more chaotic circumstances, unplanned interaction, messiness' (p 24), and 'creativity flourishes neither in complete chaos nor in complete order – it appears to require a combination of the two' (p 29), resonating with Brock's (2011) view that solutions to traditional educational rigidities may be easier to develop in disaster situations. Competition and property rights, including legal protection of intellectual property, are also stimuli (p 29), together with bringing young people into leadership, acceptance of initial failures, and readiness to challenge prevalent beliefs (p 30). In summary:

> History, therefore, points to inclusive, pluralistic institutions which allow extensive debate of ideas…combined with a consumer society whose demands are met by continuously competing and therefore innovative businesses whose property rights are protected in law.
>
> (Barber, Donnelly and Rizvi 2012 pp 28–29)

This analysis certainly has relevance to education, especially its emphasis on inclusivity, pluralism and freedom of debate, but much of the argument is based on facts relating to technological and commercial innovation. As previous chapters have suggested, education is an intrinsically valuable 'charitable purpose' bound up with the livelihoods and well-being of individuals and communities. In the field of education, humanitarian consciousness, and commitment to social reform need to be added to the lessons of history quoted above: a point the writers imply elsewhere in the essay.

To take forward how school leaders can generate the conditions for educational innovation, attention must be given to how and by whom developments in education are funded; how new developments should be evaluated; and the relationship between educational innovation and educational values.

Financially sustainable innovation

I argued earlier that it will prove necessary to think about the resourcing of education in new ways, because it is simply unaffordable to make universal education available using the funding and delivery models that are regarded as normal in mature school systems. Two examples in Leadbeater's (2012) collection – Cristo Rey, where students are placed in paid employments for part of their time, and Fundacion Paraguaya, where schools are attached to income-generating farms – offer models of financial sustainability. To these may be added the pioneering work of ARK (Absolute Return for Kids), with its partner PEAS (Promoting Equality in African Schools) to create a new model for the provision of secondary schools in Uganda. These schools are set up with philanthropic capital and aim to achieve financial self-sufficiency partly through income-generating activities, including agriculture (http://www.arkonline.org/education/uganda; accessed July 2013).

Some schools in England attempt to offer casual employment to older students, and make an effort to offer employment to the local community alongside other forms of community engagement. Also in the UK, some 'extended school' activities such as commercial letting of premises and the provision of certain forms of adult education have been undertaken specifically to generate income streams. Vocational further education colleges provide fee-charging training restaurants, hairdressing salons and travel agencies as part of their curriculum. Looking forwards, there is potential to see schools as hubs within their communities becoming engaged with enterprises which generate income to extend participation in learning and to enhance its quality.

Apart from income-generating activities, another approach to affordability is to make resources go further. 'Highly leveraged' initiatives are those where a given level of investment achieves disproportionately beneficial outcomes in comparison with the normal 'input-output' equations of schooling.

A good example of a highly leveraged innovation is one of the projects run by the Bangladesh Rural Advancement Committee (BRAC), a wide-ranging philanthropic organization much involved in supporting education in Bangladesh. The scheme in question develops and supports village-based primary education in locations where girls' participation is low. The school has to be supported by the village authorities; it is based in the village and constructed from the same materials and in the same style as people's homes. A girl resident in the village who has completed ten years of schooling is appointed as the teacher and is given some basic training, materials and ongoing support. Of the children enrolled, 70 per cent must be girls until equal numbers of girls and boys are in school. A large number of these schools have been established. Academic achievement and progression have been good, despite the schools following a distinctive curriculum. As well as offering a low-cost form of education, the scheme scores highly on integrating school with families and the community. Without that factor, the girls would not be able to attend school.

The Citizens Foundation (TCF) in Pakistan, one of Leadbeater's examples, uses a combination of philanthropic funding and good management to provide very low fee independent education. I visited a TCF school serving an illegal squatter settlement in a shanty town on the outskirts of Karachi. A fleet of minibuses collected the female staff for each of the two shifts in the school day. Water was brought in on a lorry so that the children could wash. Despite evidently very low levels of resources, the smartness and punctuality of the children, and strong community support, were impressive. TCF schools are substituting for the failures of the Government of Pakistan to achieve such basic provision through its own school system.

The examples above incorporate some of the trade-offs that have to be accepted to devise pragmatic solutions to educational problems in specific contexts. One concerns the development of professional standards in teaching, and how that agenda meshes with reliance on undereducated, undertrained, and often unpaid or underpaid community-based individuals who, to their great credit, do their best to carry out the role of teacher. Secondly, where a government or other official agency is failing to carry out its statutory obligations, there is the dilemma of whether, in the long run, it is good for philanthropic initiative to 'let them off the hook' by making the provision which they should have made. Another concerns the widespread way in which an innovation developed by a philanthropic organization expands with the help of government subsidies, so that over time the organization becomes in effect a service provider operating under a government contract, with some potential loss of independence and responsiveness. Many philanthropic organizations do manage to act as contracted service delivery agencies while also maintaining their advocacy functions, but from a purely financial point of view, the philanthropic contribution becomes much diluted.

Beyond financial sustainability is the broader sustainability of innovative projects, which is connected to effective management of change. Barber (2013) expresses impatience with the way in which questions about sustainability can be used to discourage initiative. He prefers the more demanding concept of 'irreversibility' (p 28). He emphasizes the role of key individuals and policy continuity in the following example:

> In November 2010, Madhya Pradesh was 'Exhibit A': serious progress in a big Indian state between 2006 and 2008. However, with a change of Chief Minister and a change of policy, the results changed too. By 2011, results in Madhya Pradesh were below where they had been at the start of the improvement journey five years earlier.
>
> (Barber 2013 p 29)

Worthwhile innovation: Some evaluation criteria

Schools and school leaders are accountable, so innovators must expect, at least in principle, that their innovations will be subject to evaluation. Indeed, when a new development is conceived as a pilot, then evaluation is central to that concept. This raises the problem of how to evaluate something which is new, or more specifically, what measuring rods to apply. When evaluating mainstream provision, the measuring rod is good practice being achieved in comparable cases. Where there are no comparable cases, there is a danger that an evaluator's judgements become too subjective. Some other measuring tools are needed to inform judgements about the 'validity' of educational innovations. I offer the following checklist to support that process:

1. How developed was the rationale for the innovation at the start of the process? What problem was it addressing? What range of possible solutions, including tried and tested methods, were considered before developing the innovative solution, that is, does it have process validity?

2. What was the innovator's evidence or rationale for believing that this particular innovation would address the problem, and do so more effectively than other possible solutions, with due regard for opportunity costs?

3. Were success criteria and internal and external monitoring and evaluation arrangements put in place at an early stage in the development?

4. Has the innovation impacted on the problem in the way and to the extent intended, that is, does it have outcome validity?

5. Among relevant interest groups, how widely and deeply has the innovation been supported at each key phase of its development, that is, does it have democratic validity?

6. Is the innovation, including its progress and evaluation, the subject of debate within and beyond the organization: debate in which different viewpoints are tolerated? That is to say, does it have dialogic validity?

7. Has the innovation been supportive of other related developments, and of organizational learning, that is, does it have catalytic validity?

8. Has the process of implementing the innovation been managed effectively and efficiently?

9. Has the innovative practice been integrated effectively into the organization's wider operating systems?

10. To what extent is the continuation of the innovation dependent on the presence and/or active involvement of the innovator in person? Is there an exit strategy or succession plan?

11. Has the innovator, or the organization, assessed how and to what extent the innovation could be applied in other contexts and produce comparable results?

The different types of 'validity' included in points 1, 4, 5, 6 and 7 above are taken from work by Anderson and Herr (1999) on new ways of applying the concept of 'validity' used in academic research to practitioner research contexts. Assuming that innovations in school contexts often have some of the qualities of an experiment which is being monitored to create new knowledge, this is an appropriate application of Anderson and Herr's 'new validities'. Of course, while a checklist like that above can provide a framework for generating factual information and perceptions, evaluating innovations still requires the making of professional judgements regarding the interpretation of that information. Whatever progress was made, whether targets were not met or exceeded, it remains an open question how that matches what might reasonably have been expected given the specifics of the context. Similarly, assessing the significance of particular factors, and what improvements could be made, do not lend themselves to empirical evidence but require the exercise of professional judgement informed by relevant experience. Evaluation works best where there is complementarity between external and internal evaluation. Peer evaluation can be insightful, inexpensive, credible and can foster a sense of professionalism. The cause of innovatory schooling is helped when innovators surround themselves with an evaluative professional network.

What can school leaders do to create the conditions in which school staff can initiate or support significant innovation? Supposing a school in England is interested in making a difference to wider educational needs, through an activist community outreach project either locally, or in another country through the medium of an international school-to-school partnership?

First, to take practical account of the English context, such a strategic development would require the key staff of the school to be able to take both a long-term view, and a broad perspective. This means that the school would need to be secure in relation to day-to-day pressures and expectations, such as short-term concerns about students' attainment, or the possibility of an adverse inspection report, or acute difficulties regarding students' behaviour, or breakdowns in any important relationships, or any other immediate problem. Schools facing acute problems must focus on them and avoid distractions. This means that innovatory outward-facing activity is likely, in practice, to be an option only for schools at a certain point in their trajectory of development. They must at least have reached the stage where everything is running smoothly and new challenges are needed as a stimulus to stepping up to the next level of aspiration and achievement.

Innovation and values

Chua (2013), reflecting on a recent policy change in Singapore which appears to represent a shift to valuing less competitive and more rounded educational goals, draws attention to two meanings of the word 'reform'. This, especially when given connotations of progress, can mean replacing the 'old' with the 'new'. Chua points out that 'reform' can also mean the 're-gathering of something that was once valued, but which has, over time and for a variety of reasons, become neglected or misinterpreted' (Chua 2013 p 8). In the first sense, 'reform' is 'the revolutionary abolition of old paradigms to create space for new intentions', whereas in the second, it is concerned 'with retrieving the old' (Chua 2013 p 8). In the context of this chapter's discussion, Chua's insights are helpful to understanding the complex nature of innovations in education. I return to them again in the next chapter in the context of considering how to measure what is valued.

Significant innovation ('transformation') involves revisiting collective understandings of the purposes of education. Traditionally, these have been taken to include passing on culture from one generation to the next; making society more open to new ideas and knowledge; personal and social improvement; economic development; and social justice. Views will vary between contexts regarding which of these purposes should have greater priority over the next five or ten years, and how those prioritized purposes are to be translated into performance indicators.

From time immemorial there have been two 'agendas' for education, deriving from the two different meanings of the word 'education' in its classical roots. In the modern context, one of these 'agendas' may be summarized as socialization and training: transmitting customs and culture and producing a workforce suited to the current known economy. The other agenda concerns the 'blossoming' of the individual, and may be summarized as educative empowerment: enabling each child to develop to the full extent of their aptitudes. Both agendas are necessary but they represent contrasting mindsets and convey contrasting messages to the next generation. A proponent of the first agenda is saying to the next generation, 'We know the future, the future belongs to us, we know the place that you will hold in that future, we know the skills you will need, and our job is to give you those skills (and if you object, you have the problem called "disaffection").' A proponent of the second agenda is saying:

> We do not know the future, the future belongs to you not to us, we do not know the position you will occupy in that future – he possibilities are endless. We do not know the skills you will need. Our job is to give you the attitudes and confidence to make the very best of your own potential in that unknown future, and perhaps to create a better future than we can currently envision.

These are contrasting messages, and on this matter education leaders simply have to make a personal choice about where they will stand. In the seminal words of Karl Popper:

> Neither nature nor history can tell us what we ought to do. Facts cannot determine the ends we are going to choose. It is up to us to decide what shall be our purpose in life.
>
> (Popper 1966)

Perhaps many educationists would agree that the core agenda for education might be summarized in the following words: 'To enable each individual to achieve their full potential'. This definition has worked well enough for centuries, but the context of the modern world invites challenging questions that must be addressed. How and where is this 'enabling' to take place? Using what technologies, pedagogies, subject content and what range of learning places? Who defines – who has the right to define – what is a person's 'full potential', and what evidence supports that judgement? What contextual limitations are being assumed in arriving at that judgement?

These questions point towards a re-appraisal of how educational innovation is conceived. In popular usage, the dimensions of educational innovation might commonly include changes to school design, changes to curriculum and changes to the 'technologies' of teaching and learning, including the use of ICT which of course is having profound implications for how learning takes place. There is a case for looking beyond these dimensions, to understand 'innovation' as also applying to the aims and purposes of education, and the nature of the interpersonal relationships through which it happens. In nineteenth-century England, education for the masses was introduced not for the purpose of educative empowerment, but to the contrary to keep the children of the labouring classes in their place. Schooling was to teach them to accept their station in life, to respect their betters and to learn the skills they would need in the menial occupations to which they were destined. The method used for this depended on fear and intimidation, and the use of physical violence.

Modern schools in England aim to support children to blossom to the full extent of their aptitudes, and to do so using methods that foster the child's well-being and positive engagement in their learning, and that respect the child's rights and dignity as a human being. The schoolhouse benefits from modern design, curriculum and technologies, but the change that has made the most profound difference to children's lives has been this innovation in aspirations for children and in the way they are treated. In many parts of the world, this innovation, which costs nothing but changes to hearts and minds, is still to be addressed. In this way, agendas of educational innovation may be understood to include co-creating new spaces in which people have positive experiences of learning, and which enable new choices and mobilities.

CHAPTER SEVEN
Evidence, Beliefs, Standpoints and Power

Knowledge, power and direction

Ideas become prevalent and spread across national boundaries. The politics of knowledge concerns the power dynamics that operate at the interfaces between standpoints and facts. The old adage that 'knowledge is power' is certainly true for school system leaders at all but the highest levels. The ability to generate information through research, and to exercise independent and critical access to a range of published research findings, bestows confidence and agency: by those means, the person *in* authority becomes *an* authority.

On the other hand, at the highest levels the relationship between power and knowledge may be reversed. Here, power can be used to confer special status and prominence on certain selected ideas and research findings, especially those that support the policies of governments or of powerful international organizations. Subtle use of 'smart power' can airbrush out, or accord lower status to, alternative versions of 'truth'.

Many factors influence whether school leaders find themselves in tune with, or concerned by, the prevailing patterns of belief that form the context for their work. My wish is that school leaders should be conscious of these differences of standpoint, and of the different beliefs and reasons underlying them. Part of this consciousness concerns a balanced appreciation of the extents to which factors in self and in system contribute to the perceived mismatch in beliefs. Other parts are a sense of agency; and developing the attributes necessary to be able to turn spaces of prescription into spaces of negotiation, where to do so is in the interests of legitimate educational aims.

Power (2008) has explored the contemporary challenges to professionalism in education, identifying three perspectives. The perspective of the 'distressed' professional focuses on the pressures and problems faced by individuals, which are seen in terms of the shortcomings of the individual, their colleagues and the organization within which they work. This perspective on the nature and location of the problem invites a 'therapeutic' response, addressing shortcomings on a case-by-case basis. Power's (2008) second perspective is that of 'oppressed' professional, which focuses on the impact on educators of large-scale changes in society:

> Since the late 1980s, professionals have experienced a whole range of further changes that have impacted on their work. At an international level, there are claims that we are in a new era of social history – couched variously in terms of globalisation, modernity, post-Fordism and/or the 'information age'. All these aspects have impacted on the lives of professionals in different ways.
>
> (Power 2008 pp 150–151)

Power points out that this perspective is essentially deterministic, in that whether the developments described are seen through Marxist or post-structuralist understandings, there is little that education leaders can do about them. While I agree that for this occupational group, revolution is clearly not an option, the exploration of activism in Chapter 4 demonstrated that education leaders may be far from passive in their response to global developments. An active stance is found in Power's third perspective, in which she advocates the stance of the 'imaginative' professional, based on the thinking of C. Wright Mills (1970). This perspective enables the individual professional to gain a balanced appreciation of the interrelationships between private troubles (such as personal shortcomings), and public issues (such as counterproductive policies). Applying the work of C. Wright Mills, Power (2008) identifies relational, temporal and dispositional questions for education.

My interpretation of this thinking is that the 'imaginative professional' will not take up a position that implies that prevailing orthodoxies are necessarily ill-judged; or that top-down initiatives are by definition bad, and bottom-up initiatives good; or that prescription is always wrong, and self-determination is always right. In systems where headteachers lack education, skills, vision and experience of other contexts, and whose work consists only of basic administration, developments are not going to take place unless a top-down initiative imposes them. Just as students need to be assisted towards a threshold of capability beyond which they can function as independent learners, so school leaders in certain contexts need to be taken along a journey of school improvement and professional development before they have much to offer as autonomous local leaders of education. Different contextual conditions, including the level of development of organizations and individuals, call for different types of leadership and different power relations. Emergencies, disasters or over-stable 'stuck' complacency call in different ways for directive intervention. Where systems are mature, dynamic and generally in forward motion, more enabling and collegial strategies become options. Of course there will be differing perceptions of which of these conditions apply, and whether directive behaviour is motivated by the aim of longer term empowerment, or simply by a preference for ongoing coercion.

Whatever its circumstances, significant and complex change in a people-centred activity such as education requires capacity-building among those who must effect the change at operational level. 'Capacity building' includes a combination of motivation, and knowledge and skills, and opportunity, and efficacy. Those of whom significant and complex change is required need to sense seven conditions: they need a sense of desirable destination; of motivation to progress towards that destination; of navigable steps and milestones; of ability and confidence to do what is required; of permission to work differently; of support from the organization and the wider system; and a sense that success will be marked by recognition in desirable ways. Those leading change must be mindful of the need to work both with rationality and emotion: appealing both to people's thoughts and to their feelings. Relevant and reliable management information such as statistics are one of the main means of appealing to people's thinking and their rationally based motivation. Giving people experiences and bringing them into contact with people with relevant stories to tell is one of the main means of appealing to people's feelings, and their emotionally based motivation.

Combining the ideas in the two paragraphs above, there may be a logical sequence to change, starting with top-down direction in which numerical analysis is dominant, and then progressing to more local-level subsidiarity and agency, in which experience and human interaction become more significant shaping factors.

Subjectivity is unavoidable and constructive

This book's argument that school leadership benefits from an international perspective raises the questions of how leaders 'look' at other national contexts, and with what frames of reference they interpret what they see. The migration of ideas across national boundaries is relevant to the practice of international professional development. Few people would doubt that international observation and dialogue can be informative and developmental, but an enduring question concerns the nature and status of the learning that takes place, and whether and how what has been learnt from one system can be applied to another. It is necessary to steer a course between two extreme positions. At one extreme is the view that the transfer to one country of various educational practices from totally different contexts is unproblematic: a stance adopted by politicians when it suits them. At the other extreme is the view that international dialogue and professional development generates learning of a kind that does not progress beyond educational tourism. To find a middle ground means looking carefully at how other systems might be observed and interpreted, and how the transferability of practices in other systems might be appraised.

True objectivity in any form of educational research is such an elusive concept that it is better to set it aside as an expectation. Even quantitative empirical work involves subjective judgements about what it is that is worth measuring. Observation of an education system by professionals from another system will inevitably be subjective. The observer or analyst brings to their work their own experience, beliefs and conceptual frameworks. These will influence what is noticed and regarded as interesting in the other system. Also they will provide the yardsticks against which to interpret what is observed. Observers of other nations' education systems bring their own interests, agenda and 'baggage' to the task.

Provided that this subjectivity is acknowledged, and that meaningful communication takes place, subjectivity can be an advantage rather than a disadvantage. The people with whom the observer interacts in the country hosting the observer's visit will also have their interests, agenda and 'baggage'. Dialogue can help the parties to understand each other, and also, to understand themselves: for example, to become more conscious of why particular issues are problematized, and why particular solutions are preferred to other possible solutions.

There is not space here to say much about the vast and varied field of study labelled 'comparative education', but earlier in its culturalist strand, mainly European writers identified certain national traits and characteristics which they believed had explanatory value in relation to features of national education systems (see, for example, Halls 1973; Chapter 2 of McClean 1995; and the critical review by Crossley and Watson 2011). That kind of thinking, while grounded in understandings of cultural identity and history, risks stereotypical and deterministic assumptions, which are of declining applicability in a globalized world. Traditional comparative education did not ignore the issue of change, but the main focus of some strands of study tended to be on education systems as they currently were, as they had become, almost in the sense of being in a near-completed state. The significance of history as part of culture encouraged this retrospective view. There is an overlap between the disciplines of comparative education and the history of education: Glenn (2011), for example, provides a comparative historical study of parental choice and state control of schooling in the modern territories of Austria, Germany, Belgium and the Netherlands, from the sixteenth century to modern times. That example notwithstanding, change is such a dominant characteristic in education policies everywhere, that many contemporary comparativists tend to view school systems as being normally and permanently in a state of dynamic development, as systems on trajectories, as systems in a state of becoming.

The key issues for education today have more of an international dimension than used to be the case. While international trends in education are not new (think, for example, of the development of universities across late medieval Europe), the scale and depth of their impact on policy-making at national level has never been greater, and that trend will continue. Consequently, national education systems can no longer be seen, as they could in earlier historical periods, as being largely self-contained. A significant part of current agendas of policy development and change is connected with international and global factors, although the nature of national responses will be influenced by local factors. Trends and issues at global level have generated some of the conceptual frameworks which analysts use to interpret the unique features of national systems, as manifested in the different impacts upon them from, and their reactions to, those wider global patterns of change.

Localities, nations and networks

Everyone, including every school leader, operates from a current specific locality, whether that locality is the city from which a large territory is governed, or a rural area distant from the seat of power. Each individual's pattern of affinities, however, derives not from their physical location but from the networks they occupy. In the same village, there might be one person for whom the village is the extent of their network, and another, perhaps employed by an aid agency, who has a sophisticated global network. Often socio-economic status correlates with wider and stronger networks. Just as extremes of wealth and poverty are perhaps most stark in some developing countries, the same is true of the range and strength of individuals' networks. The steepness of this gradient of 'networked-ness' of different sectors of society, including those working in schools, has a direct bearing on the spread of new ideas. The extent to which individual networks overlap has a direct bearing on the extent to which people in different parts of the system 'speak the same language'.

On the first point, extending and upgrading people's networks may be a relatively inexpensive prerequisite to getting much else done. An example of this, discussed below, is the communications dimension of a school improvement project led by Michael Barber in Punjab (Barber 2013).

On the second point, in England, in the 'Westminster village' from which the country is governed, the language of school improvement is dominated by talk of test scores in a narrow academic curriculum, league table positions, opening up markets in school provision, producing a skilled but compliant workforce to compete in the global economy, and taking the 'control' of schools away from people who have been elected and giving it to people who have not. All three of the main political parties are fixated on the same issues, from only slightly different stances. The average parent collecting their six-year-old at the end of the school day is interested in none of those matters. They want a good local school in which their child will be happy, known, cared for, given a broad education, and enabled to blossom to their full potential.

That example of how two important parties to the educational process can be apparently uninterested in each other's agendas illustrates the importance of the relationships between local, provincial, national and global spaces in educational development. Rigg (2007) emphasized how place matters and localism/globalism is a false dichotomy, citing Agnew and Duncan's (1989) distinctions between location, locale and sense of place, and Lefebvre's (1991) distinctions between the spaces of planners, lived spaces and spatial flows. 'Places' have cultural and material implications for the learning spaces created within them. The factors of place, space, mobility and culture combine to complicate and in some cases counterbalance globalization and internationalism in education.

El-Ojeili and Hayden (2006) offered a selection of critical theoretical perspectives on globalization, which included questioning the actual extent of economic globalization. They also drew attention to the stratification and widening of socio-economic differentials within countries that has accompanied globalization. Ozga and Lingard (2007 pp 65–66) analysed 'the dynamics of the relationship between globalising, economising forces and technologies of education governance, and mediating vernacular forces and resources that affect the ways in which these play out and are made real in people's lives in schools ... [a] struggle over meaning, resources and power.'

School leaders operate at a key spatial scale at the meeting point between these top-down and bottom-up forces, and, if they are 'imaginative professionals' (Power 2008), their networks include a global professional community through whom they can access alternative versions of 'truth' from those that may be promulgated by actors directly involved, whether from global, national or local standpoints – not with the aim of standing aloof or contradicting local dynamics, but to support both consciousness and rapprochement.

Schools are both derivative and constitutive

The issues of globalization can be seen from the standpoint of school leaders interested in adopting an outward-looking viewpoint: making the connection between 'big picture' issues and the specifics of their own situation, with a view to practical action. Kraftl (2013), citing and developing the work of Hanson Thiem (2009), draws attention to the internal or external orientation of spatially focused studies of educational settings. His point is the extent to which studies treat schools as the dependent variable, so that what is going on in schools is seen as affected by and responding to factors that are outside the school, making school a derivative of society.

Kraftl (2013), following Hanson Thiem (2009), advocates a more outward-looking geography of education that identifies the forces at work in the opposite direction: 'to afford more constitutive power to education spaces over the modes of governance and socio-economic structures that seem simply to (have) produce(d) them' (Kraftl 2013 p 26).

School education is a global activity and a global industry; a global need; and an aspect of human living that is as old as civilization. Like homes, works of art, occupations and mobilities, school education is indicative of a society's stage of development, values and preoccupations. Currently, global educational developments are a response to, as well as a reflection of, the issues of our time. In school systems around the world, leaders are operating in contexts of challenge and change, with more complexity and uncertainty than in any previous period, but also with more opportunity.

What is really happening within the broad terminology of 'education globalization'? One perspective is to explore the dynamics of the 'problems' to which various national and global developments seek to provide 'solutions'. This question was introduced in Chapter 3 and developed further in Chapter 6. Chapter 4 addressed more specifically why and how school leaders may choose to make a difference to wider education concerns, and the implications of such a re-conceptualization of their role for how the school leaders of the future might approach their own professional development.

The curriculum is central to these explorations. In Chapter 4, examples were given of community action projects within the curriculum, which will tend to have, by definition, an intensely local focus. The point of the local focus, and the activist pedagogy, is its relevance to students' lives and contexts, and this is seen as helpful to motivating students and engaging them in learning. The opposite end of the spectrum is the increasingly common inclusion of global perspectives in the curriculum. This focus is not incompatible, and indeed may be complementary, insofar as an activist pedagogy can be applied to issues in another country, and through communication, involvement and impact, achieve relevance and engagement.

These approaches form elements of international education. As well as promoting global citizenship, international education helps students to learn more about themselves, and to become more conscious of their own cultural identity. International education may contribute directly to teaching and learning in certain subjects, and may provide content material in others. In some of its forms, such as interdisciplinary project work and extra-curricular activity, it may be the vehicle for developing a wide range of generic skills, dispositions and attributes.

International links and infrastructures play an important part in international education. International Education Week, in November, has been run globally since 1999. It is supported by the British Council. It celebrates and showcases good practice in international education, and conducts debates. Of course any reference to 'good practice' raises the issue of how much consensus there is about 'standards' in international education, and what kinds of measures and expectations are used. One initiative to address these questions is the International School Award, which is operated by the British Council. The International School Award is an accreditation scheme for curriculum-based international work in schools. The scheme provides recognition for teachers, in schools that are working to instil a global dimension into the learning experience (http://schoolsonline. britishcouncil.org/International-School-Award).

Another example of support for international education is the North South School Partnerships project. This was a two-year study funded by DfID of partnerships between schools in the UK, and schools in Ghana, Kenya, Malawi, South Africa, Tanzania, The Gambia, Uganda, Zambia, India, Pakistan and Sri Lanka (Edge, Frayman and Lawrie 2009).

Emotion and logic

Power relations include the significant 'hard power' resources of the World Bank, donor countries and aid agencies, but also the very significant influence of these organizations in defining issues and agendas, and defining acceptable processes for addressing them.

Joel Spring (2009) cites Morin's (2008) notion of 'blinding paradigms' to explain the pervasiveness of certain lines of thinking, both in literature and in practice, regarding global patterns of educational change. The 'blinding paradigm grants validity and universality to its chosen logic. Thereby it gives the qualities of necessity and truth to the discourse and theory it controls' (Morin 2008, quoted in Spring 2009).

According to Spring (2009), world education cultural theorists see the globalization of education as 'the spread of Western educational ideas...accompanied by Western ideas of human rights, democracy, free markets, and constitutional government'. He contrasts this view with that of world system and postcolonial/critical theorists who are more concerned with power relations, including the ways in which 'globalisation is increasing inequalities within and between nations' (Spring 2009 p 201).

Spring (2009) draws attention to the essential differences between these standpoints regarding both the intrinsic merits of Western educational ideas, and the motives of the actors involved. The first view assumes rationality: that the Western approaches to education do indeed include 'global good practices', proven by research, and that the selection of some of these by leaders of developing countries for local implementation is intended to, and will, be beneficial. The second standpoint questions each stage of that argument, drawing attention to the dominance of emotion over reason in human behaviour, and observing that 'national political leaders are often driven by...power and greed', and that 'while they espouse techno-rational approaches to education, educational researchers often act to serve their own interests and those of their financial supporters' (pp 202–203).

Governing by numbers

Ozga and Lingard (2007 pp 75–77) applied the term 'governing by numbers' to the overuse of performance data. Countries with developing education systems, supported by international donors, feel prompted to adopt and apply performance indicators which are amenable to international comparisons. This makes it possible to see whether and how far the education system concerned is moving up league tables. Comparative attainment data include OECD's Programme for International Student Assessment (PISA) and Trends in International Mathematics and Science Study (TIMSS). The more that weight is given to such measures, and the greater the number of countries taking part, the more the measure itself comes to define what is 'good'. While improving league table performance may be desirable, each context will vary with regard to whether this may skew educational development towards the measurable factors, and whether that is an advantage or a disadvantage. High-performing parts of countries may be entered: for example, Shanghai is in PISA but China as a whole is not, raising the question of in-country disparity. It is important to continue to try to develop forms of educational assessment which are also able to measure aspects of education that are valued within the local culture but which may not lend themselves to comparative league tables.

Achieving a high position in every league is not necessarily desirable. William Stewart, writing in the *Times Educational Supplement* (Stewart 2012), reported comments by Andreas Schleicher, the OECD official who runs PISA, that high ranking in Progress in International Reading Literacy Study (PIRLS) and TIMSS in England would be a worrying sign, for the following reason. TIMSS tests children at ages 10 and 14. The PIRLS tests children at 10. The PISA tests students at age 15. The issue pointed out by Schleicher is that if England's rankings in PIRLS and TIMSS are higher than in PISA, this suggests that the value added by England in the later years of schooling is less than in other countries (Stewart 2012).

Measuring what is valued

In the last chapter's discussion of innovation, I introduced Chua's insights regarding the nature of educational reform. Writing about recent reforms in Singapore, Chua (2013) draws attention to an apparent official rediscovery of some old educational values, according to a Ministry of Education press release dated September 2012, cited in Chua (2013). This announced the abolition of the banding of secondary schools by academic results with immediate effect, reduced school competition, and increased emphasis on recognizing best practices by schools in delivering a well-rounded education. The ministry had explained this in the following terms:

> The most crucial part is ... developing the values and character that will enable [the student] to succeed in life and contribute to others. Knowledge and skills can become outdated, but a mature social-emotional core, deep values and strength of character will enable our children to continue to thrive as they grow. It is not cognitive skills alone, but character traits of empathy, graciousness, responsibility and integrity that will enable our students to succeed.
>
> (Minister Mr Heng Swee Keat
> 12 September 2012, quoted in Chua 2013)

The question Chua raises is whether value statements of this kind derive from intrinsic or instrumental foundations. That they are, in this case, instrumental is suggested by coverage of the same development by Stewart (2013b). Writing in the *Times Educational Supplement*, Stewart reports the Director of Singapore's National Institute of Education, Lee Sing Long, as explaining that the move to 'holistic child development, student-centric curriculum and "flipped learning" ' is to create 'a more equal and caring society', and a drive for '21st Century learning skills' (p 9). As noted earlier, there are hard and soft forms of instrumentality, the latter being compatible with agendas of empowerment and agency. Approaches to measuring what is valued are explored further in the next chapter.

'Deliverology' in Punjab

Michael Barber wrote a personal narrative (Barber 2013) of his work in support of the Government of Punjab in respect of key education reforms. Central to this approach was generating management information for certain prioritized performance indicators, setting and monitoring targets for their achievement, and recommending strategies to assist their achievement, based on thinking from the stable of the school effectiveness movement: 'evidence based reform', top-down, 'what works': the 'one right way' mindset.

This approach had been epitomized by the imposition in England of the National Literacy Strategy by the New Labour government of 1997–2010, in which Michael Barber was much involved. Prescriptive, managerialistic and riding roughshod over the constitutional distribution of responsibilities of which, for much of my career, I was a champion, this approach was one to which I would, in 2010, have described myself as being profoundly opposed. Travel broadens the mind, and in Lahore the evidence of my own eyes led me to adopt a more balanced, tolerant and eclectic standpoint.

In Spring 2012, I first met the then head of the Programme Monitoring and Implementation Unit (PMIU) in Punjab. She showed me a presentation which astonished me for the level of ICT and management information which had connected every school in that vast area of difficult terrain. Data may be used well or badly, but that level of connectivity has to be a great asset on any modern journey of reform. Over the coming months it became apparent that in some of the regular District-level meetings, a friendly and motivating competitive spirit existed among the headteachers in relation to the sharing of performance indicator scores. In August 2012, Michael Barber invited me to drop into a session he was running with District officials on improving school attendance. Data-driven and directive, it was not the kind of session I would want to lead, but the participants were engaged and not resentful, and the programme had resulted in improved school attendance.

Reflecting on this experience, I decided that instead of regarding contrasting approaches as different 'set menus', it ought to be possible to work towards an overall 'à la carte menu' from which to mix and match one's own 'flavours' according both to the needs of the context and one's own normative values. So, while 'data-driven' is usually served up with high-pressure managerialism, it should also be possible to combine good management information with a collegial and developmental working style. In some situations an initial dose of the former, harder, style may be necessary before progressing to the latter.

From numbers to policies

A report published by the World Bank (World Bank 2010) about education in Colombia analyses Colombia's performance in TIMSS. Colombia participated in TIMSS in 1995 and then again in 2007, and the purpose of the report was to examine Colombia's performance over this period in comparison with other countries, looking in more detail at lower middle income countries participating in TIMSS deemed most comparable, including Jordan. The data collected as part of the TIMSS assessment enables analysis of the effects of factors such as gender, rurality, level of resources in schools, socio-economic composition of schools, teachers' qualifications, level of mother's education, whether the student has access to a computer at home, and how many books are in the home. This analysis enables the World Bank team to make recommendations about where to focus attention in order to improve future scores. Thus TIMSS embraces research which is deeper, more useful for policy-making, and less controversial, than the media covering of league-table rankings might imply.

The report's comparative analysis between Colombia and other countries seems, in addition to its intrinsic interest, to add breadth to the report's recommendations. Without detracting from all that is useful in the World Bank's approach, this report is representative of a genre of policy recommendations underpinned by large-scale quantitative research about which two caveats might be made. There is the age-old philosophical problem of the relationship between 'is' and 'ought': 'these are the facts, *therefore* this is the right course of action'. For World Bank and OECD, the recommended course of action usually seems to draw, in varying proportions, on a suite of remedies that includes more testing, more data analysis, more accountability, more market forces, more targeted intervention and more vouchers. I am not suggesting that these policies are not effective, only that there is insufficient exploring and testing of different policies that might be just as effective. Secondly, where the international comparisons draw attention to strategies adopted elsewhere, which Colombia might wish to consider, the guiding hand of World Bank/OECD behind those strategies seems to have been gently airbrushed from the narrative. I neither ascribe nor imply any conscious motive here, but there is a real difference between the apparently objective, open, invitational message: 'look at what some other similar countries have done that you could learn from', and the more positioned message that may sometimes represent a fuller truth: 'these are strategies we have caused to be implemented in other countries, that we commend to you also'.

Evidence as both power and constraint

The prime minister of Singapore, Lee Hsien-Loong, in the foreword to Barber, Donnelly and Rizvi (2012), said that 'The key is to combine evidence-based reforms with well-designed innovations' (p 3).

This statement draws attention to an important balance. It is good for decision-making at all levels to be informed where possible by research and evidence, provided that some of that research is undertaken in relevant local contexts, and embraces a suitable range of paradigms and standpoints. School leaders can support strategies to increase the impact of research evidence on policy, although education is always bound to be affected by political beliefs and to have a political dimension.

There is, however, an important distinction between 'evidence' and 'research'. Empirical research produces evidence; non-empirical, conceptual, research does not: instead, it produces the new ideas, new ways of looking at the world, and new questions which may lead to new lines of empirical research. Significant innovation often flows from this kind of conceptual work. Demanding, 'Where is your evidence?' stifles innovation, because, by definition, there can be no evidence proving what will be the outcome of an innovation.

No GERMS in Finland

The influential reports of McKinsey & Company (for example, Barber 2010) on the world's best-performing school systems emphasize the following 'lessons':

Lesson 1: The quality of an education system cannot exceed the quality of its teachers.

Lesson 2: The only way to improve outcomes is to improve instruction.

Lesson 3: High performance requires every child to succeed.

Lesson 4: Every school needs a great leader.

This view argues that it is important for teaching to be a high-status profession that attracts able graduates, and that once appointed and within good school leadership, teachers should have sufficient autonomy to drive forward improvements to practice and their own professional learning. One school system that exemplifies this is Finland. Sahlberg (2011), describing the distinctive approach to education reform in Finland, contrasts this with what he describes as the 'Global Education Reform Movement (GERM)' which adopts the following mix of strategies:

- Standardized teaching and learning

- Focus on literacy and numeracy

- Teaching a prescribed curriculum

- Borrowing market-oriented reform ideas

- Test-based accountability and control

By contrast, education reform in Finland, which is considered to be particularly successful, has adopted the following strategies which are the opposites of those above:

- Customizing teaching and learning

- Focus on creative learning

- Encouraging risk-taking

- Learning from the past and owning innovations

- Shared responsibility and trust

(Sahlberg 2011)

A rising tide lifts all boats

My colleague Marie Lall (2013 personal communication) has appraised the combined effects of globalization and devolution on Pakistan, with particular reference to Punjab Province. The central issue in her analysis is the 18th Constitutional Amendment of 2010, which devolved education responsibilities from federal to provincial governments. At the same time, in Article 25A, it was enacted that 'The State shall provide free and compulsory

education to all children of the age five to sixteen in such a manner as
may be determined by law'. Previous constitutions had included a right to
education but not, until this moment, a concomitant duty of the State to
provide it (Lall 2013). By devolution, the federal government 'dumped' this
new responsibility on the provinces with little additional resourcing. An
issue for some observers has been a perceived political tendency in Punjab
to invest in high-profile projects for able children at the expense of attention
to basic provision.

Under the heading 'We spent six times more on development than the last
government', the *Express Tribune*, Lahore Edition, 17 March 2013 (p 13),
reported comments by the chief minister of Punjab Province, at the end of
the government's term of office, as follows:

> The major education projects undertaken by the government included
> the construction of 16 Danish [*sic* – see below] Schools, which are
> meant to provide a high standard of education to talented students at
> low prices. The Punjab government handed out 125,000 laptops to high
> achieving students at a cost of Rs 4 billion and is currently in the process
> of distributing another 125,000. 200,000 students have received laptops
> so far. Rs 5 billion was spent on setting up IT labs in 4,286 schools, and
> Rs 2 billion was distributed via the Punjab Education Endowment Fund
> to 41,000 students. The government recruited 72,000 educators and
> regularised the services of 190,000 contractual teachers. It also launched
> a primary enrolment campaign to raise literacy. For postgraduate study,
> the government set up the Rs 100 million Resource Centre in Murree,
> which ... contains a modern digital library, connections with international
> libraries, high-speed internet and hostel facilities for researchers studying
> for PhD and MPhil degrees.

Widely reported and referred to as 'Danish Schools', giving the impression
of a connection with Denmark, these are in fact Daanish Schools. 'Daanish'
means 'deep-rooted wisdom'. These are residential schools intended for
poor but gifted children. www.daanishschools.edu.pk

The following day, the *Express Tribune*, Lahore Edition (18 March 2013
p 15), included a contrasting story regarding basic provision:

> There is only one teacher for 88 students in five classes at the Government
> Primary Girls School in Dadiyan village. A media team visited the school
> on Saturday and found that most of the students were in two classrooms,
> while the rest were made to sit in the lobby. Parents said the students'
> performance was being affected by the poor facilities. [One] said that
> water accumulated in the school building whenever it rained, it wasn't
> removed for days and made the place stink ... the classrooms were in
> poor condition with broken windows. The drinking water tank was not
> cleaned for weeks and children had been falling ill from drinking water

at school. [The] Executive District Officer [Education] said teachers were being appointed, 300 positions were advertised this year but applications on all seats were not received, and the process was still ongoing.

The idea that stretching the gifted will have the effect of a rising tide which will lift all boats also fits the Mawhiba Schools Partnership project in Saudi Arabia. In the words of its principal architect, UK expert Deborah Eyre, it:

> ... is a prestigious initiative designed to support schools to become more effective in creating a structure and a curriculum that enables students with giftedness and creativity to perform highly.

Eyre's thinking (see, for example, Eyre 1997, 2009, 2011) imported internationally derived models to be implemented in specially selected schools in Saudi Arabia, using an elaborate procurement process and teams of consultants. I and a team of colleagues led development programmes for principals and lead co-ordinators. While not without impact, the programme suffered the limitations of imposed change, typified by the Mawhiba Foundation's insistence that the programme should be in English medium only, even though some of the male principals struggled to understand.

Prioritize acute need

The opposite strategy is to direct most attention to where needs are greatest. This was the choice of the Ministry of Education in Colombia, to prioritize coaching to improve the teaching of maths and Spanish in schools with the most acute problems. At the end of a programme directed by my colleague Max Coates, Victor Lugo, a Formador working in the areas of Amazonas and Guaninia, Colombia, made the following remarks in the course of a presentation ceremony in 2012.

> Being here is a true privilege...because I am part of a major historical event in our nation...It is an audacious and courageous initiative to make our education system relevant and significant, and to contribute decisively to the development of the communities, by the communities and for the communities....The teaching profession...allows students to forge their own destiny while we seek to help them make life-changing decisions.... The true starring role in this programme is not played by us, but by the members of the educational communities we support. This conviction makes us Formadores and Tutores put up with travelling by bus, trips on cargo planes which due to their instability are called 'crazy broncos', travel by canoe, extremes of temperature, unusual food and...threats of violence.

We had the chance, only a month ago, finally to meet a group of teachers, mainly from indigenous communities from some villages in Amazonas. It had previously been impossible to arrange meetings because of their remote location. We managed to work together for an entire week and it was greatly rewarding to be able to observe their degree of commitment and the excitement in their eyes, as they felt valued, important, and especially, because they recognised themselves as learners. One of the teachers told us that when he was about to finish high school, due to the deprived conditions of his community, he had considered joining an armed group.... He thought about his role as a citizen and the impact of these terrorist groups. He rejected the recruiter: a courageous act. This demonstrates the commitment of teachers in these areas. Lack of resources is not always a valid excuse for low quality in education. Our teachers must value themselves and their contributions to achieve ... sustainable transformation.

This is the reality of our communities and these are the teachers who work on our programme. Despite the social inequality and the historical victimisation of the communities, which have supported such harmful actions as corruption and armed conflict, every day we are more convinced that the more the programme moves forward in this implementation, the more we will manage to impact the transformation of a national state with its own identity,... with confidence in its citizens and their future,... this is what we are learning,... to make Colombia the earthly paradise we dream of.

These comments concern a top-down government initiative, but convey to a remarkable degree a sense of place, a sense of emotional commitment through human encounter, and a sense of practitioner efficacy. Perhaps there is not too wide a gulf in aims and values between these government agents, and those leading the community-based learning described as follows.

Under the heading 'Born in bloodshed but living in hope', Bargent (2012) reported on the Peace Community founded in northern Colombia in 1997 following conflict and displacement. The community has eleven villages, each with an education co-ordinator. Although the government had wanted the community to end and children to leave if they wanted education, the community has established schools which are thriving, using volunteer teachers.

The new system was implemented in schools in 10 of the villages. The schools now teach 5 to 14 year olds a combination of academic subjects and lessons on community life, rural Colombian culture and the Peace Community's principles of resistance, solidarity, pluralism, transparency, freedom and justice. Lessons often take place outside the classroom. The children, who are all victims of the violence, are thereby given space to learn to cope with trauma and bereavement.

(Bargent 2012)

If it works for you, it will work for me

In 2001, the leaders of the Arabian Gulf nation of Qatar initiated a process of education reform, and engaged the RAND Corporation to examine K-12 education and to recommend options for improvement. Qatar's economic development through oil and gas wealth had, in 2001, greatly outstripped its educational development. With only a small percentage of its population being Qataris, the rest being migrants and ex-pat workers, inevitably ideas for reform, and the expertise to lead it, had to come from outside. A further contextual challenge, and the down-side of wealth, was motivating male Qatari citizens to take their education seriously.

The RAND review (Brewer et al. 2007) produced three options, the first and third of which were rejected. These were to continue with a centralized system run by the Ministry: rejected because that had not succeeded previously; and to move to a voucher system: rejected as being too risky without first developing an effective market of school provision. The chosen option – the Independent School Model – aimed to decentralize governance, encourage school autonomy and increase parental choice. This model involved what were previously government schools becoming independent but in receipt of government funding, very similar in concept to Academies in England or Charter Schools in USA.

In mature systems, the mindset of school leadership has grown with autonomy over a period of years. As Alkubaisi (2013 work in progress) is discovering, plentiful money and an imported solution cannot produce a quick substitute for that process.

Learning for 'productive practice'

An issue is how infrastructural developments are, or are not, conducive to sustainable improvements in educational outcomes. One strand of writing concerns the difficulties that affect the implementation of reforms which mean that many do not produce the full extent of the outcomes that governments intended, or that the positive outcomes may be accompanied by unintended side effects. In their influential 'Change over Time' project, which examined changes in school systems over a thirty-year period, Hargreaves and Goodson (2006) concluded that the reforms which proved to be sustainable had a number of characteristics in common. They generated significant kinds of learning; involved the whole local system and advanced social justice; they could be maintained on the basis of existing and achievable resources; sustained teachers' emotional and intellectual selves; involved shared responsibility; benefited from external advocacy and support; and accommodated diverse (rather than standard) local approaches. The research noted that these features of long-term sustainable change were often weak or absent from government-led reform programmes.

Many countries have been pursuing strategies to improve schools by raising the quality of teachers and teaching, and Jensen et al. (2012) report successful examples from south-east Asia, two of which are summarized next.

In Hong Kong, school reform has included school-based curriculum development, assessment for learning, professional development, and leadership. The leadership reforms have included the appointment of curriculum and/or pedagogy leaders to work with every teacher; and school principal training to create role models with high-level skills in the new pedagogy (Jensen et al. 2012).

In Shanghai, a successful teacher mentoring scheme has been developed, which includes the following characteristics:

- All teachers have mentors

- Frequent feedback is provided, based on classroom observation

- Outstanding teachers do more mentoring

- Beginning teachers have several mentors covering subject skills and classroom management

- Substantial time is invested in the mentoring system, and the cost of doing so has been accepted: for example, class sizes have been increased to enable teachers to have increased non-contact hours.
                                                          (Jensen et al. 2012)

The Institute of Education (IOE), University of London, entered an agreement with Save the Children UK, and Save the Children India (Bal Raksha Bharat), to make a partnership contribution of technical assistance throughout the life of a three-year project funded by the European Union to address the challenges in India of poor teacher cadre management, limited models of inclusive education, weak capacity and disjointed systems for monitoring teacher performance and managing schools.

Specifically the project aimed to build the capacities of national and state level institutions and education departments in India, by identifying and learning from international models of best practice in the areas of teacher cadre management and leadership, with a particular emphasis on inclusive education in a decentralized context. The capacity of local education structures was to be developed through selected districts in each of five states developing inclusive learning environments based on a decentralized and participatory planning process. The stages of the project involved learning from an inventory of international practice; the constitution of various groups working at national, state, district, cluster and village levels; and the reinforcement of the capacity of policy-makers and implementers at national and state levels. The IOE's contribution is summarized in Wilkins et al. (2013) from which this section draws.

The project, of which IOE's technical assistance formed part, was conceived from a particular philosophical standpoint which emphasized local capacity-building in the Indian education system especially at State level, to be achieved through a *learning* process. The technical assistance provided by IOE inevitably, and rightly, had an organic relationship with that process of learning. Of course, the sharing of ideas and information by IOE through publications and workshop presentations is in itself a direct contribution to learning. More importantly, the pattern, nature and emphasis of these contributions evolved responsively to take account of the actions and learning journeys being undertaken by project participants on the ground.

The fact that the project established strong local ownership, in which individual participating States made choices about the scale, direction, pace and focus for development, reflecting local contextual considerations, set a significant design imperative for the ways in which technical assistance should support learning. The fact that some States adopted an action-learning approach in which the learning process was punctuated by real executive decision-making gave further emphasis to the same consideration.

Terano et al. (2011) reported some important considerations, derived from research, regarding the nature and dynamics of 'productive practices' identified within certain global examples of school systems. These practices are 'productive' because they are productive of student learning outcomes; and what enables them to be productive of that student learning is that they provide spaces and processes which support professional learning. This research formed part of the technical assistance provided by the IOE. This insight, right at the heart of the subject content of the technical assistance, combined with the professional adult learning strategies which governed the design of the processes of the technical assistance, together gave the technical assistance what might be described as a distinctive 'signature pedagogy'. This was the outcome of interactions within an organic partnership relationship, rather than a conceptual framework unilaterally adopted at the outset by the IOE. The result was a coherent philosophy underpinning a process of facilitated cross-system learning for capacity-building.

Terano et al.'s (2011) terminology 'productive practices' reflected their conclusion that the key element that causes certain practices to produce exemplary outcomes is not so much the practice itself, as the ways in which practitioners learn from their experience and from each other. If the practices are simply transferred to another setting without engendering an equivalent process of professional learning, the outcomes are likely to be disappointing (Terano et al. 2011). The productive practices they identified, related to teacher cadre management, school-based management, and inclusive education, which in all cases were the outcome of infrastructural developments, were as follows:

- England: approaches to teacher recruitment, deployment, pre-service training, professional development and networking

- Finland: developing high-quality teachers by making the profession attractive and setting high standards

- Ontario: approaches to leadership development. Their conception of leadership embraced shared vision, collaborative learning approach and effective communication among all stakeholders.

- Queensland: approaches within a federalized system to strengthen inclusive education to meet the needs of a diverse student population, mainly through improvements to teacher quality

- New Zealand: approaches within a highly decentralized school system, with high levels of teacher autonomy and professionalism, to synthesizing evidence and developing evidence-informed practices

- Indonesia: curriculum development at school level, within national guidelines, to enable schools to reflect the needs of their diverse local populations.

The conclusion of this study was that a central focus of education reform should be to improve the capacity of the teaching workforce, which in turn required the following preconditions:

- Establishing and articulating a vision for reform

- Focusing on teaching and learning

- Capacity-building through pre-service and in-service training

- Building the educational credibility of the civil service

- Adapting to local needs

- Developing coherent monitoring systems

- Developing teachers to be advocates of the reform process

- Adopting a constructive approach to the distribution of resources

This research report (Terano et al. 2011) eschewed the notion of 'international best practice' in the sense that those words imply practice which is replicable across different national and cultural contexts. It did, however, identify the centrality of teaching and learning in the classroom to educational reform, and hence the importance of improved teacher capability and improved school leadership. The report also addressed policy-making, including the need to determine priorities, and to share the policy-making process across a wide range of different levels of decision-making, involving those as close to practice as possible. Often merits have been found in de-centralization and educational democracy; in structuring decision-making to give clear areas for professional autonomy; and in encouraging distributed leadership. This suite of strategies for effective decision-making is completed by the encouragement of a culture of enquiry, promoting critical thinking, reflection and research-informed practice.

Terano et al. drew attention to research which indicated that effective communication strategies are necessary to successful education reform. Successful communication not only informs: it creates involvements, dialogues, roles and relationships. In the context of education, it also, essentially, engenders learning.

These examples of recent research point towards the importance of professional learning of teachers and school leaders, within systems that achieve a successful combination of local autonomy and systemic coherence and shared purpose. The key is, of course, the nature of 'learning'. There is a big difference between learning how to implement someone else's ideas and agenda, and truly professional learning which advances thinking, practice and agency. There is considerable scope for school leaders to draw on global developments in education in a discerning and productive manner (Wilkins 2010), provided that the interfaces between schools and centralized infrastructures enable this. The final two chapters explore how professionalization and leadership development can help to convert spaces of prescription to spaces of negotiation.

CHAPTER EIGHT

Towards a Pedagogy
of School Leadership

Working towards the idea of a 'pedagogy' of school leadership requires a number of mental steps. School leadership is educational work, not just for the learning of the students, but also for the learning and development of the staff. An important part of this role is the work that school leaders do in their capacity as senior and influential members of the teaching profession. The externally orientated work of school leaders, whether with parents, civil society, industry or official agencies may also embrace an educational dimension: not formal instruction, but more in the tradition of informal adult and community education.

School leadership and leaders

Who are school leaders? The first point to make is that they are growing in number and influence – there is growing recognition that school leadership makes a difference. There is a growing number because the world population of children and young people is growing, of whom an increasing proportion are in formal schooling, so there are more school leaders, even if many of them have yet to progress from administration to leadership of learning. In many school systems, leadership has become more widely distributed within schools, creating a substantial population of 'middle leaders'. The scope of individuals' leadership remits may be nested from individual classrooms to national and international spans of responsibility. A question for leadership development is, how 'leadership' is different at different scales of operation, and whether those differences are ones of degree and emphasis or fundamental differences of kind.

Worldwide, there are no neat characterizations of those exercising senior leadership responsibilities for schools. The position of headteacher or principal is held by people who do, and who do not, hold a professional qualification as an educator; some of whom are also either the proprietor or a senior entrepreneur within a business of which the school forms part. Many headteachers are also political activists. Some are important community leaders. In England, there is a long tradition of some individuals combining school leadership with religious ministry. In some systems, appointment to a senior school leadership position depends on good standing in the ruling political party, or on trade union backing. In some systems, being a headteacher is a major stretch of a professional career; in others it is an interlude after which the individual returns to classroom teaching.

There is even greater variety at school system leadership level, where the leader may be a senior headteacher (or 'super-head'), a district school superintendent or other local government official, an entrepreneur, a philanthropist, an official in a religious organization, or a member of a university department in systems where universities are also providers of schools. In addition, a range of policy advisers, opinion-formers and prominent academic researchers could also be said to count as school system leaders. On another dimension, students and parents can contribute significantly to school leadership. Certainly the school leader of the future, however they are defined, will need the skills and dispositions to work among a very diverse group of other individuals exercising leadership roles and influences.

It is important to open up the narrow conceptions that can attach to school leadership in the English context, where often the term is used to refer to headteachers leading state schools in the achievement of politically specified priorities. Even in England school leadership is much wider than that! On the other hand, the scope of leaders and leadership under discussion could become so diffuse that it becomes impossible to theorize.

To deal with this, I advocate professionalism in school leadership. This book is not written for the particular interests of business entrepreneurs or political activists. Its focus is the leadership of schools and school systems for the purpose of enabling learning. My target audience is anyone who shares that focus. If they also want their school to make a profit, or if they hope that educating (as distinct from indoctrinating) people will support particular kinds of political change, then in an open society that is their own business. I offer no advice in support of such aims because I focus on school leadership as a professional activity.

Agency as an end in itself

To talk of pedagogy requires consideration of aims, means, methods and relationships between teachers and learners. It is logically consistent to want to see the pedagogic principles set out in Chapter 4 being applied both to the leadership of schools as organizations, and to the leadership of the teaching profession. These are two different aims which draw on different ways of thinking. In particular, those principles include a focus on the intrinsic justification of education, on enabling people to arrive at their own informed opinions and choices, and on learner agency in respect of the learning journey. They include a focus on activist problem-solving which, while being inevitably 'political', is de-coupled from agendas based on particular political ideologies; and an openness to finding 'ways and means' of resourcing education that are not constrained within conventional models.

The conceptual frameworks that school leaders place around school, family and community partnerships should be consistent with the cultivation of mutual respect, educative development and agency. The Epstein model of partnership respects the agendas and concerns both of school and community, identifies different forms of partnership which require balanced attention, and provides a forum for sharing accumulated research about successful partnership practice (Epstein et al. 1997).

Within the school leadership role, the principles above are advanced through a combination of professionalism, which provides quality assurance for public trust; knowledge generation, which provides expert authority; community relationships which promote agency; and financial leverage which increases the beneficial impact of available resources. It is worth emphasizing, however, that the core aim of these activities is the educational aim of opening up the opportunities available to people and enabling them to make their own informed choices of which options to follow. Thus for the educator, agency is an end in its own right. This involves the development of criticality in relation to imposed 'soft power' agendas; a self-denying ordinance for educators to restrain the imposition of their own preferences on their learners; and, within acceptable moral limits, tolerance of a wide range of choices on the part of learners and their communities about the ends to which they will direct their learning. 'Agency' may embrace the ideas expressed by words such as educative empowerment, capacity-building and consciousness. If these principles guide work with students, what might be the equivalent and consistent principles for the professional leadership of teachers, and the organizational leadership of school staffs? This question highlights the problematical nature of 'education leadership': a puzzle at the heart of the enterprise. If leadership requires followers, and if education is about people making up their own minds, is 'education leadership' a contradiction in terms? A pedagogy of school leadership must provide a solution to that conundrum.

The professionalization of teaching and school leadership

In England, and internationally, the term 'leadership' has been emphasized by central governments, perhaps partly because it conveniently blurs the distinctions between policy-making, policy implementation, governance, and the professional direction and development of educational practice, each of which have their own constitutional and legal bases of authority and accountability. Government-directed 'leadership' has enabled a command and control culture to cut through the constitutional checks and balances of the English system, and to undermine notions of professional judgement and autonomy. Internationally, complex multi-agency development projects, short-term funding, donor agencies' love of project management, and the increased involvement of the private sector have all combined to emphasize approaches to education leadership which are essentially managerial rather than professional. This has its shortcomings: for example Ali (2006) examined why policies fail in Pakistan, and in addition to factors conventionally cited (goals, politics, governance, centralization, resources and foreign aid), found that implementers 'do their own sense-making'.

The same tendency is seen in many countries where governments are seeking to raise standards through top-down interventions. This managerialism is being balanced in part by school leaders and practitioners not only 'sense-making' (Ali 2006), but also asserting their professionalism through the networks to which they belong; through reflective practice and the ability to generate and access independent sources of information.

The concept of professionalism in school leadership enables 'multi-hatted' individuals to be more conscious of the different roles that they exercise, and commentators to choose the aspects of a person's activity that should be seen as falling within their role as a school leader. Some school leaders have other roles such as business entrepreneur, political activist, religious or community leader, or government official. There are not sharp boundaries between roles. For example, professional practice as a school leader is likely to involve some business management, some lobbying and some community leadership. That is different from someone who might perhaps hold a generic public office (not concerned with education) and who runs a chain of schools as a business in their spare time. Multi-hatted people do not cease to have one of their roles when they turn their attention to another, but there is a sense in which at any one moment, one of their roles will provide the dominant mindset governing their behaviour. The other roles have not gone away but at that moment they play a supporting rather than leading part. Incidentally it could be argued that in the modern world, with greater autonomy, and greater complexity both of organizations and issues, there will be greater need for school leaders generally to become more multi-hatted, combining educational expertise with being business-savvy and politically adept.

How to decide the boundaries of the school leader's role

Any global-level mapping of education leadership exposes the variety of space-time contexts for leadership. It is not just a matter of different places, with different levels of educational provision, socio-economic development and political stability: vast though the range of such circumstances may be between, for example, a flood-relief camp at Tatta in Sind and the playing fields of Eton. There is also the matter of the interpretations and meanings that the players involved attach to what they are experiencing or observing: what they regard as the 'problem' (How big a problem? Why is it a problem? To whom is it a problem?), and what they envision as a satisfactory 'solution'. This will be linked to expectations, motivations and aspirations, and hence also to perceived success criteria. In the example of the flood-relief camp, do any of those involved, such as the volunteers providing make-shift education in the 'school tent', or the Pakistan Navy who run the camp, or Western agencies, believe (perhaps on the ground of global equity) that the ideal model to aspire to *ought* to be something like the education offered at Eton? Or something like a madrasah in Islamabad?

Where there are no universal rules – but instead dynamic change, fluidity, the constraints and opportunities of local contexts, and many interweaving agendas – school leaders have to work out their stance afresh in each situation. They will have their identity and their high-level beliefs and values, forged through the significant moorings and mobilities which have punctuated their journey. That identity sets a general outlook, but the diagnosis of what needs to be done in a particular situation, and what kind of leader to be, reflect a range of dispositions and motivations. School leadership with a globalized mindset needs to cultivate greater consciousness, and less reliance on instinct and intuition, in the choice of aims, strategies, tactics and behaviours considered appropriate to particular contexts.

The focus of this chapter is how school systems operate organizationally, by blending four organizational orientations. These, in shorthand, are professionalism, knowledge generation, activism and management, and it is assumed that the school leaders of the future, like those of the present, will need to fuse elements of all four. 'Management' must be distinguished from 'managerialism'. The latter is the currently fashionable term to describe a style of directive, demanding, bullying, blaming management that has wholly negative connotations, and which is incompatible with some fundamental educational principles. That is different from 'management' which describes the honourable art and science of getting things done, which every educational leader needs. Because professionalism depends for its authority on evidence and hence on research, it has a connection to knowledge generation, especially to the extent to which the teaching profession is able to engage in research and make cumulative and worthwhile contributions to the field.

Organizational leadership which emphasizes professionalism is concerned with the ongoing enhancement and application of standards of practice: standards which will assure quality, and which embed the application to practice of knowledge gained from research and from experience. Professionalism tends to emphasize a broad, generalized view of time and space. The authority accorded by the general public to professional standards and recognitions normally has to be earned over the long term, and the structures of a profession need to be constant enough to form a basis for planning a whole career. Similarly there is an element of universality in the notions of competent professional practice by, say, a doctor, engineer or accountant: people in many countries would share broadly similar expectations of what these roles entail. Professionalism implies support for the gradual evolution of standards which are widely recognized over time and place. All professions have specialisms, and just as medicine has the specialism of emergency medicine, supported by a recently formed College of Emergency Medicine, so in education, designing teaching and learning practices in extremely challenging geographical contexts is evolving towards a distinct professional specialism, and Karpinska (2012) writes about an 'education-in-emergencies community' in terms which identify this as a community of professional practice.

An orientation towards activism carries a different emphasis. This concerns the ends and purposes to which the professional applies their skills. Here the focus is essentially social and political. Typically the activist leader wants to right a wrong; address a social injustice; or administer humanitarian relief. Their agenda involves enabling an identified group to improve their circumstances, and often, to bring about a change in power relations. Activist education leaders are conscious of the empowering purposes and effects of education, and are drawn to give particular attention to vulnerable and disadvantaged groups, intending to bring about a long-term improvement in their chances and quality of life.

One of the issues for the preparation and ongoing development of school leaders is to recognize the political dimension of educational activism and to have recourse to conceptual frameworks and rational justifications for deciding where to draw the proper boundaries between a role as a professional school leader and a role as politically active individual. When leaders support the application of educational professional skills to activist purposes; when they enable the development of appropriate means and methodologies to pursue those purposes; and when they provide an organizational context for practice which is conducive, then it becomes meaningful to talk about a 'pedagogy' of school leadership, recognizing that the educational purposes are enabled through processes which are themselves fundamentally of an educational nature.

School leadership and teacher professionalism

Discussion about the status of teaching as a profession is receiving a fresh wave of attention. Understandings of teacher professionalization are centrally relevant to issues of school leadership. Andy Hargreaves and Michael Fullan (2012) wrote a new book called *Professional Capital*. In the UK, in 2011, the Independent Review of Teachers' Standards produced recommendations concerning the replacement of the government-designated 'Excellent Teacher' and 'Advanced Skills Teacher' standards. The UK government is encouraging the leadership teams of Teaching Schools to become effective in fostering practitioner action research, within a context of ever-increasing school autonomy. A debate has started in the UK (see, for example, Exley 2012, Woolcock 2012, Leslie 2013 and Wilkins 2013) about whether there should be a new Royal College of Teaching.

Internationally projects are moving forward to define and enhance the practice and recognition of teachers' work. An International Summit on the Teaching Profession took place in New York, involving twenty-three countries, on 14–15 March 2012, organized by Education International, which is the global federation of teachers' unions. The OECD report *Preparing Teachers and Developing School Leaders for the 21st Century: Lessons from Around the World* (Schleicher 2012b) was produced to support this event, as its Foreword explained:

> To help governments effectively address these and other key issues, placing teachers and school leaders at the centre of improvement efforts, the US Department of Education, the OECD and Education International are bringing education ministers, union leaders and other teacher leaders together in the second International Summit on the Teaching Profession in March 2012. This publication summarises the evidence that underpins the Summit, bringing together data analysis and experience for better education for better lives.
>
> (Schleicher 2012b p 3)

What links these examples of recent developments? They are all concerned with the tension between professionalism and managerialism in education. Professionalism is represented by attempts to describe the complex skills and judgements needed in teaching, and to encourage creative, thoughtful, self-motivated innovation by practitioners, individually and collaboratively. Managerialism is represented by a focus on the organizational concept of 'school autonomy', which means increasing the executive powers of headteachers; combined with data-driven 'school improvement' in which the school as an institution is the unit which is deemed either to succeed or fail. A new way of looking at professionalism would serve as a lightening-conductor to deal with this tension, and a knowledge-base derived from a certain kind of school-based practitioner research could be catalyst, indicator and product of this 'reaction': helping to bring it about, showing it is working, and forming a substantive benefit.

Teachers as 'craft operatives' or professionals

In the UK, whether teachers should be treated as 'craft operatives' or professionals is hotly contested, and as often occurs, governmental stances seem to back both positions at once. Official support for teachers' engagement in practitioner research is a good indicator of attitudes, and it is interesting to compare the UK with some other systems.

In China, which has an authoritarian education system, Article 7 of the Teachers Law provides that

> Teachers shall enjoy the following rights: to conduct education and teaching activities and carry out reform and experiment in education and teaching; to engage in scientific research and academic exchanges, join professional academic societies and fully express their views in academic activities.
>   (http://www.moe.gov.cn/publicfiles/business/htmlfiles/moe/moe_280)

In Shanghai, the Shanghai Education Commission (SEC) is responsible for basic, higher and vocational education for twenty-three million people. SEC employs the school principals. The schools are large and there are three levels of leadership, headed by the principal and by the party secretary (who is similar to a chair of governors). They are supported by three directors: for teaching and learning; student affairs; and logistics. There are thirteen levels on the teaching career ladder with professional development attached to each. The school staff is organized into teaching and research groups: teaching groups are subject based, and spend two hours per week planning and reviewing. Research groups do and publish research, led by a Lead/Master Teacher. Publishing research is a requirement to become a Master Teacher (Asia Society 2012).

In Chile, the Ministry of Education is developing 'Headteachers of Excellence' who will, among other things, foster practitioner research.

In Ontario, the Ontario College of Teachers produced in 1999 a statement of standards of practice for the teaching profession (which has legislative force) and which included the commitment to 'reflect on their practice and learn from experience; and draw on and contribute, where appropriate, to various forms of educational research' (Ontario College of Teachers 1999 p 13).

In Fiji, standards for (basic grade) teachers have been described as including a focus on educational leadership and research (Erebus International 2008). In the USA, the National Board for Professional Teacher Standards, which is an independent professional accrediting body, has considered (since 1989) that:

> Able teachers are also students of education scholarship and are cognizant of the settled and unsettled territory in their field. They stay abreast of current research and, when appropriate, incorporate new findings into their practice.... They might conduct and publish their own research, if so inclined, for testing of new approaches and hypotheses is a commonplace habit among adept teachers, even if a normally overlooked and undocumented one.
>   (NBPTS 1989)

By contrast to these examples, the UK Teachers' Standards (DfE 2012) which came into force from September 2012 make no mention at all of the word 'research'. In relation to higher level teachers, the Second Report of the Independent Review of Teachers' Standards published in December 2011 proposed a new designation of 'Master Teacher'. The only reference to 'research' in the definition of this designation is the statement: 'They are analytical in evaluating and developing their own craft and knowledge, making full use of continuing professional development and appropriate research'. So this most senior level of teaching practitioner is to *use* research deemed by some other authority to be *appropriate* for them. The tone of the entire definition of 'Master Teacher' bears comparison with a nineteenth-century description of the perfect senior domestic servant, who diligently practises their *craft* within a system ordered by their betters, and, who, above all, knows their place.

The one place in the English system where practitioner research is officially encouraged is in Teaching Schools. This appears an act of enlightenment for which credit is due, even though there is no correlation between the factors which enable a school to achieve Teaching School status and the factors which make a school a conducive environment for practitioner research. The message conveyed is that engagement in practitioner research is not an intrinsic part of professional practice as a teacher, but a 'reward' given selectively by Government on the basis of *institutional* rather than professional criteria. Fortunately many schools and many more individuals make up their own minds to engage in practitioner research.

Yet as well as statements of teachers' standards in numerous countries, academic writing from around the world also supports the research-engagement of teachers. One example based on research in Singapore is Cheng-Yong Tan's recent advocacy of a new conceptualization of instructional leadership: 'The new model of instructional leadership proposed emphasises contextualised knowledge creation through school-wide endorsement of action research to address student and teacher needs in the unique context of the school' (Cheng-Yong Tan 2012).

In Wilkins (2011) I told the story of how, over the last decade or so, some schools have used the autonomy they already have to become research-engaged schools, using research to assert greater ownership over their educational philosophy, direction and professional culture.

The UK myth of the 'done-to' profession

Sometimes literature and debate refer to 'recent' developments and pressures within the English system that are impacting on teachers' work. Clearly the extent and pace of government-imposed change has become more acute, but it is far from new. Gill Helsby's study of changing teachers' work (Helsby 1999) identified the introduction of the Technical and Vocational Educational Initiative (TVEI) in 1983 as the start of the new era of change.

This marked the start of specific direction by a government agency of matters previously regarded as within the professional domain. TVEI established the trend followed by all UK governments since, to prefer the expediency of dodging around the constitutional safeguards of which they are the custodian rather than going to the effort of changing them. That form of prescription has increased exponentially over the intervening thirty years: a period of time that means few teachers can now remember the era of professional trust and discretion. Although the context and the intensity of pressure have changed, the frustrations reported by Helsby remain recognizable.

Whitty (2008) reviewed the changes and political pressures which have impacted on teaching in England, and the ways in which these have been critiqued – mainly from a sociological perspective – and used this to propound the concepts of traditional, managerial, collaborative and democratic models of professionalism. Collaborative professionalism is teachers working within multi-professional teams, while democratic professionalism is teachers actively engaging with stakeholders including students and parents. Perhaps in practice a mix of all four models is likely to feature in teachers' working lives.

Both Whitty's (2008) analysis and Power's (2008) depictions of the 'distressed' and 'oppressed' professional, introduced earlier, are representative in highlighting the 'beleaguered' quality of life for many teachers. This reflects the reality: many teachers are pressured, beset with impossible expectations and feel failures. There is, however, a question about who is seen to be included within the profession. Much of Whitty's analysis assumes the profession is the teachers who 'have been done to' by school managers and national level government agencies. This ignores the fact that many of the individuals in those positions who have driven these developments are themselves members of the profession. So these issues and tensions, especially those related to what Whitty called 'managerial professionalism', are being played out within the profession just as much as between the profession and other stakeholders.

Politicians in the UK do not themselves run any schools: within the teaching profession, in senior positions, are those who, for whatever motivation, have been the zealous implementers and advocates of government policies including 'managerialism'. This calls for a major re-conceptualization: from teaching as a 'done-to' profession that has been at the mercy of politicians and other external forces, to teaching as a profession that is deeply divided and troubled within its own membership.

Teaching and school leadership: Two professions or one?

In a number of jurisdictions there are initiatives to develop professional criteria for school leaders which mesh with those for other teachers. In

Alberta, this work has progressively embraced school principals and school district education administrators. The development of criteria ('criteria' because there the word 'standards' is reserved for those that can be measured and enforced) has been accompanied by associated professional development programmes (Brandon 2012). In Alberta this work is moving forward through a broad consensus among government, school leaders and the unions, of a kind that in the UK was replaced decades ago by confrontational relationships.

In Alberta, school leaders:

> must nurture and sustain a school culture that values and supports learning;... promote and model life-long learning for students, teachers and other staff; and promote and facilitate meaningful, collaborative professional learning for teachers and other staff.
>
> (Government of Alberta 2012)

In the USA, in 2009, the National Board for Professional Teaching Standards extended its scope to develop National Board Certification for Education Leaders (NBCEL) which builds upon and complements its standards for teachers.

In Punjab Province, Pakistan, the Directorate of Staff Development has been working towards the creation of an autonomous body for teacher registration and licensing which will by deliberate policy embrace headteachers as well as other teachers, although progress is being obstructed by the teachers' unions.

In Ontario, the Ontario College of Teachers makes the following important statement:

> The professional learning programmes accredited by the Ontario College of Teachers must address the professional growth needs of members from the time they prepare to enter the teaching profession to the time they retire.... In the College of Teachers Act, Regulations under the Act, and in this statement of standards of practice, 'teacher' means a member of the Ontario College of Teachers. This definition requires that the College accredit professional learning programmes for not only classroom teachers but also for members in a broad range of roles such as principals, occasional teachers, superintendents and directors of education.
>
> (Ontario College of Teachers 1999)

The significance of this statement is the way it embraces principals not only within the definition of 'the teaching profession', but also within the spirit of a coherent, united professional learning community.

In the history of the teaching profession in England, fragmentation within the profession has been one of the obstacles (but only one among several) that has limited the perceptions and realities of teaching as a 'proper profession' (see, for example, Willis 2012). In earlier times the fault-lines were, for example, between primary and secondary teachers, and between different sectors of education. More recently, a number of factors have led to the impression that the fissure is hierarchical: between teachers as the 'operatives', and the newly distinctive profession of education leaders who manage them. Any advance of professionalism in teaching must counter this wholly negative impression, and it is encouraging that headteachers' leaders have been in the forefront of supporting a new Royal College of Teaching. This distinction is not an issue in other professions: accountants, architects, engineers and surgeons have professional identities and belong to professional bodies regardless of the level of position-power they have achieved in their careers.

School autonomy or professional autonomy?

In *Professional Capital*, Hargreaves and Fullan (2012) present a persuasive argument both for professionalism and for reflective practice as antidotes to managerialism. They promote the concept of 'professional capital' as a function of human capital (the capacities of an individual), social capital (the capacities derived from interrelationships), and 'decisional capital'. The latter is based on case law and on clinical practice in medicine, and the equivalent in teaching is the accumulation of professional judgements. The book offers advice on promoting a change in this direction which is as well-researched, refreshing and inspiring as one would expect from those authors. They do not extend its argument fully into some of the areas with which this chapter is concerned.

Hargreaves and Fullan (2012) do not specify the relationship between the three kinds of capital: are they additional to each other, or overlapping, or concentrically nested, with decisional capital at the centre and human capital being the largest circle? Perhaps the latter because, presumably, the other forms of capital also manifest themselves in individual capacity, i.e. human capital. Hargreaves and Fullan acknowledge that teaching is different from law or medicine but do not describe what the equivalent would be in teaching to legal and clinical records: what practical steps does a teacher take to access the decisional capital of their profession? The same problem arose in David Hargreaves' argument in *Education Epidemic* (D. Hargreaves 2003) for a 'babbling bazaar' of laterally spreading teacher innovation: how to provide an infrastructure to enable such innovation without falling back on incompatible managerialism? In his more recent work, D. Hargreaves (2010) postulated a self-improving school system based on 'local solutions' 'co-created' by 'family clusters of schools'. This put even greater emphasis on organizational and managerial mechanisms and concepts, typified by phrases such as '*schools* take ownership of problems' (my emphasis), and again relied on some unspecified, shadowy 'Big Brother'-like figure guiding and controlling these developments. Like

D. Hargreaves, A. Hargreaves and Fullan (2012) continue to imply that the autonomous school is the fundamental organizational unit for professional leadership, supervision and collaboration. They do not offer a developed model of professionalism, nor discuss the actual and potential role of professional bodies, of the kind that maintain standards and advance practice in other professions.

In the UK, professional status has not featured on most teachers' radar either as an end in its own right, or as a means to achieve, in the longer term, more control over professional matters and more cushioning from constant political interference. A significant minority do, however, choose to invest their own time and money in the wide range of subject associations, phase and specialized associations and learned societies which go a long way towards, and in some cases fully succeed in, offering professional standing and support to their members. A new Royal College of Teaching would go much further.

When government talks about giving decision-making back to the profession it refers to 'school autonomy', which is fundamentally about organizational administration. The autonomy that matters is professional autonomy, which reaches its fullest expression through a professional body structure. Such professional autonomy reduces the significance of the school as the organizational unit for collaborative professional learning. When that is achieved, the issue of school autonomy would seem less significant, because it would be exposed as being concerned with administrative systems rather than with professional practice.

Practitioner research as the cement in the structure

Power (2008) identified that the realities of transparent access to information, accountability and pressure to perform had permanently changed the context for modern professionals. Even if teaching is professionalized and there is a genuine increase in professional autonomy, there could be no going back to traditional professionalism, with its lack of transparency and accountability. This is why practitioner research is so central to the development of the new emergent forms of professionalism in teaching. Conducting and sharing practitioner research is a way of turning modern access to information from being a threat to teachers' professional autonomy to being its driving force and justification. Ultimately, rational argument based on relevant evidence is what underpins expertise and authority when systems move away from the 'do it because I say so' culture.

Access to accumulated evidence must be an element in decisional capital (Hargreaves and Fullan 2012). Involvement in undertaking practitioner research, and collaborative use of research, provide the structure and language for dialogue within the profession (of teachers and headteachers) which is different from a dialogue dominated by positional authority. Information gained by using or undertaking research enables teachers under pressure to become Power's (2008) 'imaginative professionals' who can distinguish between, and see the connection between, their private problems and systemic issues. Research enables teachers to contextualize their work and to evaluate it more objectively, and gives them the facts and confidence to challenge unreasonable expectations. It gives them the knowledge and processes to develop their own efficacy in improving educational outcomes for students. Research engagement, especially if combined with active participation in professional bodies and learned societies, gives teachers a supportive professional community which is independent from their employing institution.

Practitioner research is also the means to answer the question, raised in previous chapters, of how to measure aspects of education that are valued, but which do not lend themselves to statistics or league table rankings. The ideas used in quality assurance provide pointers to forms of evidence which could be gathered through practitioner research for this purpose.

The leadership of quality assurance, in any industry, involves making sure that answers are available to the following four questions: Are there clear standards? How and by whom are standards set? How and by whom are standards monitored? How and by whom are judgements made about whether or not standards have been met? For many aspects of running a school, standards are set externally, for example through laws and regulations, and through external examinations.

There are also success criteria where standards are set internally. Some are easy to measure, such as examination results, student attendance, staff attendance and financial viability. In relation to more complex criteria, most schools in England could give sophisticated answers to the four quality assurance questions posed above on the matter of how much progress students are making in core subjects, using assessment data. For some other kinds of success criteria where standards can be set internally, it is much harder to give satisfactory answers to the quality assurance questions: for example in relation to the school's mission statement and values, and in fields such as good school-home relations, extra-curricular activities and broader education, and the dispositions and attributes that the school seeks to foster in its students. The school's leaders may say, and believe, that these are held to be important. So how are they quality assured?

Some more questions need to be added to the four quality assurance questions posed above, regarding how those questions are asked and answered. Who is involved? Does this include those who deliver the standard and those affected by it? What information supports the process? Where does it come from? Who can see it? It soon becomes clear that measuring the softer aspects of education that are valued is an ongoing research project: one that involves students, parents and teachers as co-researchers, increasing each others' understanding of what good looks like, generating evidence, and interpreting that evidence into judgements about the extent of success achieved – judgements backed by sufficient evidence to stand up to external scrutiny.

Surrey Square Primary School in Southwark, London, is highly successful, and attributes this success in part to a set of core values that are held dear and are prominent in daily work and conversations. These are, in summary form: responsibility, perseverance, compassion, respect, enjoyment, community and excellence. Members of the school community have a shared understanding of these words, and a visitor will observe a distinctive ethos. The question is how the practices which cultivate these values can be professionalized, quality assured, and replicated elsewhere. One of the school's two co-headteachers, Liz Robinson, is leading a series of practitioner research projects to add depth of meaning to the core values, and evidence of the practices and outcomes associated with them.

In these ways, undertaking and supporting practitioner research represents the surest alternatives to managerialism, and the strongest endorsement and cultivation of teacher professionalism.

Routes to professionalism in different contexts

There are only two routes to professionalization – the shift towards more self-governance of standards and practice. The first is by legislation, to transfer functions from bodies under direct government control to autonomous status amounting to professional self-governance. Legislation created the Ontario College of Teachers, and globally it is the dominant model for raising professional standards. Its disadvantages are that it depends on political patronage, and it can be repealed, creating expedient solutions that last only until future politicians take a different view. That was the case with the creation and subsequent abolition of the General Teaching Council for England.

The second route to professionalization is professional activism: a collective self-motivation to do, to be, to achieve. In a profound sense, true autonomy is taken, not given. This was how the old professions grew their structures and identities. Whereas legislation can produce mass regulation, professional activism has to concentrate on what can be done 'in the spaces', without requiring permission. This includes professional development, professional networking, and collective advancement of standards of professional practice.

Professionalism and the unions

In the UK, the teachers' trades unions ('professional associations') have striven to improve the professional standing of their members, by undertaking educational research, providing professional development and advice, and publishing journals. The campaign current at the time of writing to establish a new Royal College of Teaching is supported by the General Secretaries of several of the professional associations. The new professional body's constitution would, incidentally, specifically exclude it from any involvement in matters of pay and conditions of service. So in the UK, there is no fundamental incompatibility between trade unionism and professionalization. At a global level the same may be said of Education International, cited earlier.

This is not so elsewhere. As noted, teachers' unions are obstructing the establishment of an autonomous professional body for teachers' standards and development in Punjab Province, Pakistan. Also, in Mexico, from my observations in 2010 it seemed that the teachers' union operated a closed shop, having complete control over who could be appointed to teaching posts, with the consequence that salaried positions were bought and sold without regard for suitability or performance. In countries where the teachers' unions wield great political influence, with the effect that schools are organized for the convenience of teachers rather than for the learning of students, and where politicians dare not pass laws to upset those arrangements, the expansion of private-sector or community-based school provision offers the best way out of the impasse. On the other hand, responsible trade unionism can be a counterbalance to the problem discussed next.

What to do about underqualified teachers

A problem for professionalization is what to do about unqualified teachers. In developing countries such as India and Pakistan, governmental desires to introduce universal standards relating to this and other topics, which in political terms are hard to resist, meet an impossible problem at the point of implementation, because of the wide range of circumstances on the ground. Administrators at the regional level ask: 'What good will it do to apply a standard when we know that all of the schools in a locality will score zero against that standard?' 'Do we have to set the standard so low that everyone has a chance of achieving it?' 'Do we apply different "national" standards to different situations?' 'Do we have to keep changing the standards as things improve?'

The issue is significant because so much community-based education in developing countries is provided by teachers with limited education and rudimentary training, often on low pay or no pay. It is relevant to school leaders in mature developed systems because establishing teaching and school leadership as a profession requires, in the modern world, working within globally comparative frameworks, and towards globally convergent standards.

In China, former Vice Premier Li Lanqing (2004) commented on the long-standing problem of community school teachers which had supposedly been resolved by the Teachers Law of 1994.

During the Cultural Revolution (1966–1976), education had been seriously disputed and teacher training suspended. Rural schools employed people without proper training, of whom there were 4.91 million by 1977. They did not count as state employees, and received allowances much lower than teachers' wages. The disparity in pay was addressed in stages following 1979, but 2.3 million were still underpaid in 1993. Li Lanqing described a personal encounter in 1994 with a community teacher with seventeen years' experience, who was paid one tenth of the teachers' wage, and was representative of many others in the locality. Li Lanqing's response was to orchestrate a national media campaign to win the support of local leaders. With government investment, the issue of differential pay was gradually addressed, but meanwhile regulations for minimum qualifications were also introduced: without these, people could not be employed in teaching posts. As demand for education expanded in rural areas, shortages of qualified teachers meant that local authorities once again resorted to employing large numbers of 'substitute teachers' on lower rates, without sufficient funds, so salary arrears once again became a problem (Li Lanqing 2004 pp 29–31).

If achieving a paid and qualified teacher workforce is proving a problem in China, then it is a safe assumption that it will be a bigger problem in many smaller developing systems. In Africa, comparable issues are reported by Marphatia et al. (2010), and Edge et al. (2009). The latter publication is a literature review which formed part of the project reported by the former. The research examined the role of teachers in Burundi, Malawi, Senegal and Uganda, concluding:

> Understanding what is happening with teachers' availability, training and quality is one of the most pressing issues facing education in Africa today. Over the past decade, many African countries have been reducing their investments in teacher training and recruiting non-professional teachers, both as a cost-cutting measure and as a quick-fix solution to the teacher shortage. The full impact of this trend is only now being felt as the teaching profession fragments and learning outcomes deteriorate.
>
> (Marphatia et al. 2010 p 6)

The report notes the confusing terminology which in different contexts describes teachers as being variously 'contract', 'unqualified', 'underqualified', 'undertrained', 'untrained', 'volunteer' or 'para-teachers', and that these terms have different meanings in different jurisdictions (Marphatia et al. 2010 p 15).

In a process of professionalization, it is common for a point to be reached where a decision has to be taken about how to introduce standards for practitioners, and what to do about current practitioners who do not

meet the standards now required. Sometimes it is tempting, and may be
urged by trade unions, to begin with the mass registration of the whole
current workforce into the new professional body or licensing system,
notwithstanding that many do not meet the standards required. Mass
registration in such circumstances can be almost guaranteed to turn into a
costly bureaucratic exercise, which causes resentment and does nothing to
raise standards.

If teaching is to become a true profession, comparable to other mature
professions, and if much of the education of the world's growing population
is inevitably to be community-based, this points logically towards more
precise use of the word 'teacher'. While school education in all situations
should be professionally supervised by a qualified school leader and qualified
teachers, there will be many situations where children are educated in part
or in whole by people who are not teachers. A certainty is the continued
presence of many underqualified para-professionals and lay educators, who
enable children to access forms of schooling who would otherwise have
none, but in respect of whom the designation 'teacher' is, strictly speaking,
a misnomer. Of course the term 'teacher' will always have wide popular
usage, just as 'We'll send an engineer' when equipment is faulty does not
necessarily mean a member of one of the engineering professional bodies.

This has implications for a pedagogy of school leadership. It means that
integral parts of the role include providing professional support, supervision
and leadership to para-professionals and lay educators; and being a teacher
trainer, enabling those of them who can, and who wish to, to progress
through professional development to achieve full professional status.

Moving on from managerial leadership

At the start of this chapter, a distinction was made between school leaders'
roles as leaders of educational institutions, and their roles as leaders of
professional educational practice. These roles represent overlapping circles
of responsibility. At the point of overlap, the leader leads educational
practice in their school as well as running it as an organization. Running
the organization will also involve activities which are only indirectly
concerned with professional practice. Equally, acting as a leading member
of the education profession can include activities that range beyond the
leader's institutional responsibilities. The point is that the two sides of the
leadership role have different authority bases, operate through different
kinds of relationship, and draw upon different qualities. Organized systems
for developing school leaders concentrate almost entirely on how to run
a school, and very little on how to be a leading member of the education
profession. A pedagogy of school leadership needs to redress that imbalance.

In England, the Labour government which took office in 1997 set out on
a raft of strongly managed national projects. These embraced attention to

school leadership. The government's strategies depended on schools being led not only well, but in a certain way, hence it created the then National College for School Leadership.

This drive to develop school leadership was motivated by a growing pool of evidence of the importance of leadership to school improvement: by a genuine belief in its intrinsic benefit. That notwithstanding, a feature of New Labour's working methods was that each of its initiatives would be designed to support as many as possible of its other initiatives. This policy of cross-reinforcement meant, inevitably, that 'good' school leadership development would be increasingly understood as development which produced headteachers who would implement the government's political priorities effectively.

That impetus carried on when the government changed in 2010. Practice continued in a broadly similar direction. Meanwhile, the educational landscape, in which school leaders will be leading, is changing profoundly. The present government has greatly reduced the scale of activity previously undertaken by centrally controlled national agencies. Budgets for education spending have tightened. The activity of local authorities has been sharply curtailed and that trend will continue. The growth of academy chains means that an increasing number of school leaders find themselves in the role of site- or unit-manager within a corporately cultured conglomerate. These developments are occurring in an increasingly globalized world.

This changing landscape has implications for how 'school leadership' is becoming conceived, both as a body of people and in relation to the kinds of issues with which they deal. This implies a need for a radical re-think about future approaches to the preparation and development of school leaders. The current generation of school leaders adapting to the changing landscape will have a range of professional development needs beyond previous delineations of headteachers' roles and required competencies.

The next generation of leaders

A bigger issue is school leaders for the future. Current leaders know the old landscape, and the systems that they are changing from; they have the accumulated toolkit of everything they learnt under the old regime, including many transferable skills. They know how the new is intended to differ from the old, and whether they agree with it or not, they have lived through the debate setting out the rationale for the change. They are the current wave of pioneers.

The next generation of school leaders is in a different position. They are rising professionals in early or middle leadership positions, aspiring to be headteachers in perhaps ten or fifteen years' time. They are the people whose long-term leadership development is vital to the future success of the school system. Yet when they look to their future, they will see that every existing map is out of date; that existing infrastructures for career progression and leadership development are, in the main, obsolescent; and that there is no-one outside their current employer's organization whose job it is to help them.

What skills and attributes will future school leaders need, and what development processes will help with their acquisition? How can current leaders best support succession planning, when so much of the what, why, where and how of leadership are unknown, and where the identity of 'leaders', their position in the system and the infrastructures they command are increasingly varied? Or, as school leadership becomes more professionalized, will it be up to the next generation of school leaders to help themselves, by designing and working towards the futures they want: by being the next wave of pioneering individuals?

CHAPTER NINE

Global School Leadership Development

This chapter's title deliberately embraces two possible interpretations. It could refer to examples, from different global points, of how school leaders are being developed to meet the needs of various systems. It could also refer to developing the notion of a 'global school leader' as a particular kind of world-class professional. In fact the thrust of the argument, in the book as a whole, is that these two meanings need to converge.

Current leadership development

First, it is necessary to engage critically with some established forms of leadership professional development, not to reject them but to recognize their limitations. Such development takes place within a policy context. MacBeath (2008) examined how headteachers in England talked about National Strategies, within the global contexts of international comparison, devolution to schools, central government interventions and high-stakes accountability – an agenda he saw as driven by economic rather than educational logic. He concluded that headteachers have to work out their own salvation: 'a quest for a marriage of convenience between dutiful compliance and intellectual subversion.'

More recently, MacBeath, O'Brien and Gronn (2012) studied the coping strategies of Scottish headteachers, and found these to be: dutiful compliance, cautious pragmatism, quiet self-confidence, bullish self-assertion and defiant risk-taking. This range of strategies says something about the kinds of professional development in which leaders have engaged and where it has led them, but the fact that so much 'coping' is necessary, while being easily blamed on governments, may also raise a question about the overall fitness for purpose of conventional leadership development provision.

Brundrett, Fitzgerald and Sommefeldt (2006) critiqued national programmes of school leadership development in England and New Zealand. They considered these to be designed to create orthodoxy and compliance to centrally mandated norms, and argued that fundamental questions about the nature of leadership and its knowledge base should be re-surfaced. A more recent article by Cardno and Youngs (2013) shows, for New Zealand at least, how much progress has been made since 2006.

Cardno and Youngs (2013) report their formative and summative evaluation of the Experienced Principals' Development Programme (EPDP) in New Zealand: an eighteen-month programme commissioned by the Ministry of Education from ten providers, to help experienced school principals to develop their capability to lead change to create effective conditions for teaching and learning. Cardno and Youngs comment on the appropriate forms of learning for experienced principals, noting their needs for revitalizing and reenthusing, and their individualized approaches to development. From a literature review of research, they summarize these needs as including:

- Coaching and mentoring by credible, capable coaches, providing carefully planned support in a sustained trusting relationship

- Reflection and problem-solving experience, cultivating the particular type of critical reflection needed to resolve complex problems of practice, which requires ready access to an extensive repertoire of problem-relevant knowledge

- Professional renewal, developed by a combination of intellectual challenge, and increased emotional intelligence including self-management

- Direct involvement in school improvement initiatives in their own school to provide authentic on-the-job learning though self-directed enquiry projects and action research.

(Cardno and Youngs 2013)

The structure and content of the EPDP is consistent with these findings in a number of respects. It starts with the use of a leadership assessment tool, the Education Leadership Practices (ELP) survey, which captures staff perceptions of leadership practices across the school and contributes to the assessment of participants' development needs. This may influence the direction for another element which is a school improvement enquiry project. The programme also includes professional reading and workshops, and coaching-mentoring (Cardno and Youngs 2013).

The evaluation of the programme found that the experienced principals placed a high value on the face-to-face learning with other principals, and on the key programme features summarized above. It also concluded that effective development required sufficient duration (in this case eighteen months) for the learning to be reflective, applied and sustained (Cardno and Youngs 2013).

EPDP was designed for very experienced school principals, but in the future, if not already, the forms of professional development identified might be just as appropriate to, and appreciated by, school leaders at earlier points on life's journey. The model also implies a limitation in its treatment of time and space. Experience seems to be measured mainly in time, but an alternative model might look at breadth, complexity and intensity of experience. The latter, which is becoming more relevant, might mean that a younger and, in hierarchical terms, more junior school leader is equally ready to benefit from forms of professional development conventionally reserved for those senior in rank and years of service. The model, reflective of its current context, also assumes that more experienced principals will run bigger schools, but that they are still essentially concerned with a single institution. It is likely that many of the participants of EPDP will have system leadership roles of one kind or another, but this is not foregrounded in the evaluation.

Walker, Bryant and Lee (2013) reviewed a selection of well-regarded pre-service programmes to prepare people for appointment as school principals, namely the Ontario Principals Qualification Programme, the Australian State of Victoria's Master of School Leadership, the Singapore Leaders in Education Programme, the Hong Kong Certificate for Principalship and the New York City Aspiring Principals Programme. The study showed contrasts but also extensive commonalities among these programmes in their knowledge bases, aims and methods of learning, which included frequent use of practical application projects such as action research or internship, mentoring and the compilation of a journal or portfolio. By contrast, Zheng, Walker and Chen (2013) report the policy for developing principals in Mainland China between 1989 and 2011, which spans three levels: qualification, for new principals; improving, for principals in their first five years; and advanced, for 'backbone principals'. The article notes as the dominant feature of this provision the extreme level of State control over every aspect of the design, participation in, and conduct of these programmes.

Professional standards for school leaders

Professional standards for school leaders may provide an additional proxy-indicator for the kinds of professional development taking place, because one would expect to see some correlation between patterns of development and the stated competence requirements of the role.

The UK National Standards for Headteachers (DfES 2004), notwithstanding that they are no longer current, and have not been replaced, provide a description of attributes considered necessary to succeed in school leadership. They concern shaping the future, leading learning and teaching, developing self and working with others, managing the organization, securing accountability and strengthening community. For each of these areas the standards give an explanation and define the knowledge; disposition ('is committed to'); ability ('is able to'); actions and outcomes expected.

The Alberta School Leadership Framework: Building Leadership Capacity in Alberta's Education System (Government of Alberta 2012) sets out the vision, purposes and elements of a framework of professional competencies for school leaders. As well as detailing the competencies, this defines standards for school leader professional growth, supervision and evaluation, which are not included in the UK standards.

The professional standards for school leaders in Qatar (State of Qatar 2012) are particularly structured and thorough. They differentiate between middle and senior leaders. The core standard focuses on leading and managing learning and teaching. This is supported by six other standards, focusing on strategic vision and aims; leading change; developing people and teams; school-community relations; resources; and reflection and evaluation. Each standard is broken down into statements with indicators, followed by lists of required skills, knowledge and dispositions. These are followed by an evidence guide differentiated for middle and senior leaders. Qatar's standards were formed alongside the wholesale shift of government schools to a new independent status similar to the Academy model.

Dinham et al. (2013) describe the development of the National Standards for Principals in Australia, subsequently renamed the Australian Professional Standards for Principals. The Australian Institute for Teaching and School Leadership was established by government in 2010 to lead the promotion of excellence in the professionalism of teachers and school leaders, and the Standards were among its first tasks. The thinking behind the Standards took account, among other factors, of the emergence of 'new models of leadership within and beyond the school, with school leaders taking on a range of roles within their community' (Dinham et al. 2013 p 471).

Constraints of conventional thinking

These preparation programmes and statements of standards represent the leading edge: they are good, they are appreciated, and they are sufficiently embracing to be applied in a range of contexts now and in the future. Generally, however, these frameworks move only slowly forward from a set of historically implied assumptions that are gradually being challenged and tested by the more innovative leaders. Those old assumptions were that leaders will be leading a single institution; that their concerns are limited to their own institution and its immediate community rather than embracing a sense of responsibility for wider educational issues; that there is a coherent local school system; and that the fundamental nature of the school conforms to the traditional pattern.

If a conservative view is taken of likely future changes, then those assumptions will remain valid for the majority of future school leaders. Sections of the public and some politicians want schools to become more old-fashioned rather than more modern: a 'good' school is a traditional school.

A more radical view of the potential scale of change raises the possibility that these assumptions amount to what Joel Spring (2009), building on Morin (2008), refers to as 'blinding paradigms'. A blinding paradigm

> gives privilege to particular logical operations and sets of assumptions...[and] grants validity and universality to its chosen logic. Thereby it gives the qualities of necessity and truth to the discourse and theory it controls.
>
> (Morin 2008, cited in Spring 2009 p 201)

Blinding paradigms shut doors: preventing serious attention being given to alternative ways of looking at things. There is no logical reason why notions of 'school' and 'school leadership' remain so traditional. It is only force of habit that decrees that the activity described as 'leadership' is, in fact, largely making minor efficiency adjustments to an inherited model. Many headteachers are happy with that role, including those who boast 'We've got it cracked; we know what works'. Perhaps there is also a need for other school leaders interested in pushing forward ideas about new models of schools and school leadership for a rapidly changing world.

Taking a view mid-way between these extremes, it is likely that there will be at least a minority of up-and-coming school leaders whose future careers will take them in ground-breaking directions. These will be the innovators who shape a new school system to respond to rising global expectations. In order to create conditions in which worthwhile innovation can flourish, it is worth considering what might be different about the roles, approach and attributes of these future leaders.

Nature and purpose of 'school autonomy'

In England, school leaders, individually and collectively, are to have greater autonomy (which will sometimes translate simply into 'less support'). In fact they will have more autonomy than headteachers in any other state school system in the world. They are also expected to play a major role in generating new arrangements which are intended to amount to a coherent pattern of school system governance and support to replace roles previously undertaken by local authorities. What will this mean? What new models of school leadership will England be contributing to the global field? Does 'autonomy' mean simply exchanging loose control by a local authority for much tighter control by an academy chain? Will the English contribution to global thinking simply be the most privatized state school system? Or will school leaders, collectively, use their autonomy to create new models of professional leadership of school systems? Perhaps these could be models driven by educational philosophy, and evolving new pedagogies to match new needs, rather than externally imposed business models.

These changes come at a time when the day-to-day demands of core business remain acute. Greater autonomy offers the opportunity for school leaders to assert professional leadership of school development, and to take this in directions which better reflect educational knowledge and beliefs. But unless something is done to break out of established habits and ways of thinking, then time, energy, ideas and support will all be insufficient to take full advantage of the opportunity offered by autonomy. Other organizations will fill the vacuum with their own schemes and structures. What might that 'something' look like?

The organizational patterns in this unfolding era are still hazy: they include the concepts of collaboration, school-to-school support and school-led (i.e. headteacher-led) business arrangements to enable these activities. Such thinking implies the emergence of a cadre of local school system leaders to support school development at individual schools, groups of schools and district-wide, in ways that reflect local contexts and are led by locally shared visions, and that offer professional rigour, quality assurance, transparency and accountability. These models must either grow locally or emerge from national and international dialogues within the profession itself. If 'school autonomy' is to mean anything at all, school leaders must move on from models for the exercise of 'autonomy' that are designed and advocated by central government.

Returning to first principles: Educational values, global responsibility and the long view

The kind of leadership provided by local school system leaders will evolve over time, and take different pathways. Some will want to maintain the momentum of recent government policy, including heavy-handed intervention in each other's schools based on test results, and the rigorous reinforcement of 'tried and tested' methods which discourage experimentation. Others would see this as the successful impact of the use by government of 'smart power' (Nye 2011) to achieve the unconscious and voluntary co-option of school leaders into the self-imposed continuance of the harsh and limiting regime into which they were coerced.

Much of the professional development provision specifically aimed at current or future headteachers is anchored into a policy agenda that emphasizes delivering short-term improvements in performance, and discourages debate about the fundamental purposes and design of the school system. That is why it is helpful to adopt a completely different starting point, and to explore future directions for school leadership development starting from global issues, educational values and the long view.

It has been noted that two great forces are at work on the global scene. One is the march of the education industry as one of the drivers of the global economy. The other is the growth of education as a humanitarian response to acute need. Two challenges are posed by these trends. The first is the cultural gulf between the worlds of well-resourced formal institutions of schooling, and make-shift community-based education. The second is the unsustainable escalating dependency of education as a humanitarian response on aid funding and philanthropic giving.

Colin Brock's analysis 'Education as a Global Concern' (Brock 2011) was adopted as the statement of a set of problems that need to be addressed. He argued that the solution 'depends on repairing the dislocation between the formal system and civil society wherein the non-formal and informal majority of learning takes place' (Brock 2011 p 142). His thesis was that 'Bringing the forms of education together' involves generating new partnerships to develop cultural capital, involving the 'world of formal education learn[ing] from the more organic world of civil society' (Brock 2011 p 142).

Spatial perspectives

One way to look at these possibilities is to return to the concept that school leaders manage certain kinds of spaces, and impact on or interact with other spaces. There are three principal domains to this. The school leader manages the spaces they occupy, physically and mentally, as an individual human being, as a professional, as a person with values and commitments, and as a repository of their own knowledge, resources, energies and motivations. At the next level of spatial scale, school leaders manage a school, or perhaps a group of schools, embracing all of the formal and informal learning spaces and ambiences that make up the campus. Thirdly, they in their individual capacity, or the school in its institutional capacity, interact with a diverse range of spaces within communities: from the students' homes to community groups, to businesses which have links to the school, to other schools with which the school may have various kinds of partnership.

If one of the schools in the latter group is an international link, that is, a school in another country, it may be assumed that the headteacher of that school has an equivalent network of spaces with which they interact. The nature of that network may be different, but the idea is the same. When the two networks become joined through an international link, the range of potential linkages across the combined networks is multiplied. An important part of the energy and potential capacity of each part of the linked network is the students themselves. The overall effect of the combined network is the potential for considerable synergy.

North-South school partnerships have been shown to benefit the curriculum and staff professional development in the schools concerned (see, for example, Edge et al. 2009). The next step is to extend such partnerships to include the aims of developing system leadership capacity, and impacting on wider educational problems. International professional networking can be a catalyst and capacity-builder. It can enable school leaders in England to take a stronger lead in shaping the new educational landscape, and leaders of well-resourced independent schools in other countries to contribute more to addressing wider educational needs.

School leadership of the future, as a collective entity, will need to be able to develop schools as network nodes with local and international connections. In this way, the impact of leadership spreads into four connected places: own school, own local communities, linked school and the linked school's local communities. To maximize its potential impact, school leadership of the future will need to break down the barriers between formal and informal learning, and lessen the disconnections between ongoing or mainstream education, and education to respond to the needs of emergencies and extreme situations.

School leadership reconceptualized

The key spatial considerations of preceding chapters may be summarized in the form of the following normative aspirations for school leadership:

Starting Points

- School leadership understands starting points, making discerning and empathetic assessments of contexts and obstacles to learning; also strengths, positive identities and potentialities. (Chapter 2)

- School leadership is cosmopolitan, promoting global citizenship, multi-layered affiliations and respect for and understanding of others' spaces. (Chapter 3)

Processes of Becoming

- School leadership addresses humanitarian needs, using activism to impact on spaces of exclusion and disconnection. (Chapter 4)

- School leadership creates infrastructures for capacity-building, including by connecting homes, workplaces and civic spaces through the school's networks. (Chapter 5)

- School leadership designs pragmatic solutions, problem-solving in specific contexts to co-create new spaces and mobilities. (Chapter 6)

Desired Destinations

- School leadership upholds values, engages critically with imposed values and the politics of knowledge, to transition spaces of prescription to spaces of negotiation. (Chapter 7)

- School leadership utilizes its agency in space-making on at least three scales: the leader's own personal spaces; the spaces within the institution the leader manages; and the networks of places and organizations with which the leader and the school have links. Leaders' values guide how they want to change both their own spaces and how others experience the spaces they occupy. (Chapters 8 and 9)

These statements are presented in the order in which the book's line of exploration has proceeded, and the dynamic relationships between these points fall into the same pattern. The starting points represent a rich, evidence-informed, empathetic and co-owned appreciation of local context, set against and interacting with a similar appreciation of global context. Between the starting point and the desired destination are processes of becoming, concerned with activist humanitarian problem-solving, developing the community as a learning infrastructure, and innovating in order to achieve pragmatic, context-specific solutions. All three processes are strongly interconnected and mutually reinforcing. The desired destinations give people enhanced and enriching experiences of the spaces they occupy, and create spaces in which people are free to develop their own opinions, beliefs and values. Again the factors are linked, because a space in which people can be true to their own identity is likely to be one in which they have a sense of well-being.

Chapter 2 cited Murdoch (2006) as advocating thinking about 'space' as a verb: 'spacing' as an action, event or way of being. Perhaps 'space-making' captures the same idea equally well. For ease of presentation, in the paragraphs above I have set out the dynamic relationships among seven spatial concepts as if they were in a chronological sequence of three phases: start, process, outcome. In reality, the dynamic relationship is spatial, not temporal. All seven points concern different aspects of space-making, and all seven occur concurrently and reinforce each other. So the processes of problem-solving and community-building are at the same time deepening shared understandings of context, and at the same time enriching experiences and opening up thinking.

Moving forward by striking balances

Moving towards practical application of these principles may seem a daunting prospect for current school leaders, constrained by the expectations surrounding the role they occupy, and beset with short-term pressures. Professional collaboration may be the key to breaking out of that impasse. Progress may involve striking a series of pragmatic balances between short-term pressures and longer term needs for systemic development. The following statements describe some of the aims that school leaders may be working towards:

- Combining knowledge of global, national and local productive practices in the most effective combinations. Local conditions and issues are very important, but the English school system is currently at risk of being too inward-looking. A more global perspective, including more international school links, productive international professional networking, and professional reading, will bring fresh insights, energies and solutions to local challenges.

- Interacting on the basis of a deep understanding of the processes through which professional practice evolves and spreads. The lateral spread of good practice, and applying 'what works' are popular concepts, but are often applied superficially, relying on managerial authority. There are profound differences between supporting school development, and fixing a car or television set. Peer-supported school improvement must adopt a professional rather than managerial model, and, within that, strategies that draw more on human relations thinking and less on engineering thinking.

- Supporting worthwhile innovation in appropriate combination with established methods. School staffs need to feel that they are enabled to try out new ways of working, which requires experimentation and acceptance of a heightened level of risk tolerance. On the other hand, there is little merit in innovation for its own sake, or for implying that untested methods should be preferred to tested methods.

- Combining addressing short-term needs with nurturing the conditions for longer-term 'blue skies' thinking. Undoubtedly there are needs, which will continue to arise, for urgent and acute action to ensure that current cohorts of students receive their entitlement.

Such action will be easier, less disruptive and in the end cheaper, if it is nested inside parallel work to clarify long-term educational visions. As well as building motivation and capacity, this will add depth to school self-evaluation, and eventually reduce the need for intervention.

- Generating evidence and knowledge for local and national dissemination. Broadening the generation and use of evidence, especially qualitative as well as quantitative, is one of the hallmarks of progressing from managerial to more professional leadership and development of schools and school systems. Broadly based evidence enables developments locally to be compared and contextualized with practice elsewhere; it enables rigorous evaluation of the effectiveness and value for money of school improvement strategies; and it has been shown to have a strong positive effects on staff development.

Tasks and processes

If the next generation of school leaders is going to be engaging with these agendas, leadership development needs to include a much stronger 'lateral' element, giving practitioners in early leadership positions more exposure to school-to-school networking both locally and internationally, and more opportunity to engage with 'big picture' issues and possibilities.

Two tasks are likely to be among the central foci of such developmental activity. The first is essentially practical: to work with others on the co-creation of mutually beneficial business models for taking forward school-to-school collaboration both locally and internationally, in forms that allow the partner schools to operate as network nodes. The second is to explore long-term visionary futures for the school system and its role within society. If the professional leaders of education (especially those young enough to see the vision through to reality) do not lead this work, who will?

To support development of this kind, the list of processes identified as useful in the Cardno and Youngs (2013) study are likely to be relevant. So these would include face-to-face learning such as through annual residential workshops; executive coaching; broad and deep critical professional reading; and opportunities personally to lead and reflect on innovative projects including through use of the action research methodology; and periodic opportunities for inspirational intellectual stimulation. This would provide a fitting response to Brundrett et al.'s (2006) call for a resurfacing of fundamental questions about the knowledge base and nature of school leadership. To answer the question what will the school leaders of the future need to know, and what will they need to do, in order to address society's big educational problems, the following section explores elements of the school leadership role in the light of the issues considered in previous chapters.

Elements of leadership

The statements of school leadership standards referred to earlier, developed in a number of different countries, all define school leadership as spanning a range of different types of activity, involving different sorts of working relationship, and calling upon different qualities. As always, the key to the most successful and effective leadership is to achieve the right balance in how these different elements are combined. The following sections, abstracted very loosely from the collective wisdom of leadership standards globally, describe five elements of school leadership, and three levels of activity for each. These are outlined first in relation to leading a school or a group of schools under common management. Then I explore the implications of these different elements of leadership for the most productive forms of collaboration among institutions and individuals. The elements of leadership most relevant to the development of global school leaders are:

- Leadership of efficient business organization(s): this is concerned essentially with *leverage*, to get more output and outcome from the resources available.

- Leadership of educational innovation and problem-solving: this is concerned essentially with *vision*, seeing what needs to be done and how it might be achieved.

- Leadership of knowledge generation: this is concerned essentially with the *authority* underpinning practice, strategies and standpoints.

- Leadership of professionalism: this is concerned essentially with *quality*, setting, meeting, demonstrating and enhancing standards of professional practice.

- Leadership of policy influence: this is concerned essentially with *permission* from external stakeholders.

How do these elements of leadership relate to each other, and to the seven aspects of space-making described earlier? Whereas the aspects of space-making suggested a sequence from starting points, to processes, to outcomes, the elements of leadership are perhaps most helpfully seen as concurrent and mutually reinforcing: a pentagram inside a pentagon. This figure-of-five may be seen as sitting underneath and supporting each aspect of space-making.

The second element of leadership is, however, more obviously connected to the 'process' aspects of space-making: activist, humanitarian problem-solving, community development and innovation. I make a specific point in connecting this activity to visioning. Some leadership development texts and programmes imply that visioning is the start of things, and that all else is implementation. Often reality follows a different path. Vision grows through involvement with people and situations, through insights that embrace both rationality and normative commitment. Working with contexts and issues gives leaders a growing understanding of the facts of the matter; interacting with people and understanding their viewpoints affects feelings, values and priorities. Thus the visioning element of leadership is an ongoing process.

School leadership is, in this book, a professional activity, distinguished from other roles which individuals in leadership positions may have, such as political campaigner or entrepreneur. For that reason, I focus the leadership of policy influence away from issues that are properly and primarily the concern of politicians, and towards the central concern of advocating for the removal of obstacles to the development of good educational practice, hence my choice of the summarizing word 'permission'.

Each of these elements requires activities at three levels: strategic infrastructures within which practice takes place, practice, and services in support of practice. These elements and levels of leadership activity could be visualized as a five-by-three matrix, as expanded below.

Leadership of business organization(s)

At the level of strategic infrastructure, this element of leadership sets the purpose and vision of the organization, and its overall business model. At the level of practice, it determines the shape, structure and culture of the organization, including which parts of the organization need wide or narrow spans of control, and the extent to which working cultures follow the 'loose-tight' notion of extensive trust, delegation and operational freedom within a framework of non-negotiable norms and rules. At the level of support and services, this element will employ a range of business models for the provision or procurement of infrastructural services, including in-house provision, contracting and commissioning.

Leadership of innovation and problem-solving

At the level of strategic infrastructure, this element of leadership sets an activist agenda of problem-solving and external philanthropic impact and public contribution. At the level of practice, it creates the conditions in which innovative professional educational practice can develop, including developments in pedagogy, curriculum, learning technology, modes and locations of learning, and the nature of interactions between and among staff, learners and the community. At the level of support and services, this element of leadership includes communication, external relations and co-option, the generation of data, the creation of new business entities, project management, and resource leveraging to increase the impact of the staff time and expenses invested.

Leadership of knowledge generation

At the level of strategic infrastructure, the leadership of knowledge generation involves establishing and maintaining a top-level commitment to the importance of knowledge, and its generation and application, as a non-negotiable core value. This affects the working culture, as leadership, governance and organization must be conducted in ways which exemplify this value. Attaching value to knowledge generation also involves making spaces in the life of the organization for creative conceptual development: that is to say, the generation of new ways of thinking which are not the products of empirical studies. At the level of practice, this element of leadership is concerned with creating and supporting working relationships, professional development and professional dialogues within which good quality practitioner research, and the judicious appraisal and utilization of published research, can be embedded as normal elements of professional practice. At the level of support services, this element of leadership involves creating ambiences conducive to serious study and reflection, access to research literature, and support from external experts.

Leadership of professionalism

At the level of strategic infrastructure, the leadership of the professionalism of teaching, and school leadership itself, requires establishing an organizational culture in which line management is mainly exercised as an integral, and not particularly obtrusive, ingredient of a system of professional supervision. It also requires both internal and external support for and exemplary active involvement in the affairs of relevant professional bodies. At the level of practice, it creates the conditions for individuals to take responsibility for their own continuing development and external recognition as practitioners, and for strong peer support and collaboration within a collegial organizational culture. At the level of support services, this includes systems for procuring inputs of external expertise, in relationships where the teachers and school leaders are the clients, procuring advice from external experts.

Leadership of policy influence

At the level of strategic infrastructure, the leadership of policy influence requires establishing and sustaining organizational capacity to make timely and convincing contributions to relevant policy debates, whether through public fora or more private advocacy. To do this convincingly requires strategic attention to stakeholder endorsement of positions so advocated. It is also necessary to exercise judgement regarding whether, and when, to attract attention to the school's developmental agendas. If 'policy influence' is interpreted as primarily concerned with obtaining space and permission to advance good professional practice, there will be times when it is better to keep emerging good practice 'under the radar' until its worth is proven.

At the level of practice, policy influence depends on the manner and extent to which practitioners can, individually and collectively, develop and advocate standpoints drawing on the products of other elements, especially innovative problem-solving, knowledge generation and professionalism. Policy influence involves advocacy which progresses from empirical evidence and experience to normative exhortation, and from institutional experience and insights to wider application. Leadership of this function involves establishing the range of viewpoints tolerated within the organization's corporate life of debate and opinion-forming, as well as the norms and protocols for managing the distinction between individual and organizational advocacy.

At the level of support services, leadership of policy influence includes creating opportunities for serious internal debate, and creating communications systems which combine the institution's knowledge and experience with its standpoints for advocacy; as well as maintaining networking arrangements with external opinion-formers.

Collaborations among schools and leaders

The elements and levels of leadership outlined above have been described in relation to the leadership of a single organization, or to a group of organizations under common management. This thinking can be developed and extended to consider forms of collaborative working. I have argued that new forms of networking and collaboration have the potential to develop into powerful means to address educational problems, and also to raise the profile and influence of school leadership as a global profession. The words 'new forms' are important. In the UK, school to school collaboration has long been advocated by national government and its agencies as the answer to reduced support from local government.

The experience of collaboration has, however, fallen well short of the rhetoric, presenting a mixed picture both of the actual lasting effects of collaborations which have taken place, and of the conceptual and organizational development of collaborations. One model has been the major, financially induced contrived collaboration, of which the Technical and Vocational Educational Initiative (TVEI) and Education Action Zones (EAZ) were significant examples. In both cases, the UK government offered significant financial grants lasting a number of years, on the condition that groups of schools and other agencies worked together in certain ways. Of course they did so, because additional resources are powerfully attractive. Structures of co-operation were devised that met the grant criteria. Much good work was done, which brought about some lasting changes in thinking. The overwhelming incentive for collaboration was, however, to access the funds, and when the funding ended, so did the collaboration.

Another example of collaboration of similar type is the Networked Learning Communities led for some years by the (then) National College for School Leadership. McLaughlin et al. (2008) researched the effectiveness of six of these that had been selected as examples of 'success'. McLaughlin et al. critiqued the 'taken for granted' good of school networks:

> There is, it seems, little reporting of bad or weak school networks, or evidence regarding whether networking is necessarily the best means by which to accomplish a particular set of ends. This sometimes unquestioning belief in the intrinsic rightness of school networks may detract from a more useful and rigorous critique of what does and does not work well and why.
>
> (Black-Hawkins 2008 p 65)

In fact, the study showed that three of these six 'good' examples had achieved little, and the other three had benefited from pre-existing partnerships and strong external support.

Other types of collaboration have been developed by English local authorities to enable schools to engage in the 'joint commissioning' of children's services. Typically these have involved clusters of headteachers working with local authority staff to plan the prioritization and provision of services directed to children's care and welfare in a particular geographical sub-division of the local authority. The issue often is whether in practice this form of collaboration can amount to more than an enhanced form of consultation, and if not, whether the outcomes are sufficiently different to justify the time.

A number of problems are raised by consortia of these kinds. They have been added as an additional layer of activity on top of, and without modification to, pre-existing arrangements for governance, legal liability, and the locus of powers and duties. Many collaborations among groups of schools have proceeded on an entirely informal and voluntary basis, without creating a legal entity, without any contractual obligations attached to commitments made, and informal, amateurish arrangements for covering shared costs. Where collaborative arrangements have only the status of a 'gentlemen's agreement', staff of one school working in another may enter a grey area regarding their potential legal liabilities. Collaboration can also be seen as a voluntary activity dependent upon goodwill, which will be withdrawn as soon as a headteacher has urgent issues they need to address in their own institution.

There is no particular reason for this level of informality, because there are plenty of more formal options available to schools in England, which are in the schools' own hands rather than needing to fit into a central government scheme. School governing bodies of a number of schools can form a joint committee to provide a governance structure for joint activity. Schools and groups of schools can establish limited liability companies to put a business-like framework around their collaboration. The help individuals give to another school can be contracted and paid for, bringing it within transparent project management, quality assurance and accountability. All of these options, and more, are available, but they have been taken up to a very small extent. I have the impression that most headteachers simply do not see the point of formalizing such arrangements. They like their freedom, they want their school to remain their own domain, they are alright as they are, it is what everyone else is doing, formal arrangements sound complicated and threatening, so why bother?

That approach may have sufficed for the past and the present, but it would be seriously limiting in the future. In England, if school leaders are not proactive in bringing about a step-change in the forms of collaboration that they lead, the initiative will be taken, and the vacuum filled, by other organizations, notably management consultancy companies, and by organizations managing chains of schools. The opportunity for school leadership as a profession to take genuine autonomy and to re-balance the respective roles of professionals and politicians would be lost.

Conceptual frameworks for forms of collaboration need to be developed, based on the purposes of the collaboration and the partners involved, because different functions require different forms, different skills, and different modes of professional practice. The key purposes explored in the following sections are to increase efficiency, to generate knowledge, to address wider educational problems, to promote professionalism and to influence policy. Key factors differentiating forms of collaboration include in each case the driving force, funding, business model, partners, scope and duration of the collaboration.

In addition to these factors, there are two further dimensions to collaborations. The first is whether the collaboration is between institutions or individuals. In the case of some collaborations among headteachers, in particular, this has sometimes not been sufficiently clarified. The second dimension concerns the fundamental rationale of collaboration which will tend towards one of two contrasting models. One is based on similarity and common interests and operates, therefore, as a club offering common identity, solidarity, mutual support and strength in numbers. The other is based on division of labour and the complementarity of different specialized contributions, and operates as a strategic alliance to undertake projects which would be beyond the capabilities and remits of individual members.

Where collaborations take a formalized business model, it is likely that their full benefit is only achieved where they are overlain by networks of individual and informal communication and co-operation. It is important to recognize that this will be the case, and welcome it, and to resist the temptation to try to formalize things which require their informality in order to be effective.

Collaboration for business efficiency

The most common rationale of collaboration among a group of schools for the purpose of increasing business efficiency is to generate arrangements for beneficial collective procurement of goods and services. These might range from contracts for energy supply, to making joint appointments to achieve economies of scale in the in-house provision of certain kinds of support services, to operating a pool of known and trusted external sources of expertise bought in on an 'as and when required' basis.

Essentially this form of collaboration is between institutions rather than individuals, so it needs to be operated through a formal legal entity, usually a company with limited liability, of which the collaborating schools are joint owners. The partners in the collaboration are the schools: other parties involved are suppliers, not partners. The scope of the collaboration is limited to the schools involved which are likely to be geographically proximate, so as to benefit from their bargaining power with local suppliers. Similarity in other respects relevant to service procurement, in addition to proximity, offers operational and commercial strength. The duration of the collaboration is permanent, and the costs of its operation are at least covered by the financial savings it achieves.

In this model of collaboration, there will be clear formalized linkages to each member organization, and clear processes and protocols for how the procurement business functions. That skeleton of formal legal structures is likely to be overlain by a web of informal networks of individuals, which will generate much of the collective knowledge about good suppliers and sources of expertise, and, for example, knowledge of desirable individuals to encourage to apply for key vacancies in the member organizations.

Collaboration for activist problem-solving

In line with previous chapters, the case considered here is international collaboration as a means to working on wider educational problems. The nature of these collaborations could take many forms. An example would be a partnership between two strong, successful schools, one in a developed country and one in a developing country. At the centre of the collaboration is a similarity and a difference. The partners must share the driving philanthropic vision, and have enough in common to work comfortably together. Their contrasting contexts provide the rationale for the collaboration.

To be taken seriously, it will embrace partnership between institutions as well as between individuals, and it will require some formalized structures. One approach would be a bi-centric model involving the establishment of a charitable trust in both countries, each having a primary purpose to support and collaborate with the other for wider educational benefit.

It is likely that this formal structure will 'come alive' through human relationships developed bilaterally between individuals, and that the whole will be supported by a range of informal networks in both contexts. The formal part of the structure is likely to exist permanently, to be scoped to the geographical regions of the partners, and to be funded by seed-corn investment and freely given time, leading to the development of philanthropic and grant-aided sources of support.

Collaboration for knowledge generation

Collaborations for knowledge generation require a different 'shape'. In this field there is a fair body of experience to draw upon, but except where this had additional external funding, or very substantial external expertise, the overall picture is not particularly rosy. A mistake in the past has been to assume that formally structured support *between* schools can be a substitute for properly supportive conditions for knowledge generation *within* schools.

In this form of collaboration, a starting point must be to establish that the participating schools are indeed 'research-engaged schools', within the meaning of that term as elaborated in Wilkins (2011). If that condition is in place, the day-to-day practice of collaboration for knowledge generation is unlikely to be helped greatly by a formal organization connecting the schools. If all of the member schools are encouraging the activity, then cross-school collaboration will essentially be between groups of researching individuals rather than between institutions, and will be mainly informal. The work of those individuals and groups of individuals will lead to outputs, such as publications or conference papers. At that point, after research has been done, and the issue is how to disseminate and promote its outcomes, the member schools may want to collaborate formally to sponsor and endorse the outcomes. They may also wish to collaborate to provide peer-review of each others' practice as research-engaged schools.

Collaborations for knowledge generation require like-mindedness, including shared beliefs about the value of practitioner enquiry, the nature of teaching as professional practice, and the forms of knowledge which educational practice generates and draws upon. Promoting knowledge generation is only meaningful as a long-term commitment, and insofar as formal collaboration between schools is necessary for knowledge generation, the costs of the activity are likely to be seen as a legitimate use of core funding.

Collaboration for professionalism

The focus of professionalism is on individual professional practitioners rather than on the organizations which employ them or in which they practise. This means that when school leaders promote professionalism, whether as an integral part of their management responsibilities, or separately, they are acting essentially in their capacities as senior professional practitioners. The organizational framework around professionalism is the professional bodies to which individual practitioners belong, which endorse and support their capabilities. That organizational framework for professionalism is not yet fully in place for teachers (including school leaders) in the UK, but must be worked towards as a desired destination. Any other approach will default to position-power and managerialism.

For these reasons, collaborations among schools for the purposes of supporting the professionalization agenda are likely to take the form of peer support, and are likely to be keyed into active involvement in and through professional bodies so as to provide an element of quality assurance and external endorsement. Collaborations for professionalization are based on similarity, common interests and mutual support. While commitment to professionalism is of permanent duration, it is possible for collaboration to advance the process of professionalization to take the form of a time-limited project. Regarding how such activity is paid for, the convention is that the recurrent costs of professionalism are funded by individual fees and subscriptions, and pro-bono contributions of time to peer support and to activity within professional bodies.

Collaboration for policy influence

The kind of policy influence relevant to school leaders in their capacities as professional practitioners is focused on how policy needs to change in order to extend and improve effective education. This advocacy will distinguish itself from more general political lobbying by being closely associated both with knowledge generation and professionalism. Collaboration for policy influence does, therefore, imply commitment to increasing the amount and quality of relevant knowledge generated within the profession itself, and to developing stronger professional body structures so as to give greater authority to school leaders' voices.

The game-changer in this matter is the potential offered by modern communications greatly to increase the power of international professional networks, and internationally generated knowledge, in support of such advocacy. These collaborations are likely to be issue-based, operationalized through professional bodies, individual rather than institutional and resourced through the low-cost pooling of information and ideas as part of normal professional practice.

Education in the balance

The sections above suggest that collaborations for different purposes need different structures, rationales, processes and resourcing models. These various forms of collaboration, led and 'owned' by school leaders, will develop in different locations and on different spatial scales. The extent of their development will reflect the factors which have been explored in previous chapters. To what extent will state school systems enable both increased school autonomy, and sufficient leadership development of headteachers to take proper advantage of that autonomy? To what extent will well-resourced private-sector school leaders extend philanthropic support to failing state school systems? To what extent will school leaders in sophisticated mature systems support capacity-building in developing systems? To what extent will world-class school leaders from different continents collaborate to create global professional networks, voice and impact? In these ways the global dynamics of school leadership hold education in the balance.

REFERENCES

Agnew, J. and Duncan, J. (1989) *The power of place: Bringing together geographical and sociological imaginations*, Boston: Unwin Hyman.

Alexander, T. and Potter, J. (Eds.) (2005) *Education for a change: Transforming the way we teach our children*, London: RoutledgeFalmer.

Ali, S. (2006) 'Why does policy fail? Understanding the problems of policy implementation in Pakistan: A neuro-cognitive perspective', *International Studies in Educational Administration*, 34, 1, 2–20.

Alkubaisi, H. (2013) 'Resource management in secondary schools in Qatar's educational reform initiative', unpublished post-graduate research in progress at the Institute of Education, University of London.

Amin, A. (2002) 'Spatialities of globalisation', *Environment and Planning*, 34, 385–399.

——— and Graham, S. (1999) 'Cities of connection and disconnection', in Allen, J., Massey, D. and Pryke, M. (Eds.) *Unsettling cities*, London: Routledge, 7–47.

Anderson-Levitt, K. (2003) 'A world culture of schooling?', in Anderson-Levitt, K. (Ed.) *Local meanings, global schooling: Anthropology and world culture theory*, New York: Palgrave-Macmillan.

Anderson, G. and Herr, K. (1999) 'The new paradigm wars: Is there room for rigorous practitioner knowledge in schools and universities?', *Educational Researcher*, 28, 5, 12–21.

Ansell, N. (2005) *Children, youth and development*, Oxford: Routledge.

Asia Society (2012) *Teaching and leadership for the twenty-first century: The 2012 international summit on the teaching profession*, Asia Society: Partnership for global learning, available at: www.AsiaSociety.org/teachingsummit.

Association of London Government. (2003) *Class acts: Diversity and opportunity in London schools. Report from the commission on race and education*, London: Association of London Government.

Barber, M. (2010) *How the world's most improved school systems keep getting better*, New York: McKinsey&Co.

———. (2013) *The good news from Pakistan*, London: Reform.

———, Donnelly, K. and Rizvi, S. (2012) *Oceans of innovation: The Atlantic, the Pacific, global leadership and the future of education*, London: Institute for Public Policy Research.

Bargent, J. (2012) 'Born in bloodshed but living in hope', *Times Educational Supplement*, 5022, 7 December, 22.

Bennington, J. (2009) 'Creating the public in order to create public value?', *International Journal of Public Administration*, 32, 3–4, 232–249.

Black-Hawkins, K. (2008) 'Networking schools', in McLaughlin, C., Black-Hawkins, K., McIntyre, D. and Townsend, A. (Eds.) *Networking practitioner research*, Abingdon: Routledge.

Bolstad, B. (2012) 'Curriculum development and thematic learning: Norway', in Wrigley, T., Thomson, P. and Lingard, B. (Eds.) *Changing schools: Alternative ways to make a difference*, London: Routledge.

Brandon, J. (2012) Personal communication.

Brewer, J., Augustine, C., Zellman, G., Ryan, G., Goldman, C., Stasz, C. and Constant, L. (2007) *Education for a new Era: Design and implementation of K-12 education reform in Qatar*, Santa Monica: RAND Corporation.

Brighouse, T. and Fullick, L. (Eds.) (2007) *Education in a global city: Essays from London*, London: Institute of Education, University of London.

Brock, C. (2011) *Education as a global concern*, London: Continuum.

Brundrett, M., Fitzgerald, T. and Sommefeldt, D. (2006) 'The creation of national programmes of school leadership development in England and New Zealand: A comparative study', *International Studies in Educational Administration*, 34, 1, 89–105.

Buckland, P. (2005) *Reshaping the future: Education and postconflict reconstruction*, Washington DC: The World Bank.

Burdman, D. (2003) 'Education, indoctrination, and incitement: Palestinian children on their way to martyrdom', *Terrorism and Political Violence*, 15, 1, 96–123.

Caldwell, B. (1997a) 'Global trends and expectations for the further reform of schools', in Davies, B. and Ellison, L. (Eds.) *School leadership for the 21st Century*, London: Routledge.

———. (1997b) 'Thinking in time: A gestalt for schools of the new millenium', in Davies, B. and Ellison, L. (Eds.)

——— and Hayward, D. (1998) *The future of schools: Lessons from the reform of public education*, London: Falmer.

Callon, M. (1991) 'Techno-economic networks and irreversibility', in Law, J. (Ed.) *A sociology of monsters: Essays on power, technology and domination*, London: Routledge.

Cardno, C. and Youngs, H. (2013) 'Leadership development for experienced New Zealand principals: Perceptions of effectiveness', *Educational Management, Administration and Leadership*, 41, 3, 256–271

Castells, M. (1996) *The rise of the networked society*, volume 1 of *The information age: Economy, society and culture*, Oxford: Blackwell.

Chapman, J. and Aspin, D. (1997) 'Autonomy and mutuality: Quality education and self-managing schools', in Townsend, T. (Ed.) *Restructuring and quality: Issues for tomorrow's schools*, London: Routledge.

Chua, J. (2013) 'Recent reforms in Singapore's educational landscape: What's new?', *Education Today*, 63, 2, 8–11.

Clarke, P. (2010) 'Community renaissance', in Coates, M. (Ed.) *Shaping a new education landscape*, London: Continuum.

Coates, M. (2010) 'Gateway: The ownership of education by communities', in Coates, M. (Ed.) *Shaping a new educational landscape*, London: Continuum.

Cresswell, T. (2004) *Place: A short introduction*, Oxford: Blackwell

———. (2006) *On the move*, London: Routledge.

Crossley, M. and Watson, K. (2011) 'Comparative and international education', in Furlong, J. and Lawn, M. (Eds.) *Disciplines of education: Their role in the future of education research*, Abingdon: Routledge.

Daniels, P., Bradshaw, M., Shaw, D. and Sidaway, J. (2001) *Human geography: Issues for the 21st Century*, Harlow:Pearson Education Ltd.

D'Arcy, K. (forthcoming 2014) *Travellers and Home Education: Safe spaces and inequality*, London: Trentham Books.

DCSF. (2008) *Vision for London 2008–2011: London education on the way to world class*, Nottingham: DCSF Publications.

Department for Education. (2012) *Teachers' standards*, London: DfE.

DfES. (2004) *National professional standards for headteachers*, London: DfES.

DFID. (1999) *Social capital: Key sheets for sustainable livelihoods 3*, London: Department for International Development.

Dinham, S., Collarbone, P., Evans, M. and Mackay, A. (2013) 'The development, endorsement and adoption of a national standard for principals in Australia', *Educational Management Administration & Leadership*, 41, 4, 467–483.

Drucker, P. (1993) *Post-capitalist society*, New York: Harper.

———. (1995) *Managing in a time of great change*, Oxford: Butterworth-Heinemann.

Edge, K., Frayman, K. and Lawrie, J. (2009) *The influence of North-South school partnerships: Final report executive summary*, London: Institute of Education, University of London.

———, Tao, S., Riley, K. and Khamsi, K. (2009) *Teacher quality and parental participation: An exploratory review of research and resources related to influencing student outcomes. Literature review for the improving learning outcomes in primary schools project in Burundi, Malawi, Senegal and Uganda*, London: Actionaid and the Institute of Education, University of London.

el-Ojeili, C. and Hayden, P. (2006) *Critical theories of globalisation*, Basingstoke: Palgrave Macmillan.

Epstein, J., Coates, L., Salinas, K., Sanders, M. and Simon, B. (1997) *School, family and community partnerships: Your handbook for action*, Thousand Oaks: Sage.

Exley, S. (2012) 'Arise if you like the concept of a royal college', *Times Educational Supplement*, 5014, 12 October 2012, 18.

Eyre, D. (1997) *Able children in ordinary schools*, London: David Fulton.

———. (2009) *Designing a curriculum for giftedness and creativity in Mawhiba Partnership Schools: White Paper Number 1*, Riyadh: King Abdulaziz and his Companions Foundation for Giftedness and Creativity.

———. (2011) *Room at the top: Inclusive education for high performance*, London: Policy Exchange.

Fielding, M. (2009) 'Public space and educational leadership: Reclaiming and renewing our radical traditions', *Educational Management Administration & Leadership*, 37, 4, 497–521.

Fleure, H. J. (1919) 'Human regions', extracts reproduced, in Agnew, A., Livingstone, D. and Rogers, A. (Eds.) (1996) *Human geography: An essential anthology*, Oxford: Blackwell.

Freire, P. (1970) *Pedagogy of the oppressed*, New York: Continuum.

Glenn, C. (2011) *Contrasting models of state and school: A comparative historical study of parental choice and state control*, New York: Continuum.

Government of Alberta. (2012) *The Alberta school leadership framework: Building leadership capacity in Alberta's education system*, Edmonton: Government of Alberta.

Gulson, K. (2005) 'Renovating urban identities: Policy, space and urban renewal', *Journal of Education Policy*, 20, 2, 141–158.

Gutstein, E. (2012) 'Using critical mathematics to understand the condition of our lives', in Wrigley, T., Thomson, P. and Lingard, B. (Eds.) *Changing schools: Alternative ways to make a world of difference*, Abingdon: Routledge.

Habermas, J. (1976) *Legitimation crisis*, London: Heinemann Educational.

Halls, W. (1973) 'Culture and education: The culturalist approach to comparative studies', in Edwards, R., Holmes, B. and Van de Graaff, J. (Eds.) *Relevant methods in comparative education*, Hamburg: UNESCO Institute for Education.

Hanson Thiem, C. (2009) 'Thinking through education: The geographies of contemporary educational restructuring', *Progress in Human Geography*, 33, 154–173.

Hargreaves, D. (1994) *The mosaic of learning: Schools and teachers for the new century*, London: Demos.

———. (2003) *Education epidemic: Transforming secondary schools through innovation networks*, London: Demos.

———. (2010) *Creating a self-improving school system*, Nottingham: National College for Leadership of Schools and Children's Services.

Hargreaves, A. and Fullan, M. (2012) *Professional capital: Transforming teaching in every school*, Oxford: Routledge.

——— and Goodson, I. (2006) 'Educational change over time? The sustainability and non-sustainability of three decades of secondary school change and continuity', *Educational Administration Quarterly*, 42, 1, 3–41.

Harley, J. B. (1989) 'Deconstructing the map', reproduced, in Agnew, A., Livingstone, D. and Rogers, A. (Eds.) (1996) *Human geography: An essential anthology*, Oxford: Blackwell.

Harris, A. (2009) *Improving schools in challenging circumstances: Inaugural professorial lecture*, London: Institute of Education, University of London.

Hart, J. (2011) 'Young people and conflict: The implications for education', in Paulson, J. (Ed.) *Education and reconciliation: Exploring conflict and post-conflict situations*, London: Continuum.

Harvey, D. (2006) 'Space as a keyword', in Castree, N. and Gregory, D. (Eds.) *David Harvey: A critical reader*, Oxford: Blackwell.

Helsby, G. (1999) *Changing teachers' work*, Buckingham: Open University Press.

Hofkins, D. (2009) 'East side story', *London InstEd*, Issue 9, Autumn 2009, 22–23.

Holmes, B. (1981) *Comparative education: Some considerations of method*, London: Allen and Unwin.

Hoque, A. (forthcoming 2014) *British-Islamic identity: Third generation Bangladeshis from East London*, London: Trentham Books.

Houellebecq, M. (2012) *The map and the territory*, London: Vintage.

http://www.moe.gov.cn/publicfiles/business/htmlfiles/moe/moe_280 *Teachers Law of the People's Republic of China* (enacted 1993–1994), Ministry of Education of the People's Republic of China, accessed September 2012.

International, Erebus. (2008) *Report to the department of education, employment and workplace relations: Scoping study on the development of teaching standards in the broader Asia-Pacific Region*, Brisbane: Erebus International.

International Network for Education in Emergencies. (2013) *Strategic plan*, www.ineesite.org/en/strategic-plan

Ireson, J., Mortimore, P. and Hallam, S. (1999) 'The common strands of pedagogy and their implications', in Mortimore, P. (Ed.) *Understanding pedagogy and its impact on learning*, London: Paul Chapman.

Jensen, B., Hunter, A., Sonneman, J. and Burns, T. (2012) *Catching up: Learning from the best school systems in East Asia*, Melbourne: Grattan Institute.

Karpinska, Z. (Ed.) (2012) *Education, aid and aid agencies*, London: Continuum.

Kearney, J. (2011) 'A unified Rwanda? Ethnicity, history and reconciliation in the Ingando solidarity camp', in Paulson, J. (Ed.) *Education and reconciliation: Exploring conflict and post-conflict situations*, London: Continuum.

Kirschner, B. (2008) 'Guided participation in three youth activism organisations: Facilitation, apprenticeship and joint work', *The Journal of the Learning Sciences*, 17, 60–101.

Knowles, M. (1970) *The modern practice of adult education: Andragogy vs Pedagogy*, New York: Association Press.

Knox, P. and Pinch, S. (2000) *Urban social geography: An introduction (4th Edition)*, Harlow: Pearson Education Ltd.

Kraftl, P. (2013) *Geographies of alternative education: Diverse learning spaces for children and young people*, Bristol: Policy Press.

Kumar, S. (2005) 'Human scale education', in Alexander, T. and Potter, J. (Eds.) *Education for a change: Transforming the way we teach our children*, London: RoutledgeFalmer.

Lanqing, Li. (2004) *Education for 1.3 billion (English edition)*, Beijing: Pearson.

Law, J. and Mol, A. (Eds.) (2002) *Complexities: Social studies of knowledge practices*, Durham NC: Duke University Press.

Lawton, D. and Gordon, P. (2002) *A history of western educational ideas*, London: Woburn Press.

Leadbeater, C. (2012) *Innovation in education: Lessons from pioneers around the world*, Doha: Bloomsbury Qatar Foundation Publishing.

Lefebvre, H. (1991) *The production of space*, translated by D. Nicholson-Smith, Oxford: Blackwell.

Leslie, C. (Ed.) (2013) *Towards a royal college of teaching: Raising the status of the profession*, London: The Royal College of Surgeons of England.

Luke, A. and Hogan, D. (2006) 'Redesigning what counts as evidence in educational policy: The Singapore model', in Ozga, J., Seddon, T. and Popkewitz, T. (Eds) *World yearbook of education 2006: Education research and policy: Steering the knowledge-based economy*, London: Routledge.

MacBeath, J. (2008) 'Stories of compliance and subversion in a prescriptive policy environment', *Educational Management, Administration and Leadership*, 36, 1, 123–148.

———, O'Brien, J. and Gronn, P. (2012) 'Drowning or waving? Coping strategies among Scottish headteachers', *School Leadership and Management*, 32, 5, 421–437.

Marphatia, A., Legault, E., Edge, K. and Archer, D. (2010) *The role of teachers in improving learning in Burundi, Malawi, Senegal and Uganda: Great expectations, little support*, London: Actionaid and the Institute of Education, University of London.

Martin, J. (2011) *Education reconfigured: Culture, encounter and change*, New York: Routledge.

Massey, D. (1999) 'Cities in the world', in Massey, D., Allen, J. and Pile, S. (Eds) *City worlds*, London: Routledge, 99–175.

McEwan, C. (2009) *Postcolonialism and development*, London: Routledge.

McKenzie, J. (2001) *Changing education*, Harlow: Prentice Hall.

McLaughlin, C., Black-Hawkins, K., McIntyre, D. and Townsend, A. (Eds.) (2008) *Networking practitioner research*, Abingdon: Routledge.

McLean, M. (1995) *Educational traditions compared*, London: David Fulton.

McMahon, M. (2011) *International education: Educating for a global future*, Edinburgh: Dunedin.

Mongon, D. and Leadbeater, C. (2012) *School leadership for public value*, London: Institute of Education, University of London.

Moos, A. and Dear, M. (1986) 'Structuration theory in urban analysis: Theoretical exegesis', *Environment and Planning, A*, 18, 231–252.

Morin, E. (2008) *Seven complex lessons in education for the future*, Paris: UNESCO.

Murdoch, J. (1998) 'The spaces of actor-network theory', *Geoforum*, 29, 357–374.

———. (2006) *Post-structuralist geography: A guide to relational space*, London: Sage.

National Board for Professional Teaching Standards. (1989) *What teachers should know and be able to do*, Arlington: NBPTS, available at www.npts.org.

Nye, J. (2011) *The future of power*, New York: Public Affairs.

Ontario College of Teachers. (1999) *Standards of practice for the teaching profession*, Ontario: Ontario College of Teachers.

Oyler, C. (2012) *Actions speak louder than words: Community activism as curriculum*, New York: Routledge.

Ozga, J. and Lingard, B. (2007) *The RoutledgeFalmer reader in education policy and politics*, Abingdon: Routledge.

Pacione, M. (2001) *Urban geography: A global perspective*, Routledge: London.

Parker, L. and Raihani, R. (2011) 'Democratising Indonesia through education? Community participation in Islamic schooling', *Educational Management Administration & Leadership*, 39, 6, 712–732.

Paulson, J. (2006) 'The educational recommendations of truth and reconciliation commissions: potential and practice in Sierra Leone', *Research in Comparative and International Education*, 1, 4, 335–350.

———. (2011) *Education and reconciliation: Exploring conflict and post-conflict situations*, London: Continuum.

Pennac, D. (2011) *School blues*, London: MacLehose Quercus.

Popper, K. (1966) *The open society and its enemies, 5th edition*, London: Routledge and Kegan Paul.

Power, S. (2008) 'The imaginative professional', in Cunningham, B. (Ed.) *Exploring professionalism*, London: Institute of Education Bedford Way Papers.

Pratt-Adams, S., Maguire, M. and Burn, E. (2010) *Changing urban education*, London: Continuum.

Psacharopoulos, G. (1981) 'Returns to education: An updated international comparison', *Comparative Education*, 17, 321–341.

Ranson, S. (1994) *Towards the learning society*, London: Cassell.

Rigg, J. (2007) *An everyday geography of the global south*, Abingdon: Routledge.

Rizvi, F. and Lingard, B. (2010) *Globalizing education policy*, Abingdon: Routledge.

Robertson, S. (2009) 'Spatialising the sociology of education: stand-points, entry-points, vantage-points', Centre of Globalisation, Education and Societies, University of Bristol, at http://www.bris.ac.uk/education/people/academicStaff/edslr/publications/28slr

Sahlberg, P. (2011) *Finnish lessons*, New York: Teachers College Press.

Schleicher, A. (2012a) 'You must emulate and innovate to keep pace', *Times Educational Supplement*, 5019, 16 November, 44–45.

——— (Ed.) (2012b) *Preparing teachers and developing school leaders for the 21st Century: Lessons from around the world*, Paris: OECD Publishing.

Sergeant, H. (2009) *Wasted: The betrayal of white working class and black Caribbean boys*, London: Centre for Policy Studies.

Shaw, M. (2005) 'The cultural context of educational leadership', in Coleman, M. and Earley, P. (Eds.) *Leadership and management in education: Cultures, context and change*, Oxford: Oxford University Press.

Sheppard, E. (2013) *Ethical leadership, culture and identity in international schools: The implications of teaching a culturally specific curriculum to multicultural students*, unpublished MA dissertation, Institute of Education, University of London.

Shotton, J. (2002) 'How pedagogical changes can contribute to the quality of education in low income countries', in Desai, V. and Potter, R. (Eds.) *The companion to development studies*, London: Arnold.

Soja, E. (2000) *Postmetropolis: Critical studies of cities and regions*, Malden MA: Blackwell.

Spring, J. (2009) *Globalisation of education: An introduction*, New York: Routledge.

State of Qatar. (2012) *National professional standards for teachers and school leaders*, Doha: Supreme Education Council Education Institute.

Stewart, W. (2012) 'Not all high scores are good', *Times Educational Supplement*, 5022, 7 December, 16–17.

———. (2013a) 'Can business teach the world?', *Times Educational Supplement*, 5043, 10 May, 24–28.

———. (2013b) 'Singapore heads in a bold new direction', *Times Educational Supplement*, 5062, 20 September, 8–9.

Tan, Cheng-Yong. (2012) 'Instructional leadership: Towards a contextualised knowledge creation model', *School Leadership & Management*, 32, 2, 183–194.

Taylor, C. (2009) 'Towards a geography of education', *Oxford Review of Education*, 35, 5, 651–669.

———. (2011) 'Towards a geography of education', in Furlong, J. and Lawn, M. (Eds.) *Disciplines of education: Their role in the future of education research*, London: Routledge.

Terano, M., Slee, R., Scott, D., Husbands, C., Naoum, D., Zotzmann, K. and Kingdon, G. (2011) *International productive practices in education: Research report to the international best practices exchange leading to innovation in Sarva Shiksha Abhiyan (SSA) Project*, New Delhi: Save the Children.

The Independent Review of Teachers' Standards. (2011) *Second report of the independent review of teachers' standards: Post-threshold, excellent teacher and advanced skills teacher standards*, London: Department for Education.

Townsend, T. (1997) 'Schools of the future: A case study in systemic educational development', in Townsend, T. (Ed.) *Restructuring and quality: Issues for tomorrow's schools*, London: Routledge.

Tuan, Y. (1996) 'Space and place: Humanistic perspective', in Agnew, J., Livingstone, D. and Rogers, A. (Eds.) *Human geography: An essential anthology*, Oxford: Blackwell.

Urry, J. (2007) *Mobilities*, Cambridge: Polity.

Volansky, A. (2006) 'Education leadership in pluralistic societies: The case of Israel', *International Studies in Educational Administration*, 34, 1, 106–117.

Walker, A., Bryant, D. and Lee, M. (2013) 'International patterns in principal preparation: Commonalities and variations in pre-service programmes', *Educational Management Administration & Leadership*, 41, 4, 405–434.

Ward, H. (2013) 'The Arab teachers who will work in Jewish schools', *Times Educational Supplement*, 5057, 16 August, 14–16.

Webley, K. (2012) 'Leadership: Save the children's global challenge', in Karpinska, Z. (Ed.) *Education, aid and aid agencies*, London: Continuum.

Whitty, G. with Sally Power (2002) *Making sense of education policy*, London: Paul Chapman.

———. (2008) 'Changing modes of teacher professionalism: Traditional, managerial, collaborative and democratic', in Cunningham, B. (Ed.) *Exploring professionalism*, London: Institute of Education Bedford Way Papers.

Whitworth, D. (2013) 'Guangzhou to Eton: Why Chinese parents are sending their children to British schools', *The Times*, 27 May, 1–3.

Wilkins, R. (1986) 'Gaining insights from foreign studies: A catechism for review', *Educational Management and Administration*, 14, 49–59.

———. (2010) 'The global context of local school leadership', in Coates, M. (Ed.) *Shaping a new educational landscape*, London: Continuum.

———. (2011) *Research engagement for school development*, London: Institute of Education, University of London.

———. (2013) 'A road-map for teacher professionalisation in the UK', *Education Today*, 63, 1, 10–12.

———, Terano, M., Scott, D., Husbands, C., Lall, M. and Kingdon, G. (2013) *Report of the technical assistance provided by the Institute of Education, University of London, to the international best practice exchange leading to innovation in Sarva Shiksha Abhiyan (SSA) Project, India*, London: Institute of Education, University of London.

Willis, R. (2012) *The development of primary, secondary and teacher education in England: A history of the College of Teachers*, Lampeter: The Edwin Mellen Press.

Woodhall, M. (1997) 'Human capital concepts', in Halsey, A., Lauder, H. Brown, P. and Wells, A. (Eds.) *Education: Culture, economy and society*, Oxford: Oxford University Press.

Woolcock, N. (2012) 'Heads in challenge to union power with plans for a royal college of teaching', *The Times*, 8 October 2012, 6.

World Bank (2010) *Quality of education in Colombia – Achievements and challenges ahead: Analysis of the results of TIMSS 1995–2007*. Washington, DC:

World Bank. http://documents.worldbank.org/curated/en/2010/08/12908941/
    quality-education-colombia-achievements-challenges-ahead-analysis-results-
    timss-1995-2007
Wright Mills, C. (1970) *The sociological imagination*, Harmondsworth: Penguin.
Youdell, D. (2011) *School trouble: Identity, power and politics in education*,
    London: Routledge.
Zheng, Y., Walker, A. and Chen, S. (2013) 'Change and continuity: A critical
    analysis of principal development policy in Mainland China (1989–2011)',
    Educational Management Administration & Leadership, 41, 4, 484–503.

INDEX